Disability Classification in Education

Disability Classification in Education

Issues and Perspectives

LANI FLORIAN
MARGARET J. McLAUGHLIN
Editors

CORWIN PRESS
A SAGE Company
Thousand Oaks, CA 91320

For information:

Corwin Press
A SAGE Company
2455 Teller Road
Thousand Oaks, California 91320
www.corwinpress.com

SAGE Ltd.
1 Oliver's Yard
55 City Road
London EC1Y 1SP
United Kingdom

SAGE India Pvt. Ltd.
B 1/I 1 Mohan Cooperative
   Industrial Area
Mathura Road, New Delhi
India 110 044

SAGE Asia-Pacific Pte. Ltd.
33 Pekin Street #02–01
Far East Square
Singapore 048763

Printed in the United States of America.

Library of Congress Cataloging-in-Publication Data

Disability classification in education : issues and perspectives/edited by Lani Florian, Margaret J. McLaughlin.
    p. cm.
Includes bibliographical references and index.
ISBN 978-1-4129-3876-1 (cloth)
ISBN 978-1-4129-3877-8 (pbk.)
    1. Children with disabilities—Education—Congresses. 2. Children with disabilities—Classification—Congresses. I. Florian, Lani. II. McLaughlin, Margaret J. III. Title.

LC4005.D57 2008
371.9′043—dc22   2008003605

This book is printed on acid-free paper.

08   09   10   11   12   10   9   8   7   6   5   4   3   2   1

Acquisitions Editor:	David Chao
Editorial Assistant:	Mary Dang
Production Editor:	Eric Garner
Copy Editor:	Taryn Bigelow
Typesetter:	C&M Digitals (P) Ltd.
Proofreader:	Theresa Kay
Indexer:	Kathy Paparchontis
Cover Designer:	Michael Dubowe

Contents

Acknowledgments

This book started life as a conversation about the problem of classification of children for educational purposes. We were inspired by the pioneering work of Professor Nicholas Hobbs of Vanderbilt University whose seminal review of issues in the classification of children was now thirty years old. We felt the time was right to revisit these issues in light of new developments since that time.

We would like to thank our colleagues at the University of Cambridge in the United Kingdom, and the University of Maryland in the United States, for the continued encouragement and support for cross-national work on issues of school reform and special educational needs. We have had excellent administrative support from Anne Chippindale in Cambridge and Val Foster in Maryland. Our colleagues at Corwin Press have been patient and generous in allowing us a longer period of time to work on the book than originally anticipated.

Corwin Press gratefully acknowledges the contributions of the following reviewers:

Mary Carlson
Special Education Teacher
Park Hill K–8
Denver, CO

Wendy Dallman
Special Education Teacher
New London High School
New London, WI

Sally Coghlan
Teacher and Department Head
Rio Linda Junior High
Rio Linda, CA

About the Editors

Lani Florian is Professor of Social and Educational Inclusion at the University of Aberdeen in Scotland. Previously, she was Senior Lecturer in Inclusive and Special Education in the University of Cambridge Faculty of Education, and Fellow, St. Edmund's College, Cambridge. Her research interests include categorization of children, models of provision for meeting educational needs, and teaching practice in inclusive schools. Recently, she edited *The SAGE Handbook of Special Education* and coauthored *Achievement and Inclusion in Schools.*

Margaret J. McLaughlin is Professor of Special Education and Associate Director at the Institute for the Study of Exceptional Children and Youth, University of Maryland. She has published extensively in areas related to special education and general education policy, systems change, and inclusion. She served as a member of a National Academy of Sciences Special Committee on Education Finance and the Committee on Overrepresentation of Minority Students in Special Education. She has traveled internationally under the auspices of the World Bank and the Joseph P. Kennedy, Jr., Foundation to assess services for children with disabilities.

About the Contributors

Philip J. Burke is Professor and Chair of the Department of Special Education, University of Maryland, College Park. His principal interests lie in special education policy, teacher education, and the efficacy of special education services. He has testified before the US Congress and the President's Commission on Excellence in Special Education on disability policy issues. He serves as governmental and legislative liaison for the Higher Education Consortium in Special Education and as consultant to the US District Court in Baltimore.

Louis Danielson has served in numerous research and policy roles in the US Department of Education for over twenty-five years, and has held leadership roles in the department's Office of Special Education Programs (OSEP). He is currently responsible for the Individuals with Disabilities Education Act (IDEA) discretionary grants program, including model demonstration, technical assistance and dissemination, personnel preparation, technology, and parent training priorities. He has published in numerous professional journals, and is a frequent speaker at national and international conferences and events focusing on special education. His particular areas of interest include policy implementation and national evaluation studies.

Alan Dyson is Professor of Education and Codirector of the Centre for Equity in Education in the University of Manchester. His interests are in inclusion, urban education, and educational disadvantage. He led the production of the *Open File on Inclusive Education* for the United Nations Educational, Scientific and Cultural Organization (UNESCO) and recently coauthored *Improving Schools, Developing Inclusion* (Routledge) with Mel Ainscow and Tony Booth.

Serge Ebersold is currently an analyst at the Organisation for Economic Cooperation and Development (OECD) in Paris, where he works on special needs issues in the Education and Training Policy Division. His PhD in sociology focused on the concept of handicap in France. Between 1993 and 2006, he taught disability sociology and conducted extensive research on inclusion policies at the national as well as at the international level at the University of Strasbourg. He has authored seven books and many articles and chapters.

Peter Evans is Senior Analyst at the Organisation for Economic Co-operation and Development (OECD) in Paris with responsibility for the work carried out on special educational needs in the Education and Training Policy Division. After taking a degree in psychology and anthropology at the University of London, he completed his PhD in mental handicap at the University of Manchester. From 1976 to 1989, he taught courses for teachers of children with learning difficulties at the Institute of Education, University of London. He has written some twenty books and many articles and chapters and has traveled extensively studying special education systems in both OECD and non-OECD countries.

Michael L. Hardman is Dean of the College of Education at the University of Utah. He also serves as Chair of the Department of Teaching and Learning, Professor in the Department of Special Education, and University Coordinator for the Eunice Kennedy Shriver National Center for Community of Caring. He has numerous publications in national journals throughout the field of education and has authored several college textbooks, of which two, *Human Exceptionality: School, Community, and Family* and *Intellectual Disabilities Through the Lifespan,* are in their ninth editions. His newest coauthored text, *Research and Inquiry in Education,* was released in fall 2007.

Kelly Henderson is Adjunct Faculty at George Mason University, Fairfax, Virginia, and a consultant to national special education policy projects. She has worked as Special Education Policy Specialist for the Council for Exceptional Children, as Research Assistant at the University of Maryland, College Park, and, most recently, as Research Analyst at the Office of Special Education Programs at the US Department of Education, where she served as Project Officer for national evaluation studies. She is a former teacher of students with emotional and behavioral challenges.

Judith Hollenweger is Professor of Special Education and Head of the Department of Research and Development, Zurich University of Applied Sciences, School of Education. She is Swiss National Representative for the European Agency for the Development of Special Needs Education and Swiss representative for the Organisation for Economic Co-operation and Development Project to Improve Statistics and Indicators in Special Needs Education. She is Consultant to the World Health Organization for the revision of the *International Classification of Functioning, Disability and Health* (ICF), and is working on the development of a children's version of the same classification.

Elizabeth B. Kozleski is Professor in the Mary Lou Fulton College of Education at Arizona State University and the United Nations Educational, Scientific and Cultural Organization Chair in Inclusive International Research. Her expertise is in the areas of systems change, inclusive education, and professional development in urban education. Her research interests include teacher learning in urban education, multicultural educational practices in the classroom, and the impact of professional development schools on student and teacher learning. Currently, she directs the National Center for Culturally Responsive Educational Systems, the National Institute for Urban School Improvement (NIUSI), and the NIUSI program, LeadScape.

John McDonnell is currently Professor and Program Coordinator in Severe Disabilities in the Department of Special Education at the University of Utah. His research interests include effective instructional practices, inclusive education, and transition. He has published numerous journal articles, book chapters, and books on these topics.

Katherine Nagle is Research Social Scientist at SRI International. Currently, she works on the National Study of Alternate Assessments, which focuses on the development and impact of alternate assessments measured against alternate achievement standards for students with significant cognitive disabilities. Previously, she was Program Director of the Education Policy Reform Research Institute at the University of Maryland.

Brahm Norwich is Professor of Educational Psychology and Special Educational Needs at the School of Educational and Lifelong Learning, University of Exeter. He was previously at the Institute of Education, University of London. He has worked as a teacher, professional educational psychologist, university teacher, and researcher.

Diana C. Pullin is Professor in the Lynch School of Education and Affiliate Professor of Law at Boston College. Dr. Pullin is former Dean of the School of Education at Boston College. She was Staff Attorney and then President of the Center for Law and Education of Cambridge, Massachusetts, and Washington, DC. She has represented students, parents, teacher unions, school districts, state department of education employees, and colleges and universities in legal disputes concerning education in federal district and appellate courts and the US Supreme Court and has published widely in the areas of education law, testing, and disabilities issues.

Sheila Riddell is Professor of Inclusion and Diversity at the Moray House School of Education, University of Edinburgh. She previously worked in the Universities of Stirling and Glasgow, and has researched and written in the field of education policy, gender, and disability. She is currently director of the Centre for Research in Education Inclusion and Diversity (CREID), launched in October 2004.

Martyn Rouse is Professor of Social and Educational Inclusion and Director of the Inclusive Practice Project at the University of Aberdeen. He has undertaken commissioned research and development work on special needs and inclusion for a number of international agencies, including the United Nations Children's Fund (UNICEF) in Bosnia and for local and national governments in several other countries. Other international work includes coordinating a Department for International Development (DFID) project with the Kenyan Ministry of Education and Kenyatta University, designed to build educational capacity at the local level.

Kristin Ruedel is a PhD candidate at the University of Maryland. Her current research focuses on examining the disproportionate representation of minority children in special education. She has experience designing and administering data collection instruments, designing and implementing data analysis plans, and conducting quantitative statistical analyses using large-scale data sets. Previously, she taught hearing impaired and deaf students in the United States and internationally.

Nancy E. Simeonsson is Dean of the School of Nursing at Barton College. Her clinical expertise covers the following specialty areas: advanced medical-surgical nursing, trauma and emergency care, psychiatric nursing, obstetrics and childbearing, family, and pediatrics. She has received training in advanced practice nursing and is certified by the American Nurses Credentialing Center in two specialty areas: Pediatric Nurse Practitioner and School Nurse Practitioner. Her research and scholarship focus on the role of health in the development of children.

Rune J. Simeonsson is Professor of Education, Research Professor of Psychology, and Fellow of the Frank Porter Graham Child Development Institute at University of North Carolina at Chapel Hill. He also holds appointments as Adjunct Professor in the Department of Psychiatry at Duke University and Professor in the School of Education, Jönköping University, Sweden. He is actively involved in research and international consultation on assessment and classification of functioning and disability in children. He has chaired a working group for the World Health Organization in the development of the *International Classification of Functioning, Disability and Health for Children and Youth*, published in 2007.

Deborah L. Speece is Professor of Special Education at the University of Maryland, where she directs the doctoral program in learning disabilities. Her areas of interest include the development of reading disabilities and identification of children with reading disabilities. She is currently Principal Investigator of two longitudinal studies funded by the National Institute of Child Health and Human Development that aim to develop screening batteries for early identification of reading disability and examine the longitudinal effects of a Response to Intervention approach to identification.

Lorella Terzi is Senior Lecturer in Education at Roehampton University. She recently completed her PhD in philosophy of education at the Institute of Education, University of London, under the supervision of Professor Harry Brighouse and Professor Terence H. McLaughlin. Her research explores the meaning(s) of educational equality in relation to the funding of inclusive education and critically relates liberal egalitarian concepts of justice as fairness and the capability approach to the area of disability studies and inclusive education.

Martha L. Thurlow is Director of the National Center on Educational Outcomes. In this position, she addresses the implications of contemporary US policy and practice for students with disabilities and English language learners, including national and statewide assessment policies and practices, standards-setting efforts, and graduation requirements. She has conducted research in a variety of areas, including assessment and decision making, learning disabilities, early childhood education, dropout prevention, effective classroom instruction, and integration of students with disabilities in general education settings. In 2003, she completed her eight-year term as Coeditor of *Exceptional Children,* the research journal of the Council for Exceptional Children, and is currently Associate Editor for numerous journals.

Klaus Wedell is Emeritus Professor at the Institute of Education, University of London, where he held the Chair for Children With Special Educational Needs until retiring in 1995. Much of his research and writing is concerned with the implementation of special needs legislation and provision in the United Kingdom and abroad. He has worked in a consultative capacity with the UK and other governments, and was particularly involved with the Organisation for Economic Co-operation and Development Centre for Research and Innovation and the United Nations Educational, Scientific and Cultural Organization. He is also involved with government-funded projects in his local rural community, through chairing an Education Action Zone and an Early Years Development and Childcare Partnership Board.

Part I

International and
Cross-National Contexts
Within the Current Use
of Disability Classification

1

Disability Classification in Education

Lani Florian and Margaret J. McLaughlin

The increase in the number of children being identified as in need of special or additional educational provision is receiving heightened attention in many countries. Whether a disability classification system is used, as in the United States, or a resource-based, "special educational needs" type of classification, as in the countries of the United Kingdom, one consequence of the increasing numbers of children who are receiving additional educational support is the cost associated with the provision of these resources. Increased identification of children with disabilities and special educational needs, however, may also be an indication of an inadequate general education system as well as increasing diversity among children in today's schools. As more is spent on services for individual students, pressure increases on the overall system. Furthermore, as more children are labeled as having special needs, there is a greater risk of those children being placed in settings away from the general education classroom and denied opportunity to learn the same challenging subject matter or attain the same important educational outcomes as their peers. Thus, three major policy concerns surround the identification of children for special educational services. First, there are the costs associated with providing these services. Second, there are grave concerns about the adequacy and equity of the resources and services provided. But perhaps the greatest challenge is the difficulty in deciding who is, or is not, eligible to receive the additional services.

Questions about how to classify children as needing special education services have long been of concern to educators and continue to generate controversy internationally. There are apprehensions that children who are entitled to receive special education services will not receive them due to classification errors. Other children may be falsely identified. Further, there are concerns that the identification of special education needs may result in a lowering of expectations. These apprehensions have led to questions about the efficacy of the classification process.

Indeed, analyses of the characteristics of the students who receive special education services in both the United States and United Kingdom reveal that the students in this group are not representative of the population as a whole. For instance, boys are consistently overrepresented in special educational programs in most education systems (Organisation for Economic Co-operation and Development [OECD], 2005; Sacker, Schoon, & Bartley, 2001; Skarbrevik, 2002). Many education systems report an overrepresentation of children from ethnic and minority groups (see, e.g., Cloerkes, 2003). Differences can also be found in which children get what label. For instance, data indicate that children with similar characteristics may be classified differently depending on family background (United States Department of Education, 2006). There is no doubt that identifying more children has created greater anxiety about both the resource implications and the wider social consequences of social marginalization of certain groups of students. What is perplexing is that these concerns are not new nor have they been ignored in research or policy. Despite these efforts, however, the classification of children as having "special education needs" or "disabilities" remains a troubling and pervasive educational problem.

In 1972, Nicholas Hobbs of Vanderbilt University in the United States undertook a systematic review of the classification and labeling of children in education, with a particular focus on the consequences of inappropriate labeling. This monumental project produced a report, *The Futures of Children* (Hobbs, 1975a), based on a synthesis of the papers prepared for a two-volume sourcebook, *Issues in the Classification of Children* (Hobbs, 1975b). This influential work presented perspectives from educators, psychologists and psychiatrists, pediatricians, sociologists, parents, lawyers, and public administrators. The findings point to the complexity and ambiguity inherent in categorizing and classifying children and youth in education in an effort to meet their learning needs. As noted in one of the chapters in the Hobbs work:

> The labels applied to children are symbols constructed by senders to serve given purposes. As time passes, as the group of listeners broadens, as the needs, intents, and subsequent responses of

listener's change, the concepts . . . change. Labels that once had technical meanings take on additional meanings. Labels which could point to . . . help for a child may come to be used arbitrarily to discriminate or derogate. . . . From time to time, therefore, we should take stock of labels and classifications and their meanings in order to determine what purposes and injustices they are serving. (Cromwell, Blashfield, & Strauss, 1975, p. 5)

Once established, however, classification systems are remarkably resistant to change. What started as *a* way of organizing information often becomes *the* way of understanding phenomena. In most educational systems, an entitlement to extra support requires that a student be classified in some manner as "different." Identifying differences has traditionally been associated with assumptions about ability as fixed and evenly distributed throughout the population. As a result, there is a tendency to view difference as "deviation from normal" with all of the negative connotations that are associated with this view. In this way, the process of classification creates what Minow (1990) has called the "dilemma of difference": the problem that arises when policies intended to compensate for perceived inequalities also perpetuate the differences they were designed to address.

Since the publication of the Hobbs report, education policies have evolved. There have been advances in understanding children and the difficulties they experience in learning, coupled with a deeper understanding of the organization and structures of schooling. These developments, we believe, require a review of current thinking about the labels and classification systems. Further, we believe that a broader, cross-national view is warranted today given the international attention and concern about how to determine which children should receive special education resources.

PURPOSE OF THE BOOK

This edited book considers current issues of classification of children with disabilities in educational systems from an international perspective, with a particular focus on the United States and the United Kingdom. The chapters are based on papers presented at a symposium held at the University of Cambridge, cosponsored by the Faculty of Education at the University of Cambridge and the Department of Special Education at the University of Maryland. This symposium, held in June 2004, brought together colleagues from special education, psychiatry, psychology, philosophy, law, and sociology to revisit issues of classification, with a particular emphasis on disability classification and its implications since the publication of *The Futures of Children* (Hobbs, 1975a). The aim of the symposium was to initiate a consideration of new knowledge and developments in the area. The papers produced for this symposium were synthesized in a two-part article in the *Journal of Special Education* (Florian et al., 2006; McLaughlin et al., 2006). Subsequently, contributors revised their original papers and they were presented at a second meeting in June 2006. These papers, assembled in this volume, aim to increase understanding of the problems associated with classification and to highlight current issues in the classification of children with disabilities for educational purposes. They are intended to stimulate debate and further discussion.

STRUCTURE OF THE BOOK

The chapters in this book are organized into three sections. Part I describes the international and cross-national contexts within which disability classification is currently used. Specific national policies are discussed from historical, sociological, legal, and current educational perspectives. Hollenweger's chapter, "Cross-National Comparisons of Special Education Classification Systems," traces the development of disability classification systems in education and makes the case for a universal classification system that would allow for comparative analyses across countries. She notes that national educational policies and practices determine which children receive additional resources and, consequently, internationally comparable data are difficult to generate. Finally, she reviews international efforts to develop classification systems that will generate good quality cross-national data on students with disabilities and those with special educational needs.

Following this, Ebersold and Evans ("A Supply-Side Approach for a Resource-Based Classification System") present details of the OECD's resource-based approach to generating cross-national data on special needs education. In this approach, the concept of special needs education as the provision of additional support permits variations in definitions of disability and learning difficulty to be subsumed within three broad cross-national categories: disability, learning difficulty, and disadvantage.

Wedell's chapter, "Evolving Dilemmas About Categorization," shows how the categorization of children reflects a variety of intentions, ranging from the quest for equity to the need for prevalence data to inform planning decisions, that sometimes conflict with one another. He traces the history of categorization dilemmas as they have evolved in the United Kingdom

Burke and Ruedel ("Disability Classification, Categorization in Education: A US Perspective") provide an overview of the history of disability classification in US law, specifically the Individuals with Disabilities Education Act (IDEA) and the influence of the Hobbs Report (1975a).

Two chapters analyze how classification is used in US social and educational public policy. In "Implications for Human and Civil Rights Entitlements: Stigma, Stereotypes, and Civil Rights in Disability Classification Systems," Pullin addresses the evolving meaning and significance of disability as a classification in US law, including recent limitations of protections and accommodations for individuals with disabilities. In her second chapter, "Implications for Human and Civil Rights Entitlements: Disability Classification Systems and the Law of Special Education," Pullin discusses the specific legal considerations of classification systems within the context of public schools and for determining eligibility for special education.

Using Scotland as a national lens, Riddell provides a social policy perspective on classification issues. Her chapter, "The Classification of Pupils at the Educational Margins in Scotland: Shifting Categories and Frameworks," notes that policy frameworks often coexist in a "state of dynamic tension." These are presented as a typology that can be used to understand classification systems. Understanding these systems is important, she argues, for what they reveal about the underlying beliefs and the responses that arise from them.

Part II of this volume examines some of the problems, dilemmas, and challenges educators face in using current disability classifications. Norwich ("Perspectives and Purposes of Disability Classification Systems: Implications for Teachers and Curriculum and Pedagogy") asks whether educators need a disability classification system. He considers the relevance of special education categories to decisions about curriculum and pedagogy and proposes a three-dimensional framework for the classification of educational needs.

In their chapter, "Disability Classification and Teacher Education," Hardman and McDonnell provide a historical perspective on how the preparation of special education teachers in the United States has been aligned with traditional medically oriented disability classification systems. They discuss how recent developments, including the move to standards-driven reform and more inclusive education, are reconceptualizing the role of special education teachers and how we prepare those teachers.

In "Disproportionality in Special Education: A Transatlantic Phenomenon," Dyson and Kozleski offer a comparative perspective on the problem of disproportionality in special education. They note that both in the United States and in England and Wales children in some social groups are more likely than others to be found in special education and they describe the nature and extent of this disproportionate representation in each country.

Concluding this section, Nagle and Thurlow ("Classification of Children With Disabilities in the Context of Performance-Based Educational Reform: An Unintended Classification System") provide an extensive overview of the new requirements for assessment and accountability in US schools that, for the first time, are including students with disabilities. Their chapter points to the challenges and opportunities afforded by the new laws as well as to a new type of classification system that is emerging in classrooms as a result of the new requirements.

The last section of this volume, Part III, considers new approaches to the classification dilemma. Simeonsson, Simeonsson, and Hollenweger provide an alternative approach to classification for educational purposes. In *"International Classification of Functioning, Disability and Health for Children and Youth:* A Common Language for Special Education," they argue that the recent developments in understanding the disablement process that are reflected in the *International Classification of Functioning, Disability and Health* (ICF) can be usefully applied to educational systems.

Speece considers the classification of children with learning disabilities within the US context. In her chapter, "Learning Disabilities in the United States: Operationalizing a Construct," she discusses the long-standing difficulties in the classification of children with learning disabilities and presents an overview of a new construct, Response to Intervention (RTI), as another alternative approach to the identification of learning disabilities.

Finally, Terzi ("Beyond the Dilemma of Difference: The Capability Approach in Disability and Special Educational Needs") suggests the capability approach, as developed by the economist Amartya Sen, provides an important perspective on disability classification in education. Although the capability approach is concerned with broad issues of inequality, its theoretical claims are being considered in many spheres of social science, and Terzi considers how this approach can be used to resolve the dilemma of difference that has plagued disability classification for educational purposes.

Rouse, Henderson, and Danielson sum up the cross-national themes and provide a cogent synthesis of the dilemmas, both politically and socially, of attempting to allocate educational resources differentially. In "Concluding Thoughts: On Perspectives and Purposes of Disability Classification Systems in Education," they make the case for new classification schemes that are more inclusive and more focused on learning outcomes.

This collection of chapters is not intended to be a comprehensive comparison of international classification in special education. The chapters are intended to question the construction and uses of disability classification in education as well as to provide some new perspectives on old problems. The chapters address both the foundations and evolution of special education classification policies in the United States and United Kingdom as well as in the broader international context. Collectively, the chapters also consider some of the challenges in today's educational systems. Ensuring access to universally challenging standards for all children in the face of daunting new accountability requirements and demands for inclusive educational systems requires us to question many of the traditional policies and practices in schools. More important than ever are decisions about how to allocate resources to children to ensure equity in educational outcomes. It may not be possible to adapt old ideas. New times call for new ways of thinking about children in schools. It is in this spirit that this book has been developed.

REFERENCES

Cloerkes, G. (Ed.). (2003). *Wie man behindert wird. Texte zur Konstruktion einer sozialen Rolle und zur Lebenssituation betroffener Menschen.* Heidelberg: Universitätsverlag Winter.

Cromwell, R. L., Blashfield, R. K., & Strauss, J. S. (1975). Criteria for classification systems. In N. Hobbs (Ed.), *Issues in the classification of children: A sourcebook on categories, labels, and their consequences* (Vol. 1, pp. 4–25). San Francisco: Jossey-Bass.

Florian, L., Hollenweger, J., Simeonsson, R. J., Wedell, K., Riddell, S., Terzi, L., & Holland, A. (2006). Cross-cultural perspectives on the classification of children with disabilities. Part 1: Issues in the classification of children with disabilities. *The Journal of Special Education, 40*(1), 36–45.

Hobbs, N. (1975a). *The futures of children: Categories, labels, and their consequences* (Hobbs Report). San Francisco: Jossey-Bass.

Hobbs, N. (Ed.). (1975b). *Issues in the classification of children: A sourcebook on categories, labels, and their consequence* (2 vols.). San Francisco: Jossey-Bass.

McLaughlin, M., Dyson, A., Nagle, K., Thurlow, M., Rouse, M., Hardman, M., Norwich, B., Burke, P., & Perlin, M. (2006). Cross-cultural perspectives on the classification of children with disabilities. Part II: Implementing classification systems in schools. *The Journal of Special Education, 40*(1), 46–58.

Minow, M. (1990). *Making all the difference: Inclusion, exclusion, and American law.* Ithaca, NY: Cornell University Press.

Organisation for Economic Co-operation and Development. (2005). *Students with disabilities, learning difficulties and disadvantages: Statistics and indicators.* Paris: Author.

Sacker, A., Schoon, I., & Bartley, M. (2001). Sources of bias in special needs provision mainstream primary schools: Evidence from two British cohort studies. *European Journal of Special Needs Education, 16*(3), 259–276.

Skarbrevik, K. J. (2002). Gender differences among students found eligible for special education. *European Journal of Special Needs Education, 17*(2), 97–107.

United States Department of Education. (2006). *26th annual report to Congress on the implementation of the Individuals with Disabilities Education Act, 2004* (Vol. 1). Washington, DC: Office of Special Education and Rehabilitative Services. Retrieved October 1, 2006, from http://www.ed.gov/about/reports/annual/osep/2004/26th-vol-1.pdf

2 Cross-National Comparisons of Special Education Classification Systems

Judith Hollenweger

Classification systems are the result of a consensus process either at the international or national level to ensure a common conceptualization of a specific domain of life relevant not only to individuals, but also to society. They are the result of a standardization process to ensure a common understanding and application of specific terms. In the domain of health—and disability—the World Health Organization (WHO) is charged with the mandate to develop and improve comparable international classification systems. The history of classification systems (see www.who .int/classifications/icd/) exemplifies shifts in society's perception of relevant conceptualizations of life, death, health, illness, and disability. The earliest system, established more than a hundred years ago, was an internationally agreed upon list of causes of death approved in 1900 that developed into the *International Classification of Diseases* (ICD). With the establishment of the WHO in 1948, the organization assumed responsibility to further develop and improve this classification. Today, the ICD includes not only disease categories like Parkinson's, but also categories of disorders—or syndromes—such as childhood autism, conduct disorders, or specific developmental disorders of scholastic skills (WHO, 1996). In 1980, the WHO published a draft version of a classification of disability, the *International Classification of Impairments, Disabilities and Handicaps* (ICIDH), which focused on consequences of diseases rather than on the etiology or phenomenology of diseases. Since then, the focus has shifted to issues associated with social participation of persons with problems in functioning.

This development reflects a shift in attitudes toward phenomena perceived as relevant to societies. In the nineteenth century, a growing understanding that some deaths may be avoided by better understanding their causes was accompanied by improvements in hygiene, water quality, and avoiding the transmission of contagious diseases. During the twentieth century, knowledge about treating diseases through understanding their etiology and progression has been at the forefront. Consequently, conceptualizations of morbidity were developed by introducing the concept of illness and by defining distinctions between different types of illnesses. As a result of an increased understanding of and knowledge about the prevention of acute illnesses and death, attention turned to chronic health conditions and disability. With longer life expectancy, the likelihood of becoming disabled during the course of one's life has increased. Thus, societies have developed a compelling interest in disability.

Until recently, disability classification systems were based on distinct, one-dimensional, and fixed concepts of problems grouped according to affected body systems. Internationally, such ideas were best epitomized by the conceptualization and epistemological background of the ICD. Although the incidence of health problems may be persistent and unchangeable, the environment is also an important factor in the experience of disability. In 2001, the World Health Organization published a new classification, the *International Classification of Functioning, Disability and Health* (ICF), that conceptualizes disability as the result of the interaction between a person and his or her environment.

Categorization systems are complex representations not only of such conceptualizations but also of the ways in which categories are used and how they relate to other phenomena. Categories such as "learning disabilities" or "dyslexia" are neither "true" nor "real" without reference to the specific social context in which they have emerged or were developed. These conditions are the result of complex aggregation processes. They culminate in an idea that is meaningful to a society in a given epoch. This can be illustrated by the fate of many categories that originated as scientific terms and subsequently assumed derogatory connotations. Only sixty years ago, "idiot," "imbecile," and "moron" were used as scientific terms to distinguish different levels of mental retardation (Karnosh & Gage, 1944). Luckasson et al. (2002) offer an excellent account of the history of the classification of this category. Today, some professionals use euphemisms such as "intellectually challenged," whereas some advocacy groups use the term "differently able."

Traditionally, teaching—as a theory and a practice—focuses upon the interaction and relationship between content (e.g., curriculum, relevance of content), learner (e.g., students, student performance), and informer (e.g., teachers, teaching quality). This "didactic triangle," which can be traced to the seventeenth-century writings of Comenius (1896/ 1967), suggests complex relationships between content, learner, and informer that are represented in three key processes, namely, presentation (informer presents content), interaction (informer interacts with learner), and experience (learner makes experiences with content). Even today, this conception lies at the heart of thinking about quality indicators in education, represented in "curriculum content standards," "student performance standards," and "opportunity to learn standards" (Ravitch, 1995). Today, standards for "opportunities to learn" are not only concerned with teacher quality, but also include other environmental factors shaped by education systems.

Therefore, educational problems of students are differently conceptualized than health problems; they are essentially relational and contextual. Problems encountered by a student may arise from the interaction between learner and informer or from the interaction between learner and content. Furthermore, students may also be affected by problems primarily related to informers and content. Social constructions of "problems" in education, therefore, seldom refer merely to the characteristics of the child, and adequate classification systems should account for this. A child may experience severe health problems or impairments yet not be identified as disabled if the condition does not cause problems in the interaction with the learning environment and the learning content.

In the eighteenth and nineteenth centuries, formative years in the development of effective practices for children experiencing barriers to learning, the focus was on techniques teachers could employ to improve the relationship between content and learner. Or to put it in another way, the focus was on methodology, to enhance a student's learning and his or her learning experiences. Individuals such as Jean-Gaspard Itard, Maria Montessori, and Louis Braille asked questions such as the following: How is a child with a hearing impairment able to communicate? How can a child who appears unable to learn, learn? How could a child with a visual impairment be trained to read? These pioneers and their colleagues contributed to the improvement of the methodology of teaching students with different disabilities. The improvement of the relationship between learner and content was the core of special education during the period when compulsory education for children with disabilities was not yet established. The trend toward conceptualizing disability in education systems was promoted and nurtured by parents and voluntary and charity organizations. These agencies, such as the Shaftesbury Society in England, Perkins Institute in the United States, or the Christoffel Blindenmission in Germany, as well as other bodies, established private institutions to cater to a variety of children with a range of problems with learning.

The focus on commonly perceived problems changed dramatically with the introduction of compulsory education for all children, including children with disabilities. In the United States in the 1960s, advocates lobbied for free and appropriate public education for children with disabilities. Eventually, the Education of the Handicapped Act, Public Law 91-230, was passed in 1970. The education of students with disabilities was no longer to be exclusively made available by private organizations or individuals, but rather by the education authorities. No longer was the relationship between content and student most important. Instead, the problems arising from the interaction between the student and the learning environment in general or with the teacher in particular became most important. Richardson and Parker (1993) describe how this development led to a conflict between the compulsory attendance mandate and practical aspects of educating everyone—a problem still unresolved today. This has led to an alteration in the perception of problems. No longer were special methodologies the center of socially relevant discussions. Instead, attention was diverted to the relationship between the school environment and learner. The predominant issue now was how children with disabilities could be better accommodated within the education systems. This shift in perspective came with the conceptual move from "disability" to "special educational needs."

More recently, another major shift in conceptualizing disability in education systems has brought the third relationship represented in the "didactic triangle" under scrutiny, namely, the relationship between learning environment and content. The inclusion debate raises questions about the adequacy of school environments and their ability to reach relevant educational goals—independent of individual characteristics of children. The present debate about inclusive education and the underlying social model of disabilities claims that educational shortcomings of the child are the result of an education system that has systemically failed them. Authors like to argue that defectively trained persons operating in an unjust environment (Slee, 2001) are trying to attain inadequate goals and are therefore unable to relate appropriately to children (for a critical analysis, see Kauffman & Hallahan, 1995). It is argued that a child unable to fulfill his or her social role as a student is the result of a system unable to fulfill its obligation to ensure participation, provide equitable learning opportunities, and contribute to social cohesion.

These major shifts in understanding health problems on the one hand and educational difficulties on the other have been underlying factors in shaping classification systems and the categories used to describe disability in education systems. The basic incompatibility between conceptualizations based on the assumption of a priori defined problems, essentially "disorders," and those based on a posteriori defined problems, essentially problems in the relationships between learner, teacher, and content, have led to complex shifts and changes in categorizations of difficulties that children may experience in their education. Until today, no classification system established in education has been able to bridge this conceptual gap and adequately represent the many facets of what constitutes a disability or a special need in an education system.

EMBEDDEDNESS OF DISABILITY CATEGORIES

Disability categories and classification systems are subject to changes not only across time, but also across domains of applications. To understand the practical applications and therefore the meaning of categories, it is important to consider what exactly they represent. As described above, two types of categorization should be distinguished: a priori categories describing target groups independently of a specific context and a posteriori categories describing a problem as a result of the interaction between a person and his or her environment. Moreover, it is suggested that all categories used in education systems are in fact a posteriori categories; their meaning is essentially embedded in the ways they are used.

Disability categories can be embedded at different levels of the education system according to practice and its applications as follows: (1) at micro levels, such as the interactions between teacher and student or teacher and parents, in classroom practice, in assessment or therapy settings; (2) at meso levels, such as schools, professional organizations, organized interactions between different settings, communities of practice; and (3) at macro levels, such as systems that organize the interaction of different communities of practice or complex services. If categories or systems of categorization are only used by individuals at micro level, the embeddedness of such categories is minimal. If, however, categories are more widely applied by groups of professionals in a system or by a community of practice (such as a school with its support systems), such categories become embedded in their practice by helping to organize the work and communications. If categories are used to organize the way different communities of practice, different groups of professionals, or different services are to collaborate and organize their work, categories become powerful tools to distribute resources.

Education systems may use different disability categories and categorization systems at these levels and only a specific set of categories in a given education system will actually be used to administer or govern the system. Categories of this type may be linked to eligibility criteria or they may be reflected in professional identities or in the structure of the education system. Due to their embeddedness in a specific context, disability categories emerge through complex social processes and may guide educational practice and professional cooperation as well as policy decisions. The meaning of categories such as "learning disability" can therefore only be properly understood if their representation at different levels of the system is analyzed. Categories used at all levels in education systems have a tendency to assume circular definitions, such as (1) learning disability is defined as a condition that causes problems in learning (clinical level/ perspective); (2) students with learning disability need programs for the learning disabled (educational level/perspective); (3) programs for learning disabled are provided by specialists for the learning disabled (organizational level/perspective); and (4) specialists and programs for the learning disabled are made available for the learning disabled (policy or administrative level/perspective).

Such categories facilitate a self-referential application and, through this process, establish a truth that remains unquestioned by those who use the category. They represent highly aggregated knowledge that is deeply embedded at all levels of education. The way an accepted set of categories works in an education system can be compared to the process of "normal science" described by Thomas Kuhn (1970). The accepted paradigm (here the categorical approach to organizing and understanding difficulties in education systems) provides a community "with a criterion for choosing problems that, while the paradigm is taken for granted, can be assumed to have solutions. To a great extent these are the only problems that the community will admit as scientific or encourage its members to undertake" (Kuhn, p. 37).

Little is known about the process by which individual disability categories become so deeply embedded in educational practice and in the organization and administration of educational services and systems. The introduction of new administrative categories, such as "autism" in Ireland (Department of Education and Science, 2006), can shed some light on this process. It is usually influenced by the availability and distribution of financial and human resources, by philosophical and ideological preferences, and by advocacy of parents, professionals, and other groups. In the case of Ireland, a task force consisting of parents, education and health professionals, advocates, and researchers was set up in 2000 to look into the provision for children with autistic spectrum disorders (ASD; see the report of the Task Force on Autism, Department of Education and Science, 2001). Until then, such children fell under other administrative categories such as general learning disability, behavioral disorder, or speech and language impairment, and they tended to be referred to and enrolled in special schools for these disabilities. The important role that parents played in the process of the establishment of ASD as an administrative category was due in part to the recognition of the National Parents Council in the Education Act 1998. In other countries, such as Switzerland, autism is not an administrative category, although there are special services offered to children that fall under this label. In the early 1990s, only Iceland and Spain used "autism" as a category to report statistics on special needs education (Organisation for Economic Co-operation and Development [OECD], 1995). By 2005, Spain no longer used the category, but many other countries have since introduced autism as a category to report statistics, among them the Czech Republic, Germany, Greece, Hungary, Korea, Poland, the Slovak Republic, Turkey, and the United States (OECD, 2005, p. 147). Available statistics illustrate that categories so deeply embedded in their respective education systems are not necessarily representing the same target groups. Although the statistics provided by the United States report 0.2% of the school population to be in this category, only 0.002% are identified as autistic in Poland or Turkey (OECD, 2005, p. 73). The cross-national work done by the OECD to improve the comparability of national educational statistics on children with disabilities, difficulties, or disadvantages illustrates the difficulty of comparing such embedded categories. These existing categories tell us more about the systems, the professionals working in them, and the influence of advocacy groups than they tell us about the educational needs or problems of certain groups of children.

Today, a certain dissatisfaction and disappointment with the paradigm of conceptualizing disability by using a certain set of one-dimensional categories is apparent, especially in education systems. This model cannot respond to the policy concerns that education systems and the international community face today. As Kuhn (1970, p. 37) states, "A paradigm can, for that matter, even insulate the community from those socially important problems that are not reducible to the puzzle form, because they cannot be stated in terms of the conceptual and instrumental tools the paradigm supplies." There is today not only a need to develop a sound methodology to analyze and disaggregate disability categories in education systems, but also a need to develop alternative ways of classifying—not only to describe the target group, but also to organize educational programs and services. It is therefore not surprising that the discussion on cross-categorical or noncategorical approaches to conceptualizing disability has gained momentum.

BEYOND CATEGORICAL APPROACHES

Due to their embeddedness in local practice and policy, today's disability categories and classification methods cannot be compared cross-nationally. The circular thinking behind their application supports collaboration and facilitates educational choices, but it ultimately makes the meaning of disability categories difficult to understand if taken out of context. Today, it is widely accepted that disability categories are the product of social processes—focal points to organize our thoughts or aggregates to understand complex phenomena. Shifts in conceptualizations of disability usually result in reallocations of resources.

Presently, there is little known about how such shifts affect the efficiency and effectiveness of school systems and if they lead to an increase or decrease in social justice or equity (see OECD, 2003; and Riddell, Chapter 8). Sometimes, being identified as belonging to a category and thus receiving additional resources may also mean discrimination and exclusion. This is especially true for high-incidence disability, where different labels such as dyslexia, learning disability, dyscalculia, or behavior problems may be used to describe children with similar characteristics. The process of allocating children to disability categories and thereby to specific programs and interventions is shaped by social perception and contextual factors. When family background and race are relevant factors in being allocated to specific disability categories, factors other than health problems must be at work as well.

Faced with the overwhelming evidence that categorical approaches are not adequate, especially to conceptualize high-incidence disabilities, some countries have moved away from labeling this group or have changed their service provision to offer cross-categorical programs and modes of service delivery. In England and Wales, for example, the new Code of Practice (Department for Education and Skills [DfES], 2001) distinguishes only two groups of children across four areas of need, namely children with a statutory assessment (low-incidence disabilities) and children who do not need to be formally diagnosed (high-incidence disabilities). More recently, the Common Assessment Framework (CAF)

(DfES, 2006; and Wedell, Chapter 4) adopts a noncategorical approach to understanding special needs and concentrates on the development of the child (health; emotional and social development; behavioral development; identity, including self-esteem, self-image, and social presentation; family and social relationships; self-care skills and independence; learning), on parenting, and on family and environmental factors. The CAF defines children with complex needs as follows: "Of those children with additional needs, a small proportion have more significant or complex needs which meet the threshold for statutory involvement." This group includes children with disabilities but also young offenders or children in care (DfES, 2006, p. 2). Services, procedures, and conceptualizations of needs are based on a cross-categorical approach in which categorical thinking is still present, but is no longer predominantly guiding the assessment procedure and service delivery. The move away from categorical approaches can also be observed in teacher training. Many countries, such as Switzerland, use a cross-categorical approach to teacher programs or teacher certification to serve children with high-incidence disabilities, whereas a categorical approach is maintained for teachers for children with low-incidence disabilities such as visual or hearing impairment. Such approaches designed to meet the needs of students with high-incidence disabilities provide local schools with extra flexibility in hiring of teachers and placement of students (for an overview, see Sabornie, Evans, & Cullinan, 2006).

Whereas noncategorical approaches for designing programs for children with special needs, for simplifying administrative procedures, and for understanding complex health and education needs have been debated for the last twenty years, the discussion about the actual abolishment of disability categories in education systems is more recent. The movement argues, rightly, that diagnosis cannot inform educational practice because the actual level of functioning of the individual child is more relevant and, additionally, contextual factors play an important role in facilitating or hindering learning, communication, interaction, mobility, or self-care. Truscott, Catanese, and Abrams (2005) suggest that the number of categories currently used in the United States should be reduced from thirteen to three and that the special education classification process adopt a three-tier model, using an "assessment for intervention" rather than an "assessment for determining labels" approach (see Speece, Chapter 14, for an example of assessment for intervention). Naturally, assessment procedures would be more closely linked to the variables of the "didactic triangle," and especially to the content of education.

Disability advocates have claimed that traditional education systems and their practice of categorizing children is mainly a system of oppression and selection (Oliver, 1990). More recently, disability studies and educational research have been integrated to provide a new perspective on problems such as social justice and discrimination embedded in educational practice (Gabel, 2005). Generally today, more attention is given to the characteristics of the environment than to the characteristics of the child. It is claimed that education systems should accept difference as normal and assume responsibility to provide equitable and high-quality education for all children irrespective of their health or social status (see, e.g., United Nations Educational, Scientific and Cultural Organization [UNESCO], 2000). But despite these developments, categorical approaches to disabilities and difficulties are still deeply embedded in education systems and still guide professionals in understanding underlying causes as originating in student characteristics that exist independent of classroom processes.

APPROACHES TO DEVELOP INDICATORS RELEVANT TO SPECIAL NEEDS EDUCATION

International Conceptualizations

As a result of the historical shifts in conceptualizing disability in health and education, functional health and the quality of the educational provision has come into sharp focus. Traditionally, education systems are judged against the performance of their students, the quality of the environment they provide for learners, and the relevance of the curriculum or teaching content for society. There is a growing awareness that the level of embeddedness needs to be taken into account when attempting to analyze the significance of categories. Student characteristics are no longer perceived as independent factors but recognized as a consequence of the interaction between student and his or her environment. This is also the case for disabilities. Today, the requirement for a more comprehensive approach is acknowledged. Social factors such as poverty are taken into account when defining disability and student achievement is not considered independent of school factors. More comprehensive approaches can help avoid circular reasoning and simplistic notions as to the reasons why students with certain characteristics (disability, migrant background, gender) are more likely to have special needs in educational systems. Some characteristics may give rise to difficulties and their consequences, yet special educational needs are to some extent the creation of the education system. The interactions and the diverse aspects of the education systems and students are immeasurably complex. The inclination to make things easier and develop a few relevant indicators is irresistible. So, how have international organizations dealt with this problematic issue? What understanding have they developed of disability or special educational needs and which cross-national classification system or conceptualization have they employed? Which level of embeddedness do they focus upon— representation of individual practice, depiction of school organization, or portrayal of policies?

The United Nations Children's Fund (UNICEF) uses the "Ten Questions" procedure (Durkin et al., 1994; Zaman et al., 1990) to conceptualize child disability in an optional module of the Multiple Indicator Cluster Survey (MICS; www.childinfo.org/mics). The MICS is a household survey program, developed to help countries filling data gaps for monitoring the situation of women and children. The questionnaires and the appropriate methodology are made available to the countries that collect the data. The Ten Questions focus mainly on observable behavior, such as developmental delays in sitting, standing, walking; problems with seeing, hearing, understanding parents; difficulties in moving arms or legs; and loss of consciousness. Other problems include lack of ability to learn, speak, or name objects. Some of these observable behaviors are clearly linked to impairments (seeing, hearing, muscle movement, language production or reception), some to health conditions (epilepsy), and some to actual problems with activities required or desired for everyday living (walking, learning). The information is collected at the individual level outside schools and therefore not directly linked to educational factors. Preliminary analysis (Grieger & Martinho, 2006) reveals the difficulty of applying the questionnaire to young children. In some countries, the reported frequency of developmental delays and other problems for children under the age of three was as high as 100% (mainly owing to the "talking" item). Furthermore, differences in the results between age groups and countries are extreme (ranging from almost 0% in Sierra Leone, and 20% in Iran to more than 80% in Cameroon, and almost 100% in Madagascar). Sierra Leone differs from other countries as it obtains responses on a single rather than ten items, and uses the term "disability." Analyses are planned to include comparisons of disabled versus nondisabled children associated with immunization, recent illnesses, socioeconomic status, and level of nutrition, to specify but a few (Loaiza, 2005). Analysis into the type and severity of disability and the participation of children in activities of everyday life (including education) are also intended.

The approach to conceptualizing disability used by UNICEF represents a combination of categorical and noncategorical methods and assumes a clinical perspective (capturing relevant characteristics of the child). A similar methodology using five questions as a screener to identify children with special health needs (the Children With Special Health Care Needs [CSHCN] instrument developed by Bethell et al., 2002) has been successfully employed in recent surveys in the United States. The noncategorical approach brings together different characteristics of the child and his or her environment (in the case of CSHCN) that can be aggregated according to purpose or used individually.

Unlike the CSHCN, the MICS is administered in diverse cultural settings where little formal knowledge of categorization systems or disability can be assumed. The information collected is therefore not embedded in a clinical practice or tradition and responses may be dependent on situational factors (training of interviewer, social acceptability of response, developmental stage of the child). Additionally, the information collected is not embedded in a specific education system. It is assumed that information on special educational resources and the organization of services is not relevant because such services are not available to a substantial proportion of the population in developing countries. The household questionnaire administered as part of the MICS includes questions on participation at different levels of schooling. Nevertheless, it can be assumed that bias in responding and the high rate of "disabilities" identified will make it difficult to make any reliable statements on the quality of education for children with disabilities.

The OECD has approached the problem in a different way. In the main, Western countries collect data on health and disability according to their particular standards and methodology. None consider applying the "Ten Questions" to identify childhood disability. Available data at the national level are usually generated by different policy areas and represent benefits or services provided by a specific province of administration representing persons with certain characteristics. Data on disability generated by health policies or by insurance institutions cannot be used in education systems. Because education systems invest additional resources for children with special needs or disabilities, relevant organizations generally gather information on the services provided. The OECD's task was to make this information more comparable and use it to generate indicators on the performance of education systems. Because most countries customarily take a categorical approach to understanding disability, the OECD first analyzed national disability categories or categories of special needs to develop a common denominator by which they could be made comparable. Three cross-national categories were defined and countries were invited to allocate their national categories among them. These cross-national categories are described in detail by Ebersold and Evans in Chapter 3.

The creation of three cross-national categories enables a systematic aggregation of national categories. It eliminates the artificial differences that arise from different methods to classify multiple handicaps (cross-national category A) and from different conceptualizations used to describe high-incidence disabilities (cross-national category B). As Ebersold and Evans make clear, these categories do not represent clinical samples of students, but rather students receiving special or additional services in different settings made available by the education system. In other words, they do not represent prevalence data, but administrative data on services provided in a specific policy area. The categorization system developed by the OECD is based on the assumption that generally a specific reason why children receive additional resources can be identified. This categorical approach is valid because most education systems categorize their students on the same premise. Education systems recognize and are able to react to such a categorization system. Nevertheless, while it captures the reality of current policies, it does not accurately represent the complex interplay of different factors that determine why a specific student receives a particular intervention. In addition, cross-national categories A, B, and C should not be considered as exclusive categories; they are more like three different perspectives (biological, psychological, and social) relevant to understanding educational difficulties. It has been pointed out that education systems tend to be biased when allocating students to categories, leading, for example, to an over-representation of disadvantaged students (cross-national category C) in educational programs for learning disabled or emotionally disturbed students (cross-national category B). This is a major policy concern that unfortunately cannot be addressed with the data and methodology available at the international level. We do not know if children are identified in a way that provides them with adequate support. A comparative analysis of information on students and educational programs would be necessary to judge the adequacy of the intervention and to identify unmet needs.

The UNICEF and OECD have chosen different strategies to tackle the problem of developing cross-national comparisons to identify the participation of students with special educational needs in education systems. UNICEF has operated at the micro level and OECD at the macro education level. Both approaches are based on good rationales, and previously available information. If the two approaches could be combined and integrated, a new perspective could possibly be developed for cross-national comparisons. In the next section, a classification of possible elements and a methodology to bring together clinical, educational, organizational, and policy-related information is presented.

Dimensions of a Possible Classification System
for Cross-National Comparisons

Special needs education has undergone major shifts in conceptualizing disability and in conceptualizing measures of support to match the special educational needs of children. We are now at a point where we can integrate these perspectives and develop a common framework. Such a classification and indicator system would be able comprehensibly to relate relevant student characteristics (e.g., blindness, achievement) to environment (e.g., availability of specialists) and content (e.g., individual educational programs). Systems of quality indicators were developed some time ago and successfully tested in various countries. They propose a framework and a set of variables to conceptualize opportunity to learn standards (environment), curriculum content standards (content), as well as student performance standards (student characteristics; Peters, Johnstone, & Ferguson, 2005; Ravitch, 1995; Ysseldyke et al., 1998). The WHO has provided a framework for a noncategorical, multidimensional approach to disability called the *International Classification of Functioning, Disability and Health* (WHO, 2001, p. 10f). Some of its components can be systematically linked to these educational indicators:

1. *Activities:* An activity is the execution of a task or action by an individual. It describes the capacity or the highest probable level of functioning that a person may reach in a given domain at a given moment. The capacity construct can be linked to student achievement (reading, calculating, solving problems)—assuming that such instruments do really measure the true ability of a child (student performance standards). It also represents nonacademic abilities, for example, in the domains "self-care" and "mobility."

2. *Participation:* Participation is involvement in a life situation. In education, "participation domains" are defined by the (official and hidden) curriculum. Children may receive additional resources to ensure their participation or the expectation that they will participate in school life may be altered (individual educational plans). Thus, participation domains defined by schools are closely linked to content or educational programs (curriculum content standards). Participation can be understood as the lived experience of people in the actual context in which they live. This context includes the environmental factors.

3. *Environmental Factors:* Environmental factors make up the physical, social, and attitudinal environment in which people live and conduct their lives. The school environment (opportunities to learn

standards) influences participation opportunities for students and their access to the curriculum. It can compensate for functional limitations and ensure that educational goals are systematically pursued and reached or it can create difficulties and act as a barrier to learning if it does not adequately meet the needs of students. The ICF also includes a classification of body functions and structures (impairments, physiological and psychological functional problems) as well as personal factors (e.g., sex, age, socioeconomic status). Both can have a strong impact on the individual's ability to learn, communicate, and interact in education systems.

The development of such a comprehensive system of indicators is a long-term project and does not meet the immediate needs to understand today's conceptualizations and classifications of disability in education systems. A more analytical rather than a comprehensive approach is needed to understand the different levels of embeddedness and the process by which disability categories or categories of special needs are created and applied. There is broad consensus and overwhelming evidence that one-dimensional, categorical conceptualizations of disability as attributes of individuals are no longer helpful in understanding how to improve education systems and educational services, especially for students with high-incidence disabilities. Education systems need to acknowledge that interactions at different levels (micro, meso, macro) may be involved in this process, which involves (1) identification of problem (diagnosis), (2) development of an understanding of the problem (assessment), (3) resolution of a problem (assignment), (4) delivery of a possible solution (intervention), and (5) determination of the effect of the intervention (evaluation). The following matrix can be used to analyze the usage of different disability categories or types of problems:

	Diagnosis	Assessment	Assignment	Intervention	Evaluation
Policy perspective					
Organizational perspective					
Educational perspective					
Clinical perspective					

For example, "free school meals" is an important indicator for poverty in the United Kingdom. Free school meals can be understood as an intervention at the organizational level (schools) but targeted at a specific group of children. A recent report prepared by the Joseph Rowntree Foundation (Palmer, Carr, & Kenway, 2005) indicates that 40% of eleven-year-old students receiving free school meals fail to reach basic literacy standards, at twice the rate for other children (clinical level). The report also demonstrates that half of all children eligible for free school meals are concentrated in 20% of the schools—thus demonstrating a problem at the school level rather than only at the individual level. A concentration of poor children will require other interventions besides free school meals. It is anticipated that a variety of children will receive special educational support. Yet little is known about students' characteristics (other than low achievement). It may be relevant to collect and systematically link all the available information at different levels of the education system to improve understanding as to how children who receive free meals are perceived by the education system and what other interventions are necessary to help them overcome the difficulties of poverty.

Neither poverty nor free school meals are appropriate categories to conceptualize educational inequality in Switzerland, where students traditionally go home for lunch. The results of the Programme for International Student Assessment (PISA), conducted in the year 2000 (OECD, 2001), alarmed the Swiss education system. The problem was identified at the policy level when migrant children (clinical perspective) were discovered as performing at a much lower level than children from Swiss families. An exhaustive analysis (Coradi Vellacott, Hollenweger, Nicolet, & Wolter, 2003) revealed that a complex interaction of different factors, such as a high percentage of migrant children who additionally came from impoverished backgrounds and did not speak the language of instruction (clinical level), were vulnerable. The high percentage of migrants in the school population and disproportionate proportion of schools with over 50% migrants (organizational level) as well as a tendency of the school system to favor segregation (policy level) accounted for the considerable disparity in achievement.

In Switzerland, at present, assignment of special educational resources focuses on the identification of individual problems. In the case of migrant children, teachers identified problems and referred children to be assessed by the school psychologist. Thus, migration was essentially treated the same way as, for example, dyslexia. Notwithstanding other types of information (e.g., composition of the school), students were allocated to individual educational support (e.g., special classes for the learning disabled). In the Canton of Zurich, a major policy change will be implemented as a component of a new law on public education. In the future, the initial diagnosis may still be prepared by the regular teacher (educational level), but in the case of high-incidence disabilities, the assessment and analysis of the problem will be prepared jointly and the allocation of resources or assignment will be based on a consensus-oriented roundtable conference by all parties concerned.

Changes in special needs education policy essentially seek to implement an efficient and equitable way of establishing and responding when children experience difficulties in learning. The introduction of a more coherent, internationally comparable system may help us understand better the complex interactions between the learner and his or her environment. Recent policy shifts indicate a general move away from clinical to educational and organizational levels to guide the process of assessment, service provision, and evaluation. For example, the introduction of the *Special Educational Needs: Code of Practice* (DfES, 2001) or more recently the Common Assessment Framework (CAF; DfES, 2006) in England and Wales aims at making the assessment process more transparent and especially adequate for all involved. It remains to be seen whether these policy changes will achieve an improvement in service provision and outcomes.

Methodological Issues and a Possible Way Forward

Nevertheless, to propose systems of indicators and variables as well as a possible matrix to analyze processes of allocation and service provision is insufficient to chart a possible way forward. In conclusion, a few observations are warranted. A possible methodology for analyzing and comparing present practice in diagnosis, assessment for educational needs, assignment and delivery of interventions, as well as their evaluation, was outlined in the last section. Through this approach, the cross-national communication and understanding of country-specific conceptualizations and interventions may become readily available for international comparisons. This may facilitate better understanding, for example, as to why the United States reports higher incidences of children with autism than Poland or why special schools for the learning disabled are still tolerable in Switzerland but not in Italy.

It was argued earlier that disability categories or categories of special educational needs are deeply embedded in education systems and therefore do not lend themselves easily to international comparisons. A first step to overcome this challenge, therefore, would be to try to establish a methodology to cross-walk between clinical, educational, organizational, and administrative conceptualizations associated with disability or with special educational needs. There are two approaches that could be adopted: (1) begin with the entire school population or (2) begin with a specific category that is deeply embedded in the education system (e.g., learning disability). In both cases, the objective is to understand how characteristics of individual children relate to educational programs, organizational arrangements, and policy guidelines. Additionally, an analysis could be made as to what type of information is available and at what level. For example, in Switzerland, special schools are often unacquainted with exact clinical information (e.g., medical diagnosis) and do not assemble information on specific therapies provided to individual students. In regular schools, much more information is available on therapies provided to specific students, but currently no outcome data on the success rate of such interventions are gathered. Systems tend to collect information relevant for the distribution of resources but less systematically information important for an understanding of student outcome.

A further step toward generating cross-nationally comparable data on educational provision for children identified as having special educational needs would be the application of an internationally accepted classification system to conceptualize disability and functioning in education systems. The WHO has developed a framework classification based on a noncategorical approach to disability (ICF) that can be used for this purpose. But this classification is made up of over 1,400 items, and research is needed to identify the items that are relevant to education systems. More work is needed to develop and implement a short list of items—similar to the Ten Questions—that countries could use as part of their data collection exercise to represent disability in their educational data sets independently of their assessment procedures or the organization of their provision. The inclusion or addition of such a set of items related to functioning can only be successful if, at the same time, international standards are developed on the applications of such a list. Otherwise, the outcome may be similar to that of the UNICEF study, in which identification rates vary as a function of the interrogator rather than children's functioning. Guidelines on how to link existing measurements or a teacher's observation to individual items of the ICF need to be developed and tested. It is evident that the inclusion of functional data, including information on problems with body functions, is the key to linking health-related data to information relevant to the education of all children.

Finally, much more cooperative research will be an indispensable factor in better understanding these complex interactions associated with special needs, to develop new internationally agreed-upon indicators that are able to link educational practice, different organizational arrangements, and policy frameworks to student participation in education systems and academic as well as nonacademic outcomes.

NOTE

The preparation of this paper was supported by EC-Contract Number SP24-CT-2004–513708 (MHADIE)–thematic priority SSP.

REFERENCES

Bethell, C. D., Read, D., Stein, R. E., Blumberg, S. J., Wells, N., & Newacheck, P. W. (2002). Identifying children with special health care needs: Development and evaluation of a short screening instrument. *Ambulatory Pediatrics, 2*(1), 38–48.

Comenius, J. A. (1967). *The great didactic* (M. W. Keatinge, Ed. & Trans.). New York: Russell & Russell. (Original work published 1896)

Coradi Vellacott, M., Hollenweger, J., Nicolet, M., & Wolter, S. (2003). *Soziale integration und leistungsförderung.* Neuchatel: Bundesamt für Statistik.

Department for Education and Skills. (2001). *Special educational needs: Code of practice.* London: Author.

Department for Education and Skills. (2006). *Common Assessment Framework for children and young people: Managers' guide.* London: Author.

Department of Education and Science. (2001). *Educational provision and support for persons with autistic spectrum disorders: The report of the Task Force on Autism.* Dublin, Ireland: Author. Retrieved October 1, 2006, from http://www.education.ie/servlet/blobservlet/sped_autism.pdf

Department of Education and Science. (2006). *An evaluation of educational provision for children with autistic spectrum disorders: A report by the inspectorate of the Department of Education and Science.* Dublin, Ireland: Author.

Durkin, M. S., Davidson, L. L., Desai, P., Hasan, Z. M., Khan, N., Shrout, P. E., et al. (1994). Validity of the Ten Questions screen for childhood disability: Results from population-based studies in Bangladesh, Jamaica, and Pakistan. *Epidemiology, 5*(3), 283–289.

Gabel, S. L. (2005). *Disability studies in education: Readings in theory and method.* New York: Peter Lang.

Grieger, L., & Martinho, M. (2006). The effects of questionnaire design and survey methodology on child disability measurement: Evidence from the Multiple Indicator Cluster Survey II. Retrieved October 1, 2006, from http://paa2006.princeton.edu/download.aspx?submissionId=60840

Karnosh, L. J., & Gage, E. B. (1944). *Psychiatry for nurses* (2nd ed.). St. Louis, MO: C. V. Mosby.

Kauffman, J. M., & Hallahan, D. P. (1995). *The illusion of full inclusion: A comprehensive critique of the current special education bandwagon.* Austin, TX: Pro-Ed.

Kuhn, T. (1970). *The structure of scientific revolution.* Chicago: University of Chicago Press.

Loaiza, E. (2005). *Measuring children's disability via household surveys: The MICS experience.* Retrieved October 1, 2006, from http://paa2005.princeton.edu/download.aspx?submissionId=51417

Luckasson, R., Borthwick-Duffy, S., Buntinx, W. H. E., Coulter, D. L., Craig, E. M., Reeve, A., et al. (2002). *Mental retardation: Definition, classification, and systems of supports* (10th ed.). Washington, DC: American Association on Mental Retardation.

Oliver, M. (1990). *The politics of disablement.* Basingstoke, UK: Macmillan.

Organisation for Economic Co-operation and Development. (1995). *Integrating students with special needs into mainstream schools.* Paris: Author.

Organisation for Economic Co-operation and Development. (2001). *Knowledge and skills for life: First results from PISA 2000.* Paris: Author.

Organisation for Economic Co-operation and Development. (2003). *Education policy analysis.* Paris: Author.

Organisation for Economic Co-operation and Development. (2005). *Students with disabilities, learning difficulties and disadvantages: Statistics and indicators.* Paris: Author.

Palmer, G., Carr, J., & Kenway, P. (2005). *Monitoring poverty and social exclusion.* York, UK: Joseph Rowntree Foundation.

Peters, S., Johnstone, C., & Ferguson, P. (2005). A disability rights in education model: For evaluating inclusive education. *International Journal of Inclusive Education, 9*(2), 139–160.

Ravitch, D. (1995). *National standards in American education: A citizen's guide.* Washington, DC: Brookings Institution Press.

Richardson, J. G., & Parker, T. L. (1993). The institutional genesis of special education: The American case. *American Journal of Education, 101*(4), 359–392.

Sabornie, E. J., Evans, C., & Cullinan, D. (2006). Comparing characteristics of high-incidence disability groups: A descriptive review. *Remedial and Special Education, 27*(2), 95–104.

Slee, R. (2001). Social justice and the changing directions of educational research: A case for inclusive education. *International Journal for Inclusive Education, 5*(2/3), 167–177.

Truscott, S. D., Catanese, A. M., & Abrams, L. M. (2005). The evolving context of special education classification in the United States. *School Psychology International, 26*(2), 162–177.

United Nations Educational, Scientific and Cultural Organization. (2000). *Dakar framework for action. Education for all: Meeting our collective commitments.* Paris: Author.

World Health Organization. (1980). *International classification of impairments, disabilities and handicaps.* Geneva, Switzerland: Author.

World Health Organization. (1996). *Multiaxial classification of child and adolescent psychiatric disorders: The ICD-10 classification of mental and behavioural disorders in children and adolescents.* Cambridge, UK: Cambridge University Press.

World Health Organization. (2001). *International classification of functioning, disability and health.* Geneva, Switzerland: Author.

Ysseldyke, J., Krentz, J., Elliott, J., Thurlow, M. L., Erickson, R., & Moore, M. L. (1998). *NCEO framework for educational accountability.* Minneapolis: University of Minnesota, National Center on Educational Outcomes. Retrieved November 10, 2006, from http://education.umn.edu/NCEO/OnlinePubs/Framework/FrameworkText.html

Zaman, S. S., Khan, N. Z., Islam, S., Banu, S., Dixit, S., Shrout, P., & Durkin, M. (1990). Validity of the "Ten Questions" for screening serious childhood disability: Results from urban Bangladesh. *International Journal of Epidemiology, 19*(3), 613–620.

3 A Supply-Side Approach for a Resource-Based Classification System

Serge Ebersold and Peter Evans

INTRODUCTION

The United Nations Convention on the Rights of Persons with Disabilities (2006)[1] requires states to collect appropriate statistical and research data enabling them to implement inclusive policies and have effective measures between and among the states.[2] Thus, gathering statistics on students with special needs and developing comparable indicators of education systems are of rapidly growing importance. The developing knowledge society requires data enabling administrators and schools to plan for promoting effective and equitable rights to education. The knowledge society links social cohesion and social justice with quality assurance and institutions are expected to secure opportunities for the participation of individuals by avoiding any form of discrimination and through involving them in all dimensions of the educational process. Now, rather than teaching to the mean, schools are expected to cope with diversity and to meet each student's needs in order to enable them to be successful. Having reliable and comparable data will assist administrators and schools to monitor the educational process, to improve its quality, and to ensure students' access to rights.

The *International Standard Classification of Education* (ISCED; United Nations Educational, Scientific and Cultural Organization [UNESCO], 1997) also requires reliable and comparable data. The original version of the classification, dating from the 1970s, defined special education as the education provided in special schools. It ignored, therefore, both theory and practice developed in many countries intended to facilitate mainstream education for students with disabilities. Such a restricted definition limits the demands for obtaining valid and reliable data in this area. Thus, the most recent version of ISCED replaces the term "special education" with the term "special needs education." This change recognizes the increasing access of students with disabilities to regular settings instead of special settings and, alongside theoretical work on these issues, separates the concepts of disability and impairment. In addition, it goes beyond those who may be covered by categories of disability by extending the concept of students with special educational needs to all those who are failing in school for a wide variety of other reasons that are known to be likely to impede a child's optimal progress (UNESCO, 1997).

The separation of the concepts of disability[3] and impairment is rooted in an approach relating disability, in contrast to impairment, to the quality of education and support as well as the ability of the schools to create an enabling and stimulating environment for the pupils. Indeed, the definition indicates that "Whether or not this more broadly defined group of children are in need of additional support depends on the extent to which schools are able to adapt their curriculum, teaching, and organization and/or to provide additional human or material resources so as to stimulate efficient and effective learning for these pupils" (UNESCO, 1997). Such a definition focuses on the impact of legal frameworks in encouraging policies toward inclusion. It refers to the educational restrictions students have to face, to the modes of funding, and to the ability to create equitable education systems. It relates the need for additional resources to a lack of adaptability of the school's curriculum, to the necessity for additional human or material resources to stimulate effective and efficient learning for these pupils. Other relevant issues include a lack of trained teachers and assistants, a lack of continuity between the different levels within the school systems, a lack of cooperation between the school system and families, and so on. By relating disability to the quality of systems, it links the whole concept of disability to system change and the need to monitor policies and systems to assist in bringing this about. For instance, being able to monitor laws for compliance is a key issue, to implement consistently and appropriately the legal decisions made in order to make society more accessible and increase inclusion opportunities. Being able to monitor the implementation of individual program planning, operationalizing cooperation with the school's environment, and the transition processes within and from the school system are key issues in assuring quality education for all.

Thus, both the requirements of the knowledge society and the new ISCED definition, reinforced by the UN convention, put disability issues firmly into the camp of effectiveness and equity. By focusing on additional resources, they link students' difficulties and social inequalities to schools' ability to give all students the same chance of progressing to a particular level in the education system and to achieve successfully in an appropriate learning environment (Rawls, 1971). In addition, they include the opportunities to benefit as equally and as fully as possible from social, economic, and professional opportunities enabled by education (Brighouse, 2000; Evans, 2001).

Such a shift suggests that having impairment does not necessarily mean that there is a special need or therefore a requirement for additional resources. In contrast, having a special need does not necessarily imply the presence of impairment. This shift accepts that descriptive categories derived from a medical classification have a limited educational utility for teachers and education policymakers. Medically based categories have only partial implications for the development of teaching programs that inevitably have to take the whole child into account. Furthermore, they do not stress the requirement for additional resources to help students access the curriculum. Moreover, such a shift carries with it a requirement to take an educational policy perspective and to analyze practices in the context of a resource-based approach focusing on schools' ability to meet educational needs and thus facilitating access to employment and social participation.

A RESOURCE-BASED APPROACH FROM A COMPARATIVE PERSPECTIVE

A resource-based approach to special needs education, as given in ISCED (UNESCO, 1997), presents a number of difficulties with regard to data reliability at the international level. First, the term "special needs education" means different things in different countries. In some, it covers only children with traditional disabilities, whereas in others it includes a broader range of students, covering, for instance, disability, learning difficulty, and disadvantage. In other countries, the term "special needs education" reflects essentially a noncategorical perspective avoiding any distinction due to impairment, to a learning difficulty, or to a social disadvantage. Second, because of the wide variations in the definitions of disability and learning difficulty that are in use, the extent to which quantitative estimates for any particular category from different countries are comparable remains unclear. For example, the definition of visual impairment differs widely between Belgium, France, and New Brunswick (Canada). In Belgium, visual impairment results in a referral to a type of education that is "organized for blind or visually-impaired children who regularly need medical or paramedical treatment and/or special teaching materials." In New Brunswick (Canada), a visual impairment is referred to as a physical disability and related to "handicapped students who, because of physically challenging conditions, require mobility assistance or adaptation to the physical environment and/or personal care." Finally, in France a visual impairment is linked with a medical classification. Blindness is defined as a "serious sensory impairment" that may be "marked (very poor vision or partial blindness), almost total (severe or almost total blindness), or total (no perception of light). It may affect one eye or both." Partially sighted students suffer from "astigmatism, accommodation deficiency, diplopia (strabismus), amblyopia, and sensitivity to light."

These diverse definitions of special needs and disability may lead to significant discrepancies in data provided by various countries. Depending on the country's approach to the term "special needs" and the interest given to a type of difficulty, the number of students registered as having a difficulty may vary considerably. For example, New Brunswick (Canada) recognizes proportionally 2,720 times more students with emotional and behavioral difficulties (2.72%) than Turkey (0.001%). The different definitions of disability may also impact the number of students registered by a country, though these differences do not reflect a higher proportion of students having impairment. For instance, Poland (0.215%) registers 43 times more students who are blind and partially sighted than Greece (0.005%), and Belgium (Flanders; 0.343%) registers 343 times as many students with physical disabilities as Italy (0.001%). These diverse definitions may also lead students with similar impairments to experience different education opportunities from one country to another. For instance, in some they may be educated in regular classes, whereas in others they may be fully segregated from mainstream education. As may be seen in Figure 3.1, students with emotional and/or behavioral difficulties are fully included in regular classes in New Brunswick (Canada), whereas they are mostly schooled in special classes in Japan and registered in special schools in Belgium (Fl.).

Although all countries do not share the same definition of disability or the same understanding of the term "special needs," they all provide additional resources to help students with disabilities, difficulties, and

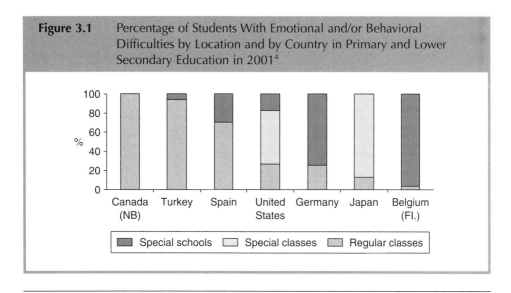

Figure 3.1 Percentage of Students With Emotional and/or Behavioral Difficulties by Location and by Country in Primary and Lower Secondary Education in 2001[4]

SOURCE: OECD, 2005.

disadvantages access the curriculum and benefit as fully as possible from education. These additional resources can be of many kinds. They can be personnel resources, such as a more favorable teacher/student ratio than that found in a regular classroom where no allowance is being made for students with special needs; additional teachers, assistants, or any other personnel (for some or all of the time); or training programs for teachers and others that equip them for work in special needs education. They can also be material resources comprising, for instance, aids or supports of various types (e.g., hearing aids), modifications or adaptations to classrooms, and specialized teaching materials. Finally, they can be financial resources, including, for example, funding formulas that are more favorable to those with special needs (including classes where it is known or assumed that there are students with special needs), systems where money is set aside for special educational needs within the regular budget allocation, or payments made in support of special needs education and the costs of personnel and material resources.

Focusing on the additional public and/or private resources provided to support special needs education helps to overcome the different definitions of special needs education that operate within countries and provides a means to identify and include all students for whom extra provision is made in order to help them make progress through the school curriculum. It offers a common comparison level between the different countries. It allows for the broadest possible numbers of students to be included, brings together students with learning difficulties with very different causes, and is not dependent on idiosyncratic categorical descriptions. Furthermore, it reduces the weight of the historical national conditions that may have led to national categorization systems. Therefore, the Organisation for Economic Co-operation and Development (OECD), in discussion with its member countries, determined that "those with special educational needs are defined by the additional public and/or private resources provided to support their education" (OECD, 2005).

Although the additional resources supplied provide a practical means of identifying the wider envelope of special needs students who are receiving additional support, it is at the same time clear that students are included in this definition for different reasons. Students with disabilities may have very different types of problems in accessing the curriculum compared with students with disadvantages, and their problems may have very different causes. Furthermore, resources provided for the different groups may be conditioned by different policies. In order not to lose sight of these differences and their significant policy implications, it becomes necessary to subdivide those covered under the additional resources definition in a relevant way. It was agreed that this could be done by a cross-national tripartite categorization system based on perceived causes of difficulty in accessing the regular curriculum and the type of needs that have to be met. This cross-national tripartite categorization system distinguishes the students according to the educational need for which resources are given and differentiates students with disabilities (category A) from those having learning difficulties (category B) and those having disadvantages (category C).

Cross-national category A refers to students with disabilities or impairments viewed in medical terms as organic disorders attributable to organic pathologies (e.g., in relation to sensory, motor, or neurological defects). The educational need is considered to arise primarily from problems attributable to these disabilities.

Cross-national category B refers to students with behavioral or emotional disorders, or specific difficulties in learning. The educational need is considered to arise primarily from problems in the interaction between the student and the educational context.

Cross-national category C refers to students with disadvantages arising primarily from socioeconomic, cultural, and/or linguistic factors. The educational need is to compensate for the disadvantages attributable to these factors.

This cross-national tripartite categorization provides a supply-side approach based on countries' own identification of those students who are perceived to need additional provision to offset or compensate for various difficulties in accessing the curriculum. In order to achieve this, countries were asked to reclassify their data into this "A-B-C" framework based on the classification and data collection arrangements used in their own national system via the operational definitions provided. The resulting reclassifications were then agreed to by all countries in a series of subsequent meetings.

A RESOURCE-BASED APPROACH FOR POLICY MONITORING

Based on the availability of resources to support students' education rather than individuals' impairment or difficulties, this categorization system offers an analytical framework enabling a policy-making perspective. Such a view reflects the availability of resources to support students' needs within the countries and, therefore, their tendency to practice positive discrimination in recognition of special needs. Even if all countries provide additional resources to students having special needs, however, the extent to which these resources are made available varies among countries. For instance, as shown in Figure 3.2, in the United States 35.5% of students receive additional resources for educational purposes in contrast to 0.56% in Korea or to 1.31% in Japan.

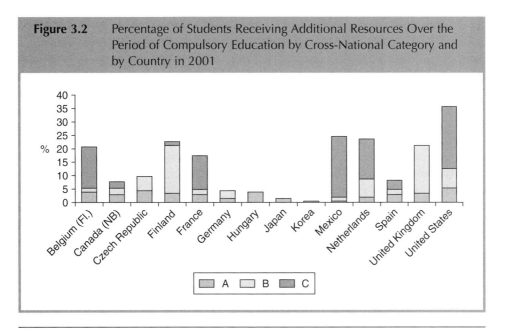

Figure 3.2 Percentage of Students Receiving Additional Resources Over the Period of Compulsory Education by Cross-National Category and by Country in 2001

SOURCE: OECD, 2005.

This categorization system also reflects the modes of distribution of these resources depending on the needs countries are focusing on. Figure 3.2 reveals the substantial differences that may exist among countries in the resource distribution to assist students having special educational needs. In Japan, Korea, and Hungary, students receiving additional resources for educational purposes are exclusively students having an educational need due to a disability (category A). In the United Kingdom and Germany, additional resources for educational purposes are exclusively given for students having a disability (category A) and students having a learning difficulty (category B). These countries differ from those where students receiving additional resources within education policies are mainly students whose educational needs are related to social disadvantage (category C), like the United States (23.9%), Mexico (22.7%), Belgium (15.3%), and France (12.6%).

Data provided by the countries show furthermore that resources are unequally distributed depending on the age of the students. Figure 3.3 reflects the important differences observed in supplying additional resources by stage of education: Students with disabilities receiving additional resources increase in proportion to the school population through preprimary and primary, peaking at lower secondary, before falling away at upper secondary level. This contrasts with the pattern followed by the

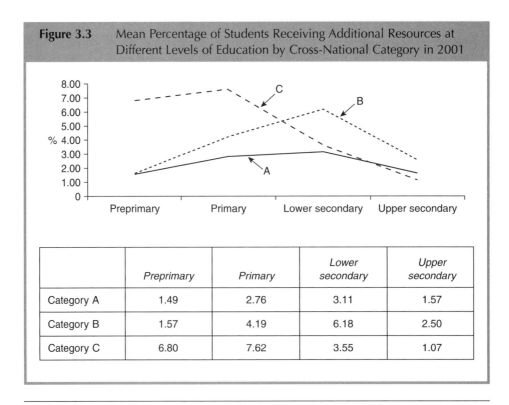

Figure 3.3 Mean Percentage of Students Receiving Additional Resources at Different Levels of Education by Cross-National Category in 2001

	Preprimary	Primary	Lower secondary	Upper secondary
Category A	1.49	2.76	3.11	1.57
Category B	1.57	4.19	6.18	2.50
Category C	6.80	7.62	3.55	1.07

SOURCE: OECD, 2005.

numbers of students with disadvantages: The peak is reached earlier at primary level, then falls successively at lower and upper secondary levels. Such a contrast reveals clearly that fewer additional resources are given to students having a disability at preprimary level than to students having social disadvantages, inviting us therefore to look at the extent to which these resources are given appropriately to students' education.

The decreasing additional resources given to all groups of students at upper secondary level revealed by Figure 3.3 invites a discussion about the cost effectiveness of the distribution of additional resources in terms of access to upper secondary education, to tertiary education, and to employment.

Features of Provision

The resource-based perspective relates also to the existing variation among the countries in regard to the features of provision and the multiple factors favoring or not the inclusion of special education needs (SEN) students. Although the median number of students receiving additional resources for disabilities for the seventeen countries reporting full data is 2.53%, there are huge variations within the countries. Figure 3.4 reveals that the numbers of students falling under category A receiving additional resources varies from 0.47% in Korea to 5.16% in the United States.

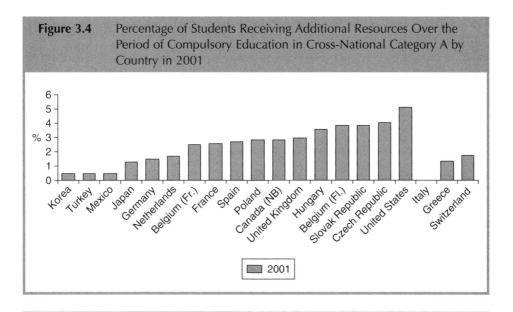

Figure 3.4   Percentage of Students Receiving Additional Resources Over the Period of Compulsory Education in Cross-National Category A by Country in 2001

NOTE: Countries are ranked in ascending order of percentage of students. Greece, Italy, and Switzerland are placed at the right of the chart because of partially missing data. For Italy, regular class data are missing due to a change in legislation on compulsory age range. Data about regular classes are also missing for Greece and Switzerland.

SOURCE: OECD, 2005.

These differences in proportion are not easy to explain. But because it is unlikely that the "organic" bases of disability differ greatly among countries, it seems most likely that the different proportions reflect national differences in policies and modes of allocating additional resources. These differences may therefore be related to the ways chosen by countries to overcome the effects of disabilities especially with regard to policy priorities, conceptualization of disability, identification procedures, educational practices, and comprehensiveness of provision.

Features of Schools With Regard to Place of Education

These data may also reflect the enabling or disabling effect of policies in terms of access to work, of participating in democracy, of acquiring social capital, and, more generally, of avoiding social exclusion. Figure 3.5 reveals that some countries educate all students with disabilities in regular mainstream classes, as is the case in the Canadian province of New Brunswick, whereas others, such as Spain and the United Kingdom, make extensive use of regular classes. These types of provision may be contrasted with the countries preferring to educate students with disabilities in special schools. More than 80% of such students are in special schools in Belgium (Fl.), the Czech Republic, Germany, and the Netherlands. In other countries, extensive use is made of special classes in regular schools, as is the case in France, Japan, Korea, and the United States.

Such differences clearly show that the same type of disabled students may have a quite different experience of schooling among the countries. In some countries they may be included in regular classes and in others in special schools, depending on the national policies followed toward inclusion. These differences may reflect the variation in the extent to which features of regular schools and curriculum, training, and attitudes of teachers facilitate or obstruct inclusion. They may also reveal the features of special schools, especially when they are viewed by parents and educators as desirable.

These differing experiences may lead to different postschool outcomes as well as different inclusion opportunities. Segregated settings provide effectively fewer opportunities than regular settings in many areas of normal life. For instance, for students being educated outside their communities, their opportunities to develop reciprocal friendship relationships may be inhibited. Separating the general public from persons with disabilities in segregated settings will not be likely to help to change attitudes toward disability, to improve employment opportunities, or to secure income and social involvement. Segregated settings also frequently deliver different curricula thereby hindering students' access to postcompulsory education.

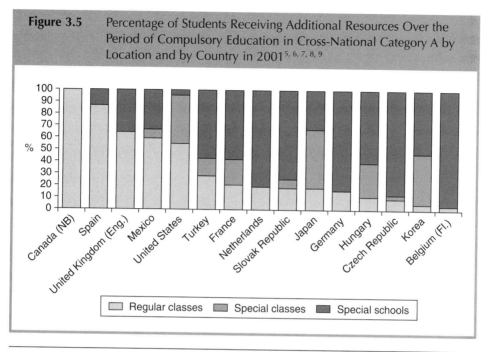

Figure 3.5 Percentage of Students Receiving Additional Resources Over the Period of Compulsory Education in Cross-National Category A by Location and by Country in 2001[5, 6, 7, 8, 9]

SOURCE: OECD, 2005.

Gender Issues

A resource-based approach may also highlight inequalities that may be linked with gender issues and the weight of educational expectations toward boys in contrast with girls. Figure 3.6 shows that in countries providing data, boys in cross-national category A are in the clear majority by a ratio of around 3:2 and by implication as a group are receiving more resources than girls to help them gain access to the curriculum. Such differences seem unlikely to be due to "natural," randomly operating biological factors, even if male children seem to be more prone to illness and trauma (Lemons et al., 2001) and, therefore, may "naturally" require more additional support.

These gender differences may reflect a tendency for boys to make themselves more noticed at school and, consequently, labeled when problems arise. They may also indicate that schools, as they currently operate, are more effective in preparing girls than boys for life in a democracy, covering such issues as willingness to take responsibility, tolerance of minority groups, solidarity with those outside the group, and attitude toward immigration policy (Hard, 1999). But these differences may also suggest that the education of boys is given greater priority than that of girls and this factor biases the distribution of the available additional resources.

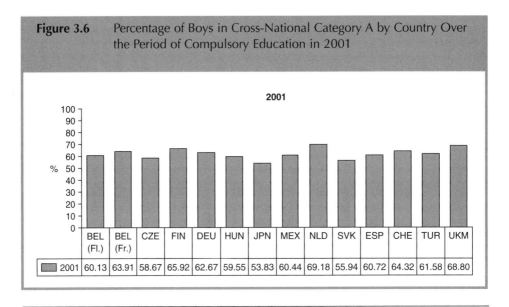

Figure 3.6 Percentage of Boys in Cross-National Category A by Country Over the Period of Compulsory Education in 2001

	BEL (Fl.)	BEL (Fr.)	CZE	FIN	DEU	HUN	JPN	MEX	NLD	SVK	ESP	CHE	TUR	UKM
2001	60.13	63.91	58.67	65.92	62.67	59.55	53.83	60.44	69.18	55.94	60.72	64.32	61.58	68.80

SOURCE: OECD, 2005.

Changes Over Time

Finally, an emphasis on the additional resources being supplied can provide a perspective on change over time directly linked with the principles underlying the modes of funding or to the changes undertaken in policy.

As an example, the decrease in the numbers of students in the Slovak Republic belonging to category A receiving additional resources between 2001 and 2003, as shown in Figure 3.7, may reflect the fewer number of students having an organic disability than changes made to their identification procedures or in the reliability level of the gathered data. In contrast, the increasing numbers of students belonging to category A receiving additional resources between 2001 and 2003 in some countries may reflect less an increase in the actual number of children with impairments and rather an increase in resources made available to support children experiencing difficulties in accessing the curriculum as a result of diagnosed impairment.

Figure 3.8 reveals the evolution of the location of education at primary level between 2001 and 2003 among the different countries. It shows that some countries increased the resources given to category A students for their education in regular classes, whereas others reduced it but invested more in special classes.

Once more, explaining these evolutions is not easy. In some countries, they may reflect a trend in policy toward inclusion at primary level or, on

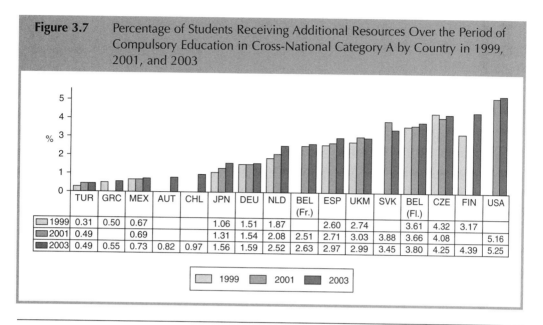

Figure 3.7 Percentage of Students Receiving Additional Resources Over the Period of Compulsory Education in Cross-National Category A by Country in 1999, 2001, and 2003

	TUR	GRC	MEX	AUT	CHL	JPN	DEU	NLD	BEL (Fr.)	ESP	UKM	SVK	BEL (Fl.)	CZE	FIN	USA
1999	0.31	0.50	0.67			1.06	1.51	1.87		2.60	2.74		3.61	4.32	3.17	
2001	0.49		0.69			1.31	1.54	2.08	2.51	2.71	3.03	3.88	3.66	4.08		5.16
2003	0.49	0.55	0.73	0.82	0.97	1.56	1.59	2.52	2.63	2.97	2.99	3.45	3.80	4.25	4.39	5.25

Legend: 1999 · 2001 · 2003

SOURCE: OECD, 2005.

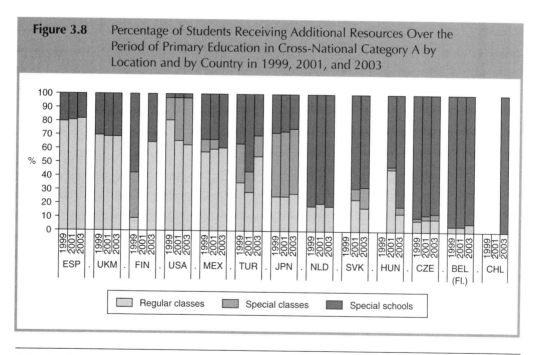

Figure 3.8 Percentage of Students Receiving Additional Resources Over the Period of Primary Education in Cross-National Category A by Location and by Country in 1999, 2001, and 2003

Legend: Regular classes · Special classes · Special schools

SOURCE: OECD, 2005.

the contrary, away from inclusion. In other countries, they may reflect an increase of data quality and may, therefore, suggest a better level of monitoring. But in any event, these changes are ultimately explicable by the policies adopted by the countries and in their implementation.

CONCLUSION

In contrast to the traditional classification systems, the resource-based approach offers an educational perspective focusing on the ability of the schools' systems to promote human capital through teaching to diversity and through the effectiveness of schools' practices in the context of general economic development. The data provided certainly do not per se allow the conclusion that a particular country's provision is more or less equitable than another's. But, by emphasizing the additional resources being supplied, they may allow policy development in this field. It should help policymakers to make rational decisions for resource distribution that will lead to an equitable education for all. It may also help special needs students themselves to claim better provision and support and to keep attention on these issues by demonstrating existing problems in access and opportunity. By determining whether additional resources are being used efficiently and effectively in school settings in achieving quality and equality of opportunity in access to the labor market, gathered data may provide essential information to improve quality of provision but also access to rights and citizenship (Orfield, 2001).

In addition, the educational perspective followed by this model leads to a focus on the capabilities given to the individuals to transform their opportunities in skills, competencies, and resources enabling them to participate actively in society. It could offer a classification system based on the enabling or the disabling effect of policies and practices toward participation and equal opportunities instead of the individuals' impairment or inability to cope with school or institutional requirements. By referring disability to the disablement process people may be involved in (Ebersold, 2004; World Health Organization [WHO], 2001), it could be helpful to avoid the stigmatization processes that may lead to exclusion and poverty. The educational perspective considers the individual in time and, therefore, as being by definition involved in personal and social development. It assumes that skills and knowledge for personal and social development can be acquired by receiving appropriate teaching and support. Difficulties students may face are fundamentally linked to the receptiveness of school systems and the quality of teaching practices and support rather than inabilities due to impairment. Associated with personal and social development, quality outcomes refer to capacity-building issues with regard to students' ability to participate in the community, to progress within the educational system, and to have parity of participation (Fraser, 2005). Quality indicators are those things that enable individuals to progress successfully and to transform their opportunities into skills, competencies, and resources in order to participate actively in society. Associated with personal development, quality outcomes refer to the impact schooling processes may have on individuals' opportunity to define themselves as stakeholders of their future. Quality indicators therefore encompass the various factors that impact individuals' identity with regard to emerging independence, the sense of coherence given by teaching practices and support (Antonowski, 1987), and the sense of existing that they both feel and express (Ebersold, 2005; Flahault, 2002). There is, however, still a long way to go to obtain the necessary data to provide the empirical support needed to develop fully many of the arguments raised here.

NOTES

1. Convention on the Rights of Persons with Disabilities, United Nations, New York, August 2006.
2. Article 31 of the United Nations Convention on the Rights of Persons with Disabilities.
3. According to the *International Classification of Functioning, Disability and Health* definition of disability proposed by the WHO, the term "disability" refers to the interaction between the individual and his or her environment and the term "impairment" refers to organic factors.
4. In Germany, the data refer to the period of compulsory education.
5. In the United Kingdom, it is not possible to compute this as students in special classes and regular classes are not counted separately.
6. Special classes: Not applicable in Belgium (Fl.), Canada (NB), and the Netherlands.
7. Special classes: Included in special schools in Germany and Spain.
8. Special classes: Included in regular classes in England.
9. Special schools: Not applicable in Canada (NB).

REFERENCES

Antonowski, A. (1987). *Unraveling the mystery of health: How people manage stress and stay well.* San Francisco: Jossey-Bass.

Brighouse, M. H. (2000). *School choice and social justice.* Oxford, UK: Oxford University Press.

Ebersold, S. (2004). The affiliation effect of participation into community: Conceptual and methodological aspects of a participative research. In J. Trossebo (Ed.), *Studying the living conditions of disabled people* (pp. 105–125). Stockholm: Studentlitteratur.

Ebersold, S. (2005). *Le temps des servitudes: la famille à l'épreuve du handicap.* Rennes, France: Presses Universitaires de Rennes.

Evans, P. (2001). Equity indicators based on the provision of supplemental resources for disabled and disadvantaged students. In W. Hutmacher, D. Cochrane, & N. Bottani, *In pursuit of equity in education* (pp. 253–266). Dordrech/Boston/London: Kluwer Academic Publishers.

Flahault, F. (2002). *Le sentiment d'exister*. Paris: Descartes et Cie.

Fraser, N. (2005). *Qu'est ce que la justice sociale?* Paris: La Découverte.

Hard, S. (1999). *Equity and democracy*. Presentation to the OECD/ONES ad hoc group on equity in education, Geneva, Switzerland.

Lemons, J. A., Bauer, C. R., Oh, W., Korones, S. B., Papile, L-U., Stoll, B. J., et al. (2001). Very low birth weight outcomes for the National Institute of Child Health and Human Development neonatal research network, January 1995 through December 1996. *Pediatrics, 107*(1). Retrieved from http://pediatrics .aappublications.org/content/vol107/issue1/

Orfield, G. (2001). Why data collection matters. In W. Hutmacher, D. Cochrane, & N. Bottani (Eds.), *In pursuit of equity in education* (pp. 165–194). Dordrech/Boston/London: Kluwer Academic Publishers.

Organisation for Economic Co-operation and Development. (2005). *Equity in education: Students with disabilities, learning difficulties and disadvantages*. Paris: Author.

Rawls, J. (1971). *A theory of justice*. Cambridge, MA: Harvard University Press.

United Nations. (2006). *Convention on the Rights of Persons with Disabilities*. New York: Author.

United Nations Educational, Scientific and Cultural Organization. (1997). *International standard classification of education*. Paris: Author.

World Health Organization. (2001). *International classification of functioning, disability and health*. Geneva, Switzerland: Author.

4 Evolving Dilemmas About Categorization

Klaus Wedell

INTRODUCTION

In this chapter, I will describe some of the evolving dilemmas about categorization, with reference to special educational provision in England. The use of categorization of children and young people with special educational needs has altered over time, as it has in other countries. It has changed, on the one hand, as a result of a developing understanding of the nature and causation of disability and its functional consequences, and, on the other hand, as the result of policy developments following transformations in both society's attitudes to special needs and conceptions of the rights of individuals. The emerging issues have generated dilemmas because the measures put in place to achieve one aim have often conflicted with the realization of another aim in meeting needs. Legislation about special education has differed between different provinces of the United Kingdom, and so I am limiting myself primarily to tracing the systems of categorization in England. My focus will be on the application of categorization as it relates to the education system, but the impact of crosscutting categorization in other systems of provision such as social care will be covered with respect to the more recent period. I will be using the general term "provision" for targeted support within the universal as well as specialist statutory services. I will generally use the term "special educational needs" rather than "disability" in this chapter for the sake of consistency, although not until the early 1970s did the former become the preferred term.

The categorization of children and young people with special educational needs reflects the variety of intentions it has served. These intentions will emerge in this chapter in the course of the account of developments in England, but it may be helpful to list some of the main varieties of intention at the outset. Historically, the main intention was to understand the nature of disability and its implications for intervention. Categorization was originally formulated in terms of the "medical model" used by doctors involved in the diagnosis of impairment and the understanding of etiological conditions. This is hardly surprising, because medical practitioners were the first to work in this field. The intention was that this "diagnostic" approach would have implications about how the individual should be cared for, and whether educational provision might be relevant. As psychological and educational methods developed, the emphasis changed to identifying the particular dysfunctions associated with impairment. Initially, this assessment approach was still used also for its implications about neuropathology. A classic example of this transition was the way in which the diagnosis of "minimal cerebral dysfunction" was based on the identification of cognitive and behavioral difficulties where the usually associated organic indicators were not evident (McKeith & Bax, 1963). Over time, assessment focused on cognitive and behavioral difficulties in their own right, because these were then regarded as having more direct relevance to the choice of educational and other interventions. The prevalence of certain conditions often followed particular interest in some developments. For example, in England in the late 1950s there was a growing awareness that some children assessed as mentally handicapped because of their motor and communication disabilities resulting from cerebral palsy were in fact intellectually able (Wedell, 1960). Progressively detailed assessment led to greater differentiation within the broader categories of disability. So, for example, notions such as "specific learning difficulties" and "autism" were separated out from general learning difficulty, with the aim of devising more differentiated educational provision. In etiological terms, there has also been an important gradual move from an emphasis solely on "within-child" organic explanations toward ones that acknowledge the interaction with environmental factors. Attention to this interaction had been stimulated by the impact of Head Start and similar programs in the United States (O'Bryan, 1975). Evidence of vulnerability and/or resilience led to recognition of the complexity of the causation of outcomes for children and young people. I have referred to this elsewhere (Wedell, 1995) in terms of compensatory interaction. The complexity derives from the interaction between the balance of resources and deficiencies in the individual, and the balance of resources and deficiencies in the individual's environment. On top of this, there is also the cumulative interaction between these balances at any one time, and also over time. Since the term "disability" was regarded as referring to a single cause, "difficulty" came to be preferred insofar as this represented the special educational need to be addressed as the result of the complex interaction (Wedell, 1970). Current trends in interactive interpretations, such as those developed by the World Health Organization, are discussed in Part III of this book.

A second intention for categorization arose from parents' concern that local education authorities (LEAs), the authorities responsible for educational provision for populations within English shires and metropolitan areas, were not making sufficiently differentiated provision to match their children's special educational needs. Parents became progressively dissatisfied with provision that they felt was too general to fit their children's needs. They used the increasingly specific differentiations to lobby for more appropriate support. These category labels then became parents' "passports" to access this differentiated provision for their children (Wedell, 2003). Much of this provision was first set up by voluntary bodies, but progressively pressure led to the LEAs taking this over (McLaughlin & Rouse, 2000). LEAs then increasingly developed the variety of their centrally funded provision in the form of specialist support staff for children in mainstream schools, specialist units in these schools, and also special schools focusing on particular forms of special needs. LEAs also set up school psychology services to support these various forms of provision.

A third intention relates to parents' concern about any stigma associated with various forms of special needs. Understandably, they preferred terms that indicated that their children's conditions did not "run in the family," and did not imply parental negligence in child rearing. For example, terms such as "specific learning difficulties" and terms with organic associations such as "dyslexia" were seen to avoid these associations, particularly when the criteria for their diagnosis were based on discrepancies with the otherwise higher levels of general ability shown by their children.

A fourth intention arises from labeling individuals in terms of the types of provision or legislative procedures to which they are subjected. For example, in the early years, those who had severely impaired intellectual function were excluded from educational provision and placed in medical institutions, and so were labeled as "ineducable." Similarly, when a "statement" procedure was established for determining the special provision for certain children, these came to be referred to as "statemented children."

A fifth intention for categorization developed around the quest for equity and accountability. LEAs are faced with the dilemmas of allocating limited resources fairly to meet children's and young people's needs.

Therefore, transparency is required in allocating finite financial resources to reflect the relative degree of special need between one individual and another. For example, some LEAs place children and young people into "bands" of funding levels, corresponding to the resources that are made available to provide the special measures to meet their needs.

A sixth intention relates to the need to collect data on the prevalence of special educational needs for planning the types of provision required, and to supply the specialist personnel to serve in them. The category terms used tend to revert to more controversial within-child labels of special needs. The administrators concerned in this activity usually justify their practice through the claim that the associated unreliability of the data obtained will be "smoothed out" within the large scale of the prevalence populations studied.

A seventh intention addresses the organization of the specialist training of teachers for children and young people with special educational needs. The chapters in this book by Norwich (Chapter 9) and by Hardman and McDonnell (Chapter 10) discuss the ways in which the specificity of the preparation of teachers has reflected both the changes in concepts about categorization and the patterns of provision over the years.

A fuller account of the implementation of these types of intention will emerge in the course of the historical review covered in this chapter. Those applying these various categorizations often appear to tackle any dilemmas they have about their validity in terms of the pragmatic demands for action to meet the needs of the children and young people concerned. As mentioned earlier, however, this expediency often generates its own further dilemmas.

CATEGORIZATION IN HISTORICAL PERSPECTIVE

The 1944 Education Act in England was the first to include special education within its general provisions. Special education was to be recognized as part of the LEAs' planned provision. The Act was prepared in the anticipation that after the war, there would be an expectation that educational opportunities should be open to all. The exception to this were children and young people who were still assessed under the Mental Deficiency Act of 1913 as not capable of being educated, and so were categorized as "ineducable."

The 1944 Act recognized that up to 17% of the school population might require special educational help (Department of Education and Science [DES], 1978, par. 2.49). At this time, assessment for special provision was carried out by doctors, and so these children and young people were described in the Act as having "disabilities of body or mind," reflecting the within-child medical model. Eleven categories of "handicap" were used: deaf, partially deaf, blind, partially sighted, physically handicapped, delicate, diabetic, epileptic, educationally subnormal, maladjusted, and those with speech defects. Although the 1944 Act recognized that children and young people within these categories would not ipso facto be educated outside the mainstream, it was apparent that the majority would be placed in schools corresponding to the label of their special need. The categorization inevitably varied in the specificity with which it was applied. For example, although schools for the "delicate" were intended for children with various medical conditions, such as severe asthma or diabetes, they also came to be used for children who might not fit into the hurly-burly of mainstream schools.

When LEAs started to set up educational psychologist services, there was an increasing switch from medical diagnoses to ones defined in terms of cognitive and other psychological functioning. A particular concern was about the children and young people who had been assessed as "ineducable." In the years following, there was a growing promotion of individual rights, which was largely led by parent groups. They persuaded the government to pass an act in 1970 that gave those previously deemed "ineducable" access to educational provision under the responsibility of LEAs.

Continued pressure to improve special needs provision induced the government in 1973 to set up a committee of enquiry. An Oxford University lecturer in philosophy, Mary Warnock (in later years ennobled to a baroness), was chosen to chair the committee, which then came to be called the "Warnock Committee." It is significant to note that the terms of reference given to the committee by the government were couched in terms that were already superseded in the context of thinking within the special needs field at the time. The committee was charged

> To review educational provision . . . for children and young people handicapped by disabilities of body and mind, taking account of the medical aspects of their needs, together with arrangements to prepare them for entry into employment; to consider the most effective use of resources for these purposes; and to make recommendations. (DES, 1978, p. 1)

The pressure to move away from a within-child medical model continued while the committee was in session up to the delivery of its report in 1978. In 1975, the government had been persuaded to issue guidance about the identification and assessment of children with special educational needs (Circular 2/75). Among its provisions was the assertion that "the recommendation whether a child needs special education, and if so, where it can best be provided, is primarily an educational matter rather than a medical one" (DES, 1975, par. 17).

Because the circular was still subject to the 1944 Act, however, a doctor's assessment was paradoxically still required for any special school placement. The circular recommended that decisions about provision should involve a teacher and an educational psychologist or an education adviser. It also recognized that assessment of special educational needs was not a one-off event (as medical assessment had tended to be), but a progressive process.

The wording of the circular quoted above reflects one of the main developments during this period—the establishment of the term "special educational needs" in contrast to the term "disabilities of body and mind" used in the 1944 legislation. "Special educational needs" was the title of a book by Professor Ronald Gulliford of Birmingham University (Gulliford, 1971). The "need" was defined in terms of the specific support necessary for the development of the children and young people involved, and so was linked to the distinction between "disability" and "difficulty" discussed earlier in this chapter. It is interesting to note that this orientation had a major impact on deliberations in the Warnock Committee, and on their adoption of the term "special educational needs" in their 1978 report. It also represents a contrast to the acceptance of the term "disability" in the United States, with its link in that country to the accountability demands associated with special educational provision.

The Warnock Report

The Warnock Report (DES, 1978) contained 224 recommendations, but I will focus on those relevant to issues in categorization. Significantly, the report states that

> To describe someone as handicapped conveys nothing of the type of educational help and hence of provision that is required. . . . We have adopted the concept of special educational need, seen not in terms of a particular disability which a child may be judged to have, but in relation to . . . all the factors which have a bearing on his educational progress. (DES, 1978, par. 3.6)

The report rejects the statutory categorization of handicapped pupils (par. 3.25) because "it perpetuates the sharp distinction between two groups of children—the handicapped and the non-handicapped" (DES,

1978, par. 3.24). Instead, the report recognized that special educational needs occur in a continuum of degree. This view was derived from a major epidemiological study of special needs (Rutter, Tizard, & Whitmore, 1970), which postulated that around 18% of the mainstream school population might be regarded as requiring some support for their special educational needs at some time, and a further 2% would require special class or school provision.

The committee was well aware of the dilemma that their rejection of a fixed demarcation of "handicap" might result in LEAs failing to identify and thus provide for children and young people's special educational needs. The committee therefore recommended that descriptive terms should still be used, but was particularly concerned to remove the stigmatizing connotations of the previous forms of labeling as much as possible. The committee made proposals about how LEAs should assess a child's needs and formulate recommendations for provision. Within the overall concept of "special educational needs," the committee suggested the following categorization (DES, 1978, par. 3.26):

- that the description of sensory and motor disabilities was acceptable;
- that "children with learning difficulties—mild, moderate, or severe" should replace terms such as "educationally subnormal";
- that specific reading disability and similar terms should be grouped as "specific learning difficulties"; and
- that "maladjusted" should be retained, while still preferring "emotional or behavioral disorders."

The committee recommended that this terminology of needs should be used in the designation of special schools and units in mainstream schools. The committee also acknowledged that data on the prevalence of special educational needs would have to be collected to help in planning provision. An appendix to the report describes proposals for carrying this out, with an illustration of a grid that groups the categorization of children's special educational needs in columns, and the respective degrees of severity in corresponding rows. These proposals for data collection, however, seem to have been forgotten subsequently.

The report was sent out for consultation, and the government then produced a white paper for further consultation on legislation. Both consultations stimulated wide consideration across the country. This had a major impact on thinking about provision in LEAs, and particularly about meeting the special educational needs of the approximately 18% of children and young people in mainstream schools (Goacher, Evans, Welton, & Wedell, 1988).

The 1981 Education Act

In 1981, the government produced legislation to follow up these developments, but the secretary of state for education delayed its implementation until 1983 because of concerns about the availability of the additional resources entailed. In the end, it was argued that the necessary resources should be sought from the supposed savings resulting from the fall in the school population that was occurring at the time.

In describing the 1981 Act, I will again limit myself to policy issues related to categorization. At the center of the Act was its definition of special educational needs, which reflected the Warnock Committee's endorsement of the interactive view: "A child has special educational needs if he has a learning difficulty which calls for special educational provision to be made for him" (Education Act, 1981, Sec. 1(1)). Correspondingly, special educational provision was defined as "provision which is additional to or . . . different from . . . provision made generally" (Sec. 1(3)(a)). One might regard this as a somewhat extreme relative formulation—pivoting on the notion of "calling for." There was an attempt at constraining the relativity with the following qualifications:

> A child has a learning difficulty if he
> - has a significantly greater difficulty in learning than the majority of children of the same age, [or]
> - has a disability which either prevents or hinders the child from making use of educational facilities of a kind provided in . . . schools. (Sec. 1(2)(a),(b))

The definition goes on to exclude learning difficulty resulting from unfamiliarity with the English language. The Act also extended to those children under five where difficulty with school learning was anticipated. Colleagues and I were involved in research on some of the decision-making aspects of the Act (Wedell, Welton, & Vorhaus, 1982). In the course of discussions with ministry officials, I was astounded when the above specification about "significantly greater difficulty in learning" was read out to me. I asked whether this indicated that, statistically, 49% of children might be regarded as having a learning difficulty.

The central concept of special educational needs in the Act has the implication that the variability of the generally available provision made for children and young people in mainstream schools will determine whether or not there will be a "call" for provision that is "additional or different." This relative criterion has continued to produce a basic dilemma for all those hankering after a more absolute criterion (e.g., Audit Commission, 2002), because of the considerable variation of provision between LEAs, and indeed within them. On the other hand, a sound argument can be made for supporting the definition, because it recognizes the reality of the situation, and so places the onus of identification on those responsible in each particular context. The phrase "calls for" thus represents an evaluation of the perceived *degree* of need *in context*, quite apart from the *identification* of the nature of the difficulty.

The Act set out procedures for making special provision for children with more complex or severe needs. The prescribed procedure involved a multi-professional assessment, which might then lead the LEA to maintain a "statement of special educational need" for a child. Such provision was described in the Act as being "determined by the LEA." This implied that the LEA would take responsibility for funding the relevant provision in a mainstream school, or for placing a pupil in a special unit in a school or in a special school. For parents, a "statement" was intended to offer "security" insofar as the proposed provision was legally binding on the LEA. In relation to categorization, these arrangements then led to children being referred to as "statemented," with the resulting dilemma that the very legislation that was intended to emphasize the continuum of need set them apart.

Further Deliberations About "Special Educational Needs"

The concept of special educational needs has continued to be debated among professionals, parents, and the individuals concerned when they became adults. An increasing body of opinion has held that the concept of "need" should itself be regarded as a social construct. The thinking behind this view was influenced by individual rights issues. In 1985, the largest LEA in the country at that time, the Inner London Education Authority, published a major review of its special needs policy. The committee carrying out the review was chaired by John Fish, who had been one of the Her Majesty's Inspectors serving the Warnock Committee. The report (Inner London Education Authority, 1985) stated its basic principles, which included the following:

> Our definition of handicap is a dynamic and relative one. Disabilities and difficulties become more or less handicapping depending on the expectations of others, and on social contexts. Handicaps thus arise from the mismatch between the intellectual, physical, emotional and social behavior and aspirations of the individual and the expectations, appropriate or otherwise, of the community and society at large. Individuals with disabilities or significant difficulties may be handicapped by their own attitudes to them, and by the attitudes of others. (par. 1.1.25)

These considerations indicate a further dilemma about the relativity of the concept of special educational needs, and have affinities to the issues of disproportionality covered in Chapter 11 and the "capability approach" discussed in Chapter 15. The Fish Report (as it came to be called) went on to observe that the education system itself might contribute to special educational needs:

> The one common factor associated with special educational needs is the present inability of schools and colleges to meet the wide range of individual needs in their population. (Inner London Education Authority, 1985, par. 1.1.35)

The Fish Committee's conclusions thus formulated a concept of special needs that recognized both children's and young people's own needs, and also the impact of the education system and society's ascriptions and expectations. It provided an interesting precursor to the subsequent move from the goals of integration, to those of inclusion.

In 1988, the government in power at that time instituted a National Curriculum and a national system of educational assessment—the first of its kind in the history of English education. The government's aim was to introduce a market economy of competition between schools in relation to their pupils' achievement in this curriculum. Those involved in special needs education welcomed the proposal that all pupils should be offered an "entitlement" to the National Curriculum. But they were concerned about the effect that competition might have on attitudes toward pupils whose achievement did not contribute to schools' standing in the aggregate academic achievement "league tables" (the comparative data on schools published annually by the government). The government responded to this dilemma by making it permissible, where relevant, to "disapply" the assessment requirement from these pupils. Needless to say, producing a category of "disapplied" pupils met with disapproval on account of its stigmatizing effect. The same government went on to increase the market economy approach to schooling in subsequent legislation in 1993. At this point, a strong lobby group called the Special Educational Needs Consortium was set up to demand assurances that mainstream schools would be required to provide support for pupils with special educational needs. The government agreed to establish a Code of Practice for special educational needs (Department for Education [DfE], 1994), but refused to enforce it beyond requiring that all concerned should "have a statutory duty to have regard to it and not ignore it" (par. 6).

The code was a substantial document, but I will again confine my account to aspects related to categorization. In this context, it promoted

a stepwise approach to identifying and meeting pupils' special educational needs, which emphasized mainstream schools' responsibility to all
their pupils. These steps were termed "stages," reflecting the *degree of concern*
on the part of teachers and others that the available resources in schools
might not be sufficient to meet a pupil's needs. The reference to degree of
need in terms of "concern" in the code thus echoes the reference to "calls
for" in the legislation. The initial stage was for classroom teachers to
respond to pupils' learning difficulty. If this was not found to be sufficient,
the next stage was for the teacher to consult with the school's special educational needs coordinator (SENCo). This was a teacher on the staff of the
school with responsibility for administering the code provisions both pro-
cedurally and professionally. The third stage was reached when the
SENCo and the school decided that help was required from the LEA and
other support services to tackle the pupil's needs. Beyond this stage, the
statement procedure could be invoked. Those lobbying for the requirement
that schools should attend to pupils' special educational needs were placed
in a dilemma by this procedure, because it clearly set up a further categorization of pupils by "stages," which once again was liable to set them apart.

The Code of Practice also set out the categories of special educational
needs of pupils to be used in the formulation of statements. In the accompanying 1993 legislation, the term "difficulty" had replaced "disability."
Eight areas of special need were specified, formulated with respect to "difficulties," "conditions," "impairments," and "disabilities."

The difficulties listed in the code were

- learning difficulty,
- specific learning difficulty,
- emotional and behavior difficulties, and
- speech and language difficulties.

Impairments and difficulties were listed as

- sensory impairments—hearing difficulties, and
- sensory impairments—visual difficulties.

Conditions referred to were

- medical conditions.

The only formulation that still included the term "disability" was

- physical disability.

Needless to say, discussion had continued about the appropriateness of using this kind of categorization within the provisions of the code. The code explicitly acknowledged the dilemma:

> This guidance does not assume that there are hard and fast categories of special educational need. . . . Each child is unique. . . . Children's learning difficulties may encompass more than one area of need. (DfE, 1994, par. 3.54)

Consideration of the dilemmas raised by categorization continued after the code came into operation. The issue also came to the fore in the deliberations about a coherent framework for the further professional development of specialist teachers for children and young people with special educational needs. The next section of this chapter addresses this issue.

Teacher Training for Special Educational Needs

The specialist preparation of teachers for children and young people with special educational needs has changed significantly over the years. The historical review in the Warnock Report (DES, 1978) states that specific training for teachers of children with visual and with hearing impairment already existed in England at the beginning of the 1900s. These two areas of specialist training, along with the later addition of multiple hearing and visual impairment, are the only ones that have been mandatory for teachers working in special schools and units. Teachers in these special needs areas are required to obtain their qualification within three years of employment. The preparation of teachers for children with visual and with hearing impairment and for children with severe learning difficulties (following their inclusion within education provision) was originally offered as initial teacher training. The Advisory Committee on the Supply and Education of Teachers recommended in its 1984 report that specialist training should only be available to qualified teachers with experience in mainstream schools (Sayer & Jones, 1985), and this then became the norm. Over the years, central government has supported LEAs with funding for the further specialist training of teachers, and, indeed, at various periods has also accredited such funded courses of training through Her Majesty's Inspectorate. Apart from these periods, it has largely been left to LEAs to develop their own criteria for qualifications demanded of those employed as teachers of children with special educational needs in their areas.

From the time of the Warnock Report onward, there have been strong recommendations that the initial training of all teachers in mainstream schools should include a basic awareness of the range of special educational needs and of provision for them. In the years following the enactment of the 1981 Education Act (in 1983), specialist teacher training was generally organized along the lines of the categories of learning difficulty specified in the Warnock Report as mentioned above. The Warnock Report also acknowledged the existence of support services for children who were "retarded" in their educational achievement through poor attendance, hospitalization, and other discontinuances in education. Help for these children was termed "remedial education," on the assumption that appropriate specialist teaching would enable them to catch up, and this was a further area of specialist teacher training. Courses providing teacher qualifications for the higher-incidence forms of special educational needs became fairly widely distributed across the country, but only certain university departments and colleges offered specialization in lower-incidence needs, such as physical and sensory impairments. Initially, courses of specialization were usually offered on an LEA-seconded, one-year full-time basis leading to an academically accredited qualification. With the development of integration policies, and later of inclusion policies, an increasing variety of patterns of provision emerged in LEAs. Central government funding for further professional development in special educational needs became less specific, and more teacher training was gradually offered on a modular part-time basis. Overall, there was a trend toward a progression of training in the general understanding and competencies of support, leading on to more specific qualifications in particular areas of special needs. Distance training also became available initially through the Open University and the University of Birmingham. Wedell (1985) called for the establishment of a coherent system of further professional development to underpin the diverse patterns of provision—reflecting both the levels and nature of responsibility of teacher posts, and their special needs foci.

By the mid-1990s, the training situation had become extremely amorphous, and so with central government funding I convened the Special Educational Needs Training Consortium with representatives of providers of further professional development and of special needs professional organizations. The aim of the consortium was to draw up a coherent conceptualization of progression and specialization in teacher education for special educational needs. The consortium's report (Special Educational Needs Training Consortium [SENTC], 1996), compiled by Professor Peter Mittler of the Manchester University education department, formulated a set of competencies covering both the established areas of special needs, and the types and levels of administrative function in which teachers were involved in LEA services. The report was presented to the government. This in turn charged the Teacher Training Agency (TTA) to consult and make recommendations, and these led to the publication of the National

Special Educational Needs Specialist Standards (TTA, 1999). These "standards" were issued as an "audit tool" for those involved in special education in mainstream and special schools and services as a means of identifying teachers' needs for further professional development. The standards reflected the administrative competencies specified in the SENTC report. They also specified "higher-level extension training" relating to the following dimensions of special educational needs:

- Communication and interaction,
- Cognition and learning,
- Behavior, social, and emotional development, and
- Sensory and physical development.

From the point of view of the categorization of special educational needs, this formulation represented a new departure, recognizing the fact that teachers would be serving children and young people who might manifest a variety of needs. From a quality control point of view of further professional development, it was presumably assumed that the standards would constitute criteria for national and local inspection as well as guidelines for courses of further professional development. This still, however, left the question about how this provision would be assured and funded. The recent report on special education carried out by the House of Commons Education and Skills Select Committee (2006) expressed concern about the variability in quality of provision for children and young people with special educational needs, and called on the government to "make training and equipping its workforce a top priority" (House of Commons, 2006, par. 318). The government's response (Department for Education and Skills [DfES], 2006b) mentions a variety of proposed measures, but, at the time of writing, a clear framework for further professional development for the whole range of special needs is not apparent.

RECENT CONCEPTUALIZATIONS OF CATEGORIZATION

In 2001, the government, after a period of consultation, issued a revised code of practice (DfES, 2001). This attempted to resolve the dilemma of placing children and young people into specific categories, by adopting the four dimensions of special needs formulated in the TTA standards mentioned above. For each of the aspects of special needs, the revised code goes on to list the type of specialist support and teaching that might be required, and specifies the levels of support to be provided by schools and by outside services. The code thus marks a definite change in the approach to categorizing special educational needs, placing a major emphasis on the various kinds of educational approach that individual children and young people require for their needs to be met. Norwich, in Chapter 9, explores the validity of such a differentiation of educational approaches.

The revised code also begins to relate the provisions for children and young people with special educational needs to the general disability discrimination legislation that had been enacted in 1995. This legislation refers to a "disabled" person as one who has an impairment that has a substantial and long-term adverse effect on the ability to carry out normal day-to-day activities. The Special Educational Needs and Disability Act of 2001, and its further formulation in the 2005 Education Act, was aimed at ensuring that a child or young person with a "disability" should have the same opportunities for *access* to education in schools as a nondisabled one. The 2005 Act thus attempts to transfer the *access discrimination* issue from the adult version onto the school context. A "disabled child or young person" is defined in within-child terminology, relating to a range of physical or mental "impairments," including "learning disabilities." It is a very interesting example of an attempt to relate a totally different conceptualization (and language) derived from a circumscribed *access discrimination* context, to the special needs conceptualization focused on educational concerns about *intervention*. How this conceptual challenge will be tackled by practitioners remains to be seen. For example, the access requirements about the noneducational concept of "disability'" raise all the familiar dilemmas about balancing the needs of individual pupils with those of the rest. The stipulations also raise more subtle issues particularly for staff in mainstream schools. For example, homework may need to be set in ways that do not bar pupils with literacy difficulties from demonstrating what they know. In relation to behavior problems, staff have to distinguish between the *can't* and *won't* interpretations.

A further crosscutting categorization has emerged from legislation arising from public alarm about failures by statutory services to prevent severe abuse of children. A few instances led to public enquiries that pointed out these failures. The government's response culminated in legislation. The Children Act of 2004 calls for health, social, and education services to be linked at the level of local authorities through the establishment of an overarching Children's Directorate. This would take overall responsibility for services to all children and young people. The stated aims for this integration of services are that they should work to achieve the following Five Outcomes for *all* children and young people, enabling them to

- Be healthy,
- Stay safe,

- Enjoy and achieve,
- Make a positive contribution, and
- Achieve economic well-being.

Now that education services come within the responsibility of these Children's Directorates in Local Authorities, the Five Outcomes have to be taken up by all schools, in collaboration with the other services involved. It is immediately evident that these Five Outcomes constitute aims for schools that extend far beyond achievement within the National Curriculum, and are particularly relevant, of course, to schools' concern for those of their pupils who have special educational needs.

The legislation is also directed at achieving early identification of, and intervention for, vulnerable children and young people. For this purpose, a Common Assessment Framework for Children and Young People is being promoted to facilitate integrated working among the practitioners in all the relevant services (DfES, 2006a). The framework is intended to be used when practitioners' concern about a child's needs is such that they judge a service other than their own should be involved—hence the use of a common assessment framework offering a "common language" to identify and deal with needs. The framework incorporates the interactive conceptualization of causation, calling for the assessment of the individual child or young person's development, the support that parents and caregivers can offer, and relevant family and environmental factors. This process can be seen as involving increasing levels of concern about a child or young person, hence generating a further categorization of needs in terms of severity. The concern can be gauged with respect to the degree of risk that a given child will fail to achieve the Five Outcomes mentioned above. The highest level of concern is one that triggers immediate action, such as in severe cases of child abuse or in relation to the complexity of needs. Within the school system, these "levels" of concern constitute a crosscutting dimension with respect to categorization in terms of the need for educational support mentioned in the revised *Special Educational Needs Code of Practice* (Department for Education and Skills, 2001). To these two dimensions, one can now add the "disability" access discrimination issue mentioned earlier. Children and young people may consequently be identified within any or all of these dimensions, and it will be interesting to discover how staff in schools deal with this complexity.

Recent Categorizations

In recent years, two issues regarding categorization have emerged, which arise primarily from administration concerns. The first issue relates to the dilemma into which the Warnock Report's rejection of categorization placed those concerned with administrative planning. As mentioned earlier, this issue was in fact anticipated in the report. It surfaced again in 2003, when the government issued a requirement that all schools should include information about the special educational needs of their pupils when making their annual returns to the national government's Department for Education and Skills. The aim was the same as that originally mentioned in the Warnock Report—to obtain data for planning and policy development. The instructions issued by the department attempt to deal with the dilemma about the relevance of the information collected, by combining the following functional and diagnostic elements:

- Cognitive and learning needs: specific learning difficulty; moderate learning difficulty; severe learning difficulty; profound and multiple learning difficulty
- Behavioral, emotional, and social difficulty
- Communication and interaction needs: speech, language, and communication needs; autistic spectrum disorder
- Sensory and/or physical needs: visual impairment; hearing impairment; multisensory impairment; physical disability

Head teachers are required to provide information on all pupils who have a statement, and on any pupils who are at the stage of support immediately below that determined by a statement. The instructions ask for individual pupils' primary need to be entered in the return, but a further significant need can be added. It is suggested that the information should be taken from the statement documentation and from the record of the support a pupil is receiving. In the light of all that has been written above, it is very obvious that data obtained in this way force the person who collects them to ignore the dilemmas about the multidimensionality of pupils' special educational needs. This also assumes that the person involved has the understanding to distinguish which data in the documentation are relevant. At a later time, further instructions were issued by the government department to discourage the use of the "other" category!

The second issue has arisen in the administrative requirements for categorization derived from the increasing demands for accountability in special needs provision. These parallel the accountability requirements in general education policy. As a result, LEAs have attempted to codify the specific funding they allocate to schools for special needs support. Some authorities, in the interest of making their allocation more "transparent," have devised a "banding" system for pupils related to their different types and degrees of special educational needs. The funding "bands" apply directly to the additional amounts of support that pupils' needs are judged to require over and above a school's own capacity to meet the diversity of needs. The additional resources may either be stated in terms of funds allocated to schools to provide this support, or in terms of hours for the employment of additional learning support assistants for the pupils concerned. This funding is then reviewed at intervals. These administrative procedures have thus generated a further system of categorization of pupils alongside those mentioned earlier in relation to the statement procedure.

CONCLUSION

The strong reaction to the perceived limitations of the "disability" categorization of the 1944 Education Act has had a lasting impact on the evolving policy and practice about special educational needs in England. The Warnock Committee's report produced a formulation of this orientation that has been sustained throughout subsequent legislation. The developments in policy and practice, however, have engendered a variety of dilemmas. It is important to note that there has been no denial of the differentiated needs of children and young people, nor that within-child factors are important to varying degrees in children and young people's special educational needs. The perception of the limitations of "disability" categorization derives from the increasing acknowledgment of the complexity of needs, and particularly of the complexity of their causation. This made it apparent that categorization by "disability" usually had neither simple nor direct implications for educational or other intervention. Differentiation continued to be the challenge for understanding the nature of need, and how to meet it. After the 1981 Education Act, categorization of "disability" consequently no longer constituted a central criterion of *eligibility* for support. The crucial criterion became the *degree of need* for "additional or different" provision from that generally offered in the mainstream school system, and, over time, a variety of administrative categorizations were developed to reflect these levels of need. The variability of levels of provision between LEAs, and also within mainstream schools, however, meant that there could not be a single quantification of need that applied throughout the country. For example, Goacher et al. (1988) already found that statementing rates differed between rural and urban LEAs. The scope for flexible response to individual needs in mainstream schools has altered over the period described in this chapter. The formulation of a National Curriculum and its related assessment procedures, while establishing the eligibility to access it for all children and young people, paradoxically constrained schools' scope for flexibility, and produced further dilemmas. It is significant to note that the dilemmas were made more apparent under the present government, because of its explicit commitment to meeting the diversity of special educational needs more effectively (DfES, 2004). In recent years, in particular, the government encouraged education and other services to promote a broader set of aims for the development of children and young people in terms of the Five Outcomes. Concurrently, the government has also promoted a more "personalized" approach to teaching and learning in schools (DfES, 2005). Both of these policies have, however, also increased dilemmas, because of the conflicting policies to promote the "standards" agenda, which is focused on requiring schools to pursue the more limited curricular outcomes of the National Curriculum and other assessments.

It is interesting to note that in late 2005, the whole dilemma about categorization and differentiated provision again erupted. Baroness Warnock published a pamphlet (Warnock, 2005) in which she maintained that the needs of children and young people within the autistic spectrum, and those with more severe social, emotional, and behavior difficulties, were not being effectively met. She felt that the disavowal of categorization in the 1978 committee report had resulted in a failure to appreciate the differentiation of needs, and that this was currently evidenced in an inappropriate extension of the government's inclusion policy. Baroness Warnock's assertion was not supported by the findings of a Department for Education and Skills–funded research project on provision for children and young people with the more severe and low-incidence forms of special educational needs (Gray et al., 2006). The research did, however, conclude that there was a wide diversity in the adequacy of provision. The research pointed to the urgent need for the formulation of national standards of provision that should be locally observed. The controversy led the House of Commons Education and Skills Select Committee to carry out a review of special educational needs as mentioned earlier in this chapter. The government in its evidence asserted that it was committed to a spectrum of differentiated provision. The committee's report (House of Commons Education and Skills Select Committee, 2006) was wide-ranging, but one of its main conclusions was to endorse the Gray et al. (2006) research recommendation on the need for national standards. The committee promoted the view that meeting the diversity of children's and young people's learning needs should be an integral part of the education system in general, and should be supported by a corresponding development of the training of all teachers as mentioned above.

This last recommendation by the select committee raises the question as to whether the current system of education is fit for the purpose of the reforms it advocates. The select committee acknowledges that the present education system in general in England still leaves a large tail of under-achievers. It points to the way in which various of the government's current policies act in conflict with one another and so impedes efforts to meet children's and young people's special needs. The committee's report stops short of recognizing that the main cause of dilemmas in meeting special educational needs is the assumption that the present education system itself is appropriate for learners in general in the twenty-first century (Royal Society for the Arts, 2005; Wedell, 1995, 2005). Limitations such as the current curriculum with its subject-based structure, and a pedagogy based on organizing learning through inflexible pupil grouping and time-tabling in mainstream schools, have imposed constraints that many now question in other countries as well. Similarly, the systems of accountability based on narrow academic standards lead to competition between schools and consequently to a distortion of their aims. Progress in special education has been based on an acknowledgment of the diversity of *all* learners and it is evident that this should be the starting point for developing a very different education system that allows a correspondingly flexible responsiveness.

REFERENCES

Audit Commission. (2002). *Special educational needs: A mainstream issue.* London: Author.

Department for Education. (1994). *Code of practice on the identification and assessment of special educational needs.* London: DfE.

Department for Education and Skills. (2001). *Special educational needs code of practice.* London: DfES.

Department for Education and Skills. (2004). *Removing barriers to achievement: The government's strategy for SEN.* Annesley, UK: DfES.

Department for Education and Skills. (2005). *Higher standards, better schools for all: More choice for parents and pupils.* London: DfES.

Department for Education and Skills. (2006a). *The Common Assessment Framework for Children and Young People: Practitioners' guide.* Annesley, UK: DfES.

Department for Education and Skills. (2006b). *The government response to the Education and Skills Select Committee Report on Special Educational Needs.* Annesley, UK: DfES.

Department of Education and Science. (1975). *The discovery of children requiring special education and the assessment of their needs* (Circular 2/75). London: DES.

Department of Education and Science. (1978). *Special educational needs: Report of the Committee of Enquiry Into the Education of Handicapped Children and Young People* (Warnock Report). London: Her Majesty's Stationery Office.

Goacher, B., Evans, J., Welton, J., & Wedell, K. (1988). *Policy and provision for special educational needs.* London: Cassell Educational.

Gray, P., Bullen, P., Duckett, L., Leyden, S., Pollard, I., & Skelton, R. (2006). *National audit of support, services and provision for children with low incidence needs* (Research Report 729). Annesley, UK: Department for Education and Skills.

Gulliford, R. (1971). *Special educational needs.* London: Routledge & Kegan Paul.

House of Commons Education and Skills Select Committee. (2006). *Special educational needs: Third report of session 2005–06.* London: The Stationery Office.

Inner London Education Authority. (1985). *Equal opportunities for all?* (Fish Report). London: Author.

McKeith, R., & Bax, M. (Eds.). (1963). *Minimal cerebral dysfunction* (Little Club Clinics in Developmental Medicine). London: Heinemann.

McLaughlin, M., & Rouse, M. (2000). *Special education and school reform in the US and Britain.* London: Routledge.

O'Bryan, K. G. (1975). Orientations in compensatory education. In K. Wedell (Ed.), *Orientations in special education* (pp. 43–58). London: Wiley.

Royal Society for the Arts. (2005). *Opening minds: Giving young people a better chance.* London: Author.

Rutter, M., Tizard, J., & Whitmore, K. (1970). *Education, health and behaviour.* Harlow, UK: Longman.

Sayer, J., & Jones, N. (Eds.). (1985). *Teacher training and special educational needs.* London: Croom Helm.

Special Educational Needs Training Consortium. (1996). *Professional development to meet special educational needs: Report to the Department for Education and Employment.* London: Institute of Education.

Teacher Training Agency. (1999). *National special educational needs specialist standards.* London: Author.

Warnock, M. (2005). *Special educational needs: A new look* (Impact Pamphlet 11). London: The Philosophy of Education Society of Great Britain.

Wedell, K. (1960). Variations in perceptual ability among types of cerebral palsy. *Cerebral Palsy Bulletin, 2,* 149.

Wedell, K. (1970). Diagnosing learning difficulties: A sequential strategy. *Journal of Learning Disabilities, 3*(6), 311–317.

Wedell, K. (1985). Post-experience training. In J. Sayer & N. Jones (Eds.), *Teacher training and special educational needs* (pp. 87–102). London: Croom Helm.

Wedell, K. (1995). Making inclusive education ordinary. *British Journal of Special Education, 22*(3), 100–104.

Wedell, K. (2003). What's in a label? *British Journal of Special Education, 30*(2), 107.

Wedell, K. (2005). Dilemmas in the quest for inclusion. *British Journal of Special Education, 32*(1), 3–11.

Wedell, K., Welton, J., & Vorhaus, G. (1982). Challenges in the 1981 Act. *Special Education Forwards Trends, 9*(2), 6–8.

5 Disability Classification, Categorization in Education

A US Perspective

Philip J. Burke and Kristin Ruedel

The classification, categorization, and labeling of children and youth with disabilities is controversial and continually debated within the United States (Deschenes, Tyack, & Cuban, 2001; Donovan & Cross, 2002; Losen & Orfield, 2002; Yell, Rogers, & Lodge, 1998). Classification of children has been used to support both the isolation and inclusion of individuals with disabilities at different times in history. Some disability advocates, international organizations, and researchers challenge the need to categorize children with disabilities because labeling children can perpetuate the medical approach to disability and lead to the stigmatization of children (Cromwell, Blashfield, & Strauss, 1975). All too frequently, a disability label does little to inform teachers or schools about what a child may need and contributes to the assumption that all children in a category function in the same way or require the same instruction.

Yet, from an educational policy-making perspective, a classification system can be very useful. In general, the purpose of the classification system used in the Individuals with Disabilities Education Improvement Act (IDEA) of 2004 is to identify and determine which students are entitled to additional educational services, interventions, and resources to address individual student needs. Here, classification can serve as a useful tool for administration and program planning. It supports a common understanding of what constitutes a "child with disability" and, therefore, can be an effective and efficient way to determine which students should receive additional educational services and how resources should be allocated and distributed to support these services (Lazerson, 1983; Losen & Orfield, 2002; Martin, Martin, & Terman, 1996). In this regard, classification systems are considered an important step to ensuring equal opportunity in the allocation of resources and instructional services.

Classification of students with disabilities for purposes of receiving special education, however, has serious implications for the educational opportunities afforded to children. As noted above, positive impacts include provision of additional opportunities, supports, services, and accommodations that meet the individual needs of a student and can help the student realize his or her full potential. Classification may also provide a structure to how supports and services are organized and how students are assigned to those resources. Nonetheless, the process of classifying students can result in negative, unintended consequences, among them, the loss of educational opportunities resulting from being tracked into segregated special educational classes that fail to provide full access to challenging subject matter curriculum. Other negative impacts can include alienation from peers, stigma resulting in a diminished sense of competence and self-esteem, and lowered teacher and parental expectations of the child (Keogh & MacMillan, 1996).

The purpose of this chapter is to provide a historical overview of the classification system used in the United States to identify students eligible for special education services. The chapter discusses (1) categorization and treatment of students with disabilities prior to 1975; (2) the landmark Hobbs Report (1975a) based on the Project on Classification of Exceptional Children; and (3) the Education for All Handicapped Children Act (P.L. 94-142) of 1975 (now referred to as the Individuals with Disabilities Education Improvement Act of 2004 [P.L. 108-446]). It concludes with a reflection on a key sentiment expressed in the final recommendation of the Hobbs Report: that policy must "nurture well all of our children."

PRIOR TO 1975

In the United States, as in other countries, there have always been students who struggle to achieve in schools. Prior to the passage of the US Education for All Handicapped Children Act (P.L. 94-142) in 1975, students who were struggling or failing were often retained in grade, assigned to lower level or vocational curricular tracks, and/or expelled (Hendrick & MacMillan, 1989). These students were often labeled as slow, backward, delinquent, or incapable of learning (Hobbs, 1975a). Within the larger group of struggling students, those with disabilities were often excluded from school entirely (Martin et al., 1996). Despite universal compulsory attendance laws, prior to 1975, school districts could choose whether they wanted to serve students with disabilities as there was no federal law and few state laws that required them to provide educational services to children with disabilities. Prior to the passing of the Education for All Handicapped Children Act (PL 94–142), not only were school districts permitted to exclude children with disabilities but these decisions were also upheld and reinforced by many courts. Children who were deemed "weak in the mind," for example, were viewed as unfit for instruction, unable to benefit from the educational system, and schools were not expected nor required to provide appropriate educational opportunities for them (Yell et al., 1998). In the state of Pennsylvania, school-aged children with disabilities were arbitrarily excluded from school. A survey conducted by the Pennsylvania Association for Retarded Children found thousands of children excluded from public schools. In response to a class action suit, Pennsylvania agreed in 1971 to provide every child with mental retardation an appropriate education from the ages of six to twenty-one. The state had maintained that children who were mentally retarded would not benefit from an education, that local school systems could provide an education if they so chose, but were not required by state law to do so.

As recently as the early 1970s, US schools educated only one in five children with disabilities (United States Office of Special Education and Rehabilitative Services, 2000). The situation did not begin to change in the United States until the late 1960s when advocates and parents brought their cases to the US federal courts, which began to issue rulings supporting the education of all children with disabilities. As discussed by Pullin in Chapter 6, the right to education was argued under the equal protection clause of the US Constitution. The basis for compelling systems to educate all children was essentially that if public tax dollars were spent on some children, all children must benefit and be educated.

In addition to lack of access, those students with disabilities that were enrolled in schools often were not given appropriate services to enable them to succeed. Typically, they were either placed in regular education classes with no special education services or were placed in special programs that did not provide them with adequate services and supports (Martin et al., 1996). It should be noted that prior to the federal government's involvement in special education, some states and local school districts had established policies that provided educational opportunities to students with disabilities. There was great variation among states and local districts, however, in how students with disabilities were included and/or excluded.

THE HOBBS REPORT

In 1972, Edward Zigler, director of the Office of Child Development in the US Department of Health, Education, and Welfare, instituted a major government initiative with the support of the Secretary of Health, Education, and Welfare Elliot Richardson and ten federal agencies, all of which had an interest in the topic of classification systems and the resultant categorization of students. According to Secretary Richardson, although research had been conducted on the use of appropriate diagnostic procedures for classifying children, the results of these studies had not been widely disseminated and appropriate diagnostic procedures still needed to by standardized and their use enforced. Thus, the purpose of this initiative was to conduct a systematic review of the policies and procedures used to classify and label children and their consequences.

What evolved from this initiative was the Project on Classification of Exceptional Children. The classification project had three objectives: (1) to increase public understanding of problems associated with classification systems and categorizing children who are handicapped, disadvantaged, or delinquent; (2) to provide a rationale for public administrative regulations and guidelines bearing on classification systems and their consequences; and (3) to improve professional practice of educators, psychologists, physicians, lawyers, social workers, and others responsible for the well-being of exceptional children (Hobbs, 1975b). Once under way, the project narrowed its focus somewhat and concentrated on four issues: (1) the technical adequacy of diagnostic and classification systems; (2) the effects of labeling on individual children; (3) the consequences (such as special class placement or institutionalization) that may ensue when a student is assigned a disability label; and (4) the social, legal, and ethical implications of categorizing and labeling children, with a view toward achieving a sensible balance between individual rights and the common good (Hobbs, 1975b).

To meet the objectives of the project, a task force of ninety-three experts was called on to summarize the existing knowledge base on the following six topics: "(1) theoretical issues in classification; (2) systems for classifying handicapped, disadvantaged, and delinquent children and youth; (3) institutional experiences that children have as a consequence of

being classified; (4) classification and its consequences from the perspective of parents, minority-group members, and children themselves;
(5) classification and the legal status of exceptional children; and (6) public
policy issues affecting exceptional children" (Hobbs, 1975b, p. viii). These
experts represented educators, psychologists, psychiatrists, pediatricians,
sociologists, public administrators, lawyers, and parents of children with
disabilities. Their review and evaluation of disability categorization was
conducted under seven general assumptions. First, it was assumed that
categorization of children with disabilities was essential to procure additional resources, supports, and services and to effectively design programs
and evaluate the progress of students in specialized programs. Second, the
task force assumed that classification policies should be designed to support children from diverse backgrounds, foster individual abilities, and
maintain the respect for all children. Third, all citizens are responsible for
the abuse of categories and labels as applied to children and unsatisfactory
programs and services provided to these children. Fourth, specialized
programs and policies for students with disabilities should be designed
to reduce the amount of time excluded from same-age peers and should
encourage inclusive participation in school, family, and community life.
Fifth, categorization of students can result in negative consequences such
as exclusion and loss of opportunity. Sixth, classification systems and
labeling students can result in positive impacts and lead to improved educational programs and legislation for students with disabilities. For example, classification systems can provide lobbying support for disability
advocates and organizations. Seventh, there is a need to develop a new
national policy to improve the educational opportunities and services provided to all students not just students with disabilities.

The work of the task force resulted in two publications: *Issues in the
Classification of Children*, edited by Nicolas Hobbs (1975b), and *The Futures
of Children* (Hobbs, 1975a). *Issues in the Classification of Children* was written
to provide a foundation for public policy and presents a systematic review
and summary about the classification of children and related problems.
The two-volume work consists of 31 papers written by members of the
task force and is divided into the six topic areas addressed by the experts
(i.e., Theoretical Issues, Classification Systems, Institutions, Special
Perspectives, Legal Aspects, and Public Policy Questions). *The Futures of
Children*, the final report of the project, synthesizes and analyzes the
reviews prepared by the task force. It addresses issues related to the legal
status of children classified as disabled, including due process, presents a
comprehensive plan for linking services to meet the needs of individual
children and reduce duplication of services, and provides numerous
recommendations to improve the classification and education of children

with disabilities. These recommendations primarily address the following seven areas: (1) helping families help children with disabilities, (2) improving classification systems, (3) reducing the unintended negative consequences of classification and labeling, (4) improving educational programs, (5) coordinating services for children with disabilities and providing training, (6) establishing patterns of funding programs for children with disabilities, and (7) conducting additional research on child development and public policy (Hobbs, 1975a).

To date, these books provide one of the most comprehensive discussions of disability classification systems in health, education, and mental health, including recommendations for addressing problems and unintentional consequences. For example, public policy issues of funding, labeling, and special education services were explored in the chapter by Gallagher, Forsythe, Ringelheim, and Weintraub (1975). Recognizing the essential role that state special education directors play in allocating funds for services to children with disabilities, Gallagher et al. administered a survey (Labeling and Special Education) to the highest official responsible for special education programming in each state. The purposes of the survey were to learn more about current policies for children with disabilities in each state and to consider the opinions of special education directors about classification and potential changes.

All forty-two survey respondents reported that children with disabilities were labeled or categorized in their state. Ninety percent of the respondents reported that their state used specific disabilities labels; the remaining 10% of the respondents reported that their state used general labels such as handicapped, developmentally disabled, or child with special problems. When asked why their state maintained the current labeling system, approximately half of the respondents said that federal laws and regulations had forced the state to establish their current labeling system or was the motivation behind continuing to support the current system. Respondents were also asked to provide their opinion regarding eliminating labeling, and more than 75% of directors of special education believed that elimination of the classification system and disability categories would result in a substantial reduction in special program funding and services delivered to students with disabilities. Some even indicated that without their use, special education would cease to exist (Gallagher et al., 1975). One respondent said that "the very survival of delivery of appropriate educational opportunities to the handicapped is based on the continuation of labels to identify target populations for which earmarked funds can be appropriated" (Gallagher et al., 1975, p. 456).

A notable exception to this point of view was manifested by the state of Minnesota. Beginning in 1957, Minnesota set aside the practice of labeling and categorizing students and developed an alternative funding system that focused on providing quality personnel and programs that would meet the educational needs of all children, including children with special needs. Therefore, the state paid two thirds of the salary costs of personnel needed to meet the individual needs of children with special needs.

In the final report for the project, *The Futures of Children*, Hobbs asserted that maintaining classification systems was politically necessary to (1) appeal to legislators with an interest in some particular handicapping condition, (2) obtain backing for epidemiological studies, (3) channel federal and state funds, and (4) marshal public and legislative support" (1975a, pp. 98–99)." Although the experts on the task force generally believed that a system for classifying children with disabilities was important for allocating resources and accessing services, alternatives for how children should be classified and systems for categorizing children were explored. To this day, researchers, policymakers, and practitioners continue to wrestle with the key challenges of classification identified in the Hobbs Report.

Today, there is wide variation among US states in the use of disability classification in education. As shown by Ebersold and Evans in Chapter 3, there is also variation internationally from country to country. Thus, it is essential to understand who is included in the various disability categories to effectively compare the educational opportunities afforded to students and to support the use of educational assessments and accountability mechanisms. A classification system can be useful to protect the educational rights of children with disabilities by requiring that schools develop the necessary capacity to provide appropriate learning supports for all children including specialized interventions and instruction, additional resources, and appropriately trained personnel. As Speece notes in Chapter 14, classification systems should meet certain criteria. In the United States, classification of students with disabilities is prescribed through federal legislation.

IDEA

The Individuals with Disabilities Education Improvement Act of 2004 (IDEA) is the primary US federal policy that defines which students are eligible for special education supports and services and protects students with disabilities against discrimination. The IDEA entitles eligible students to special education and related services as well as early intervention services for infants and toddlers. The IDEA requires states to provide a free appropriate public education (FAPE) in the least restrictive environment

(LRE). The act specifies 13 disability categories: (1) autism; (2) deaf-blindness; (3) deafness; (4) emotional disturbance; (5) hearing impairment; (6) mental retardation; (7) multiple disabilities; (8) orthopedic impairment; (9) other health impairment; (10) specific learning disability; (11) speech and language impairment; (12) traumatic brain injury; and (13) visual impairment, including blindness. Determining student eligibility for special education supports and services under the IDEA is complex and highly regulated (McLaughlin et al., 2006). The classification system under the IDEA uses a two-pronged approach. First, a child must be determined to have one of the thirteen disabilities defined in IDEA. Second, it must be documented that the disability results in an adverse impact on the student's progress in meeting the required educational standards in the classroom. Court rulings such as *Diana v. State Board of Education* (1970), *Guadalupe Organization v. Tempe Elementary School District* (1972), and *Pennsylvania Association for Retarded Children [PARC] v. Pennsylvania* (1972) have paved the way for the IDEA regulations on how students should be evaluated to determine eligibility (McLaughlin et al., 2006). According to the IDEA, the process must be individualized, address multiple domains, and include a multidisciplinary team. Limited English speaking skills and lack of appropriate instruction cannot be used as factors in determining eligibility for special education supports and services.

When a child receives special education services under the IDEA, he or she must have an Individualized Education Program (IEP). This is a written document listing, among other things, the special educational services that the child will receive. The IEP is developed by a team that includes the child's parents and school staff. The IEP is central to the provision of services under the IDEA and embodies the legal entitlement that each child with a disability has to a free and appropriate public education.

The classification system, the criteria for the thirteen disability categories, and the eligibility process to receive special education services as defined in the IDEA have evolved somewhat over the past twenty-seven years from a strict medical model that emphasized medical conditions to a model that also recognizes the social and environmental context of disability. To be eligible for special education under IDEA, a child must have a defined disability in one of the above categories and that disability must "adversely affect" his or her educational performance. Currently, eligibility for special education services continues to be primarily grounded in a disability-deficit paradigm but employs a combination of the medical and social system models of deviance (Reschly, 1987). Under the medical model, individuals with a disability are defined by their illness or medical condition. The medical model promotes the view of a person with a disability as dependent and needing to be cured or cared for, and justifies the way in which they have been systematically excluded from society. In this model, it is assumed that the person with the disability is the problem, as opposed to the environment (i.e., school). In contrast, the social model recognizes that disability is a combination of the child's abilities and the environment (i.e., interventions provided within the school) and is not considered the "fault" of an individual with a disability. Under the social model, disability is the product of the physical, organizational, and attitudinal barriers present within society that lead to discrimination. In other words, it is the societal barriers that exist in education, the workplace, health and social support services, and so on, that prevent an individual from effectively participating in society. The devaluing of individuals with disabilities through negative images in the media—films, television, and newspapers— also acts as a barrier. A primary goal of the social model is to remove the societal barriers that inhibit or prevent active participation in society and our schools so that individuals with disabilities are provided the same opportunities as everyone else.

SUMMARY

Given the efforts and results of over thirty years of toil and practice in the field of special education in the United States with respect to the issue of labeling and classification, it is useful to reflect on the final recommendation of the Hobbs Report: to increase national awareness and develop national policies that will support and nurture all children so that all children are afforded the opportunity to reach their full potential.

It appears the dilemma so eloquently posed by Hobbs in 1975, that a classification system yielding labels can have the simultaneous effect of both excluding and including children, is still with us today. Classification allows for refined systems of resource allocation and accountability in schools, at the same time it involves barriers, because the concept of all children and its definition comes with subcategories and special rules of entry and exit for students with disabilities. In a more perfect world "all" would mean *all* and not require legally defined groups, categories, and entitlements defined in a mandated system of classification. The major difference currently (in contrast with the era described by Hobbs) is the nature and extent of exclusion. Currently in the United States, it is defined by the degree of integration and inclusion children with disabilities experience in the schooling process.

In the wake of the enactment of legislation protecting the educational rights of children and youth with disabilities, as well as the No Child Left Behind legislation in the United States, one might well ask if we are nurturing all of our children well. Or, to paraphrase an eloquent speech by a most distinguished citizen of the United Kingdom: Have we merely experienced an end to the beginning of our quest to truly educate all children?

REFERENCES

Cromwell, R. L., Blashfield, R. K., & Strauss, J. S. (1975). Criteria for classification systems. In N. Hobbs (Ed.), *Issues in the classification of children: A sourcebook on categories, labels, and their consequences* (Vol. 1, pp. 4–25). San Francisco: Jossey-Bass.

Deschenes, S., Tyack, D., & Cuban, L. (2001). Mismatch: Historical perspectives on schools and students who don't fit them. *Teachers College Record, 103*(4), 525–547. Retrieved June 11, 2006, from http://www.tcrecord.org

Donovan, M. S., & Cross, C. T. (Eds.). (2002). *Minority students in special education and gifted education.* Washington, DC: National Academy of Sciences.

Gallagher, J. J., Forsythe, P., Ringelheim, D., & Weintraub, F. J. (1975). Funding patterns and labeling. In N. Hobbs (Ed.), *Issues in the classification of children: A sourcebook on categories, labels, and their consequences* (Vol. 2, pp. 432–462). San Francisco: Jossey-Bass.

Hendrick, I. G., & MacMillan, D. L. (1989). Selecting children for special education in New York City: William Maxwell, Elizabeth Farrell, and the development of ungraded classes, 1900–1920. *The Journal of Special Education, 22*(4), 395–417.

Hobbs, N. (1975a). *The futures of children: Categories, labels, and their consequences* (Hobbs Report). San Francisco: Jossey-Bass.

Hobbs, N. (Ed.). (1975b). *Issues in the classification of children: A sourcebook on categories, labels, and their consequences* (2 vols.). San Francisco: Jossey-Bass.

Keogh, B. K., & MacMillan, D. L. (1996). Exceptionality. In D. C. Berliner & R. C. Calfee (Eds.), *Handbook of educational psychology* (pp. 311–330). New York: Simon & Schuster Macmillan.

Lazerson, M. (1983). The origins of special education. In J. G. Chambers & W. T. Hartman (Eds.), *Special education policies: Their history, implementation and finance* (pp. 3–47). Philadelphia: Temple University Press.

Losen, D., & Orfield, G. (Eds.). (2002). *Racial inequity in special education.* Cambridge, MA: Harvard Education Press.

Martin, E., Martin, R., & Terman, D. (1996). The legislative and litigation history of special education. *The Future of Children, 6*, 25–39.

McLaughlin, M., Dyson, A., Nagle, K., Thurlow, M., Rouse, M., Hardman, M., Norwich, B., Burke, P., & Esquire, M. P. (2006). Cross-cultural perspectives on the classification of children with disabilities: Part 2. Implementing classification systems in schools. *Journal of Special Education, 40*(1), 46–58.

Reschly, D. (1987). Assessing educational handicaps. In A. Hess & I. Weiner (Eds.), *The handbook of forensic psychology* (pp. 155–187). New York: Wiley.

United States Office of Special Education and Rehabilitative Services. (2000). *Annual report.* Washington, DC: Government Printing Office.

Yell, M., Rogers, D., & Lodge, R. (1998). The legal history of special education: What a long strange trip it's been! *Remedial and Special Education, 19*, 32–47.

6 Implications for Human and Civil Rights Entitlements

Stigma, Stereotypes, and Civil Rights in Disability Classification Systems

Diana C. Pullin

Martha Minow, the talented legal scholar and social commentator, thoughtfully articulated the public policy dilemmas associated with disability status and other classifications used as policy tools. She described the "dilemmas of difference" associated with the policy choices required in determining when it is appropriate to create a classification and treat people differently, weighing the consequences of imposing labels, and potentially stigma, on people because of their differences against the need to label them so that they can access services and legal protections designed to address their exceptional needs (Minow, 1990, p. 20). This trade-off between the utility and the consequences of classification plays out differently in each context in which it occurs, changing over time as our conception of the common good and our notions of exceptionality shift.

Disability classifications both represent and reflect the challenges associated with the pursuit of equality of opportunity. In the United States, the last quarter of the twentieth century was marked by increasing endorsement of the public policy goals of avoiding discrimination on the basis of disability; eliminating insidious stereotypes and generalizations; promoting respect, dignity, and the worth of every individual; treating everyone equitably despite differences; ensuring that individuals with disabilities have access to educational and employment opportunities; and promoting the opportunity for those with and without disabilities to interact with one another. At the same time, public policy initiatives used disability status to distinguish people based on their differences so that they could qualify for programs, services, and protections.

At the start of the new millennium, as technology, the cognitive sciences, and medical advances present a growing array of diagnostic and adaptive approaches, there are possibilities for new types of classification determinations. In addition, the existence of a diagnosed disability is only one part of a multifaceted classification system employed by judges and legislators. Eligibility for protected status or differential treatment on the basis of disability has evolved into a complex consideration of social, public policy, economic, and educational issues extending beyond the labeling of a diagnostic disability category. At the same time, the press for performance-based, test-driven accountability creates new pressures on classification systems and on the delivery of effective and efficient educational services (see Nagle and Thurlow, Chapter 12).

In the United States, for more than thirty years, federal and state statutes, regulations, and court and administrative hearing officer decisions have played a dominant role in the education of students with disabilities (Benveniste, 1986; Chambers & Hartman, 1983; Hehir & Latus, 1992; Huefner, 2000; Pullin, 1999; Weber, Mawdsley, & Redfield, 2004). These legal mandates resulted from a civil rights movement in the early and mid-1970s on behalf of persons with disabilities who had previously been excluded from many of the educational, economic, and social benefits of society (Butts & Cremin, 1953; Cremin, 1951; Lazerson, 1983). By the beginning of the new millennium, however, legal controversies involving disability status were evolving into a struggle over the meaning of disability, not only in terms of a diagnostic determination but also in light of the impact of disability conditions on participation in the full range of educational activities.

This chapter addresses the public policy and legal uses of disability classifications. It argues that any understanding of classification systems and, in particular, classification systems with legal ramifications must be understood in light of the contexts in which classification occurs. As individuals with disabilities become more widely accepted in educational institutions and in society at large, the legal ramifications of classification are changing.

USES OF CLASSIFICATIONS IN LAW

In the United States, there are two types of legal claims addressing disability status that are significant for any consideration of the implications of disability classifications in education. First, there are constitutional provisions regarding government classification practices and issues arising under state and federal statutes providing broad civil rights protections to individuals with disabilities. Second, there are separate state and federal statutes defining the terms and conditions for the provision of special education programs and services, and recent statutes promoting test-driven, standards-based education reform and accountability. The next chapter will discuss the particular issues of disability classifications and statutes regulating the provision of special education services in the United States.

Classifications and the US Constitution

Modern legal traditions in Western nations have, for over fifty years, relied heavily upon the use of classification systems to create protections for groups traditionally disadvantaged in social or political contexts or in the provision of education or social services. The use of classification has been different in systems of judge-made law and in legislated approaches.

In the United States, for example, a traditional judicial interpretation of the provisions of the Equal Protection Clause of the United States Constitution relies upon the identification of the types of classification systems employed by government actors and agencies and the use and consequences of those classifications. The Equal Protection Clause reads, "No state shall . . . deny to any person within its jurisdiction the equal protection of the laws" (US Constitution, Amendment XIV, Section 1). This clause does not ensure equality to all people, but rather ensures equal application of the laws; thus, it is invoked by groups who feel that the laws burden them or deny them a right based on some classification, such as gender, race, or disability status. The courts enforce the Equal Protection Clause differently based upon the nature of the classification used and the consequences of the classification determination. The pre-eminent US constitutional law scholar Laurence Tribe described Equal Protection analysis during the late twentieth century as involving the identification of

> Both those fundamental aspects of the social and legal structure
> which should be equally open to all, and those criteria of government

classification most likely to reflect prejudiced reactions against various types of persons and thus most likely to deny the basic right of all persons to be treated as equals. (Tribe, 2000, pp. 14–15)

Courts in the United States have articulated a set of decision theories, and revised them over time as social and political conditions changed, to consider the acceptability (constitutionality) of classification practices. These theories were most widespread and most detailed in the consideration of classifications on the basis of race. Classifications on the basis of such factors as gender, socioeconomic status, citizenship, and residency have also been scrutinized. A growing number of cases, as well as judicial refinement of applicable decision theories, has developed concerning gender classifications. There have been constitutional law cases decided under the Equal Protection Clause regarding disability status, but these cases are relatively few in number and have not extended across the broad range of disability categories, focusing instead primarily on individuals with intellectual challenges or emotional disabilities.

Across all of the types of classification practices scrutinized under the federal Equal Protection Clause, the courts have developed over time an analytic approach that, in effect, classifies the types of government classifications under review. The more politically and socially troublesome the basis or the impact of a classification approach, the more closely courts will scrutinize a classification. Under this approach, for example, classifications that treat people differently in their access to the fundamental rights set forth in the US constitutional system (such as the rights to vote, to free expression, or to religious freedom) are looked at with particularly strict scrutiny by the courts. For classifications based on membership in a particular type of group, race-based classifications are the least likely to withstand judicial scrutiny, being regarded as inherently suspicious and able to withstand judicial review only if government can present a compelling reason for the classification and also that the means used to achieve that goal are necessary, with no less intrusive manner of approach. Government almost always loses once this level of scrutiny is applied. So, for example, deciding to consider race as a factor in admission to a state university program is only acceptable when the university can demonstrate a compelling need to have a diverse student body and, even then, only if race is used as some "plus" factor in a holistic review of an admissions application, not part of a quota system for deciding who is admitted (*Gratz v. Bollinger*, 2003; *Grutter v. Bollinger*, 2003).

On the other hand, there are some government classifications that are not subject to the type of strict scrutiny applied to race-based classifications, but are still inherently troublesome for social, political, or historic reasons. So, for example, gender-based classifications are generally regarded as less potentially troublesome than race-based classifications but still worthy of considerable attention by reviewing courts. Gender classifications are looked at closely, but not as closely as race classifications. Gender classifications are justifiable only if government can prove that it is trying to address some particularly important need and has some exceedingly persuasive rationale for utilizing the gender classification (*U.S. v. Virginia*, 1996). Thus, a rule requiring particular treatment of pregnant women in a workplace involving toxics particularly hazardous for women of childbearing ages might be allowed, but a rule barring women from participating in a military academy run by the government would not be allowed.

Disability-based classifications, at least those challenged to date before the United States Supreme Court, have not been regarded as worthy of any special level of judicial scrutiny of government activities. As a result, government classifications utilizing disability classifications will be acceptable to US courts under the Equal Protection Clause if there is some rational basis for the classification and it furthers some legitimate government objective.[1] Most government activities meet this type of standard. The interpretations of state constitutions generally follow the same approach.

Interesting public policy and legal issues arise from these standards of judicial interpretation regarding the meaning of the constitutional obligation for government to afford Equal Protection of the law in the United States, as would be the case in most nations. These legal standards have always changed over time as political, social, and economic contexts have changed. So, for example, in the United States for decades, race-based classifications were seen as acceptable and many instances of government-sponsored race-based approaches were accepted if they were seen as benefiting previously disadvantaged racial minority groups. Over time, race-based approaches became less socially and politically acceptable and an increasingly socially conservative federal judiciary began to reject many race-based classifications, striking down many previously acceptable practices used to advance the interests of traditionally disadvantaged minorities. As disability status becomes a more visible issue and closer to home to the increasing number of families who are involved with disabling conditions, will the scrutiny by courts of disability-based classifications also change, with judges becoming less tolerant of disability classifications unless there is a very persuasive reason for engaging in this type of classification? At present, given the relatively weak constitutional protections for individuals with disabilities, statutory provisions have had the greatest significance in disability classifications and their consequences.

Legislated Classifications to Protect Civil and Human Rights

Although the courts have not been particularly expansive in defining rights and protecting individuals with disabilities under the US Constitution, legislative bodies have been more active, both at the national and state government levels. Under both national and state statutes, very detailed sets of classifications have been created defining disabilities and the extent of protections for individuals with those disabilities. Although there are analogous provisions in most states and in some localities, particularly urban municipalities, this discussion focuses on statutes adopted by the United States Congress. These federal statutes can themselves be classified into two groups: civil or human rights statutes and education statutes. This chapter discusses the civil or human rights statutes; the next chapter discusses statutes specific to education.

There are two primary US statutes creating specific human rights or civil rights protections for individuals with disabilities. The first civil rights statute creating rights for individuals with disabilities defined disability categories and articulated a general nondiscrimination requirement. Section 504 of the Rehabilitation Act of 1973 provides that

> No otherwise qualified individual with a disability in the United States . . . shall solely by reason of her or his disability, be excluded from the participation in, be denied the benefits of, or be subjected to discrimination under any program or activity receiving Federal financial assistance.

The statute only applies to public or private entities that have chosen to receive federal financial assistance from the US Department of Education[2] and it creates a two-part criterion for eligibility for the protections under the statute: An individual must be "otherwise qualified" and must have a "disability." Section 504 requires nondiscrimination in education and employment; program accessibility/physical accessibility to the premises; reasonable accommodations for disabilities; and, through its regulations, the provision of free appropriate public education in elementary and secondary education.[3]

The second United States federal civil rights statute is the Americans with Disabilities Act of 1990 (ADA). The ADA defines an almost identical set of protected individuals,[4] but applies much more broadly and in more specific detail. There are three separate sections to the ADA, governing government activities and other public services, public accommodations like private schools, and employment (including activities of many private employers).[5] Among the detailed provisions Congress incorporated into the ADA are such requirements as those barring discrimination in the implementation of testing (e.g., higher education admissions testing or state elementary or secondary accountability testing).

The broad nondiscrimination provisions of both ADA and Section 504 include requirements for reasonable accommodations or modifications to meet the needs of individuals with disabilities. So, ADA is violated when an educational program fails to make reasonable modifications in policies, practices, or procedures, when such modifications are necessary to afford such goods, services, and accommodations to individuals with disabilities, and the covered program has not demonstrated that such modifications would fundamentally alter the nature of such goods, services, or accommodations (42 U.S.C. § 12182). Section 504 provides similar protections.

The disability classifications created under both these laws (ADA and Section 504) are defined in three ways, any one of which would make an individual eligible for the protections of this law:

- Any person with a physical or mental impairment that substantially limits one or more major life activities;
- Any person who has a record of such impairment; or
- Any person who is regarded as having such an impairment (42 U.S.C. § 12102(2); 29 U.S.C. § 794(d)).

Clearly, the first category covers the largest number of individuals, those with functional limitations. There has not been much judicial activity concerning the latter two categories in education, which seem particularly designed to meet the public policy goal of barring stigmatization associated with disability status for those wrongfully treated as if they have a disability when they in fact do not. The increasing level of litigation concerning the first category presents an interesting opportunity to assess the changing role of law-based disability classification. Although most of this litigation has arisen in the higher education or employment context, it provides some useful insights into the future of disability classification in elementary and secondary education.

DIMINISHING DISABILITY

Litigation in the United States over the definition of "disability" reflects an increased narrowing by judges of the number of people who have disabilities and are also eligible for protection under the national civil rights laws. There is a general presumption under both the ADA and Section 504 that there is a wide range of physical or physiological, mental, and psychological disorders that would allow a person to be covered under the statute. Hence, the regulations defining disabilities covered by the laws include a fairly broad list of diagnostic categories of "impairments."

Courts have generally engaged in thoughtful scrutiny of diagnostic data and testimony from expert witnesses to determine whether an individual seeking ADA or Section 504 protections falls within an appropriate diagnostic category for statutory coverage. Take as an example a case involving a medical student whose learning disability caused difficulties in succeeding on medical school exams due to what initially presented as "cognitive deficits and weaknesses in processing discrete units of information" (and was later formally diagnosed as "dyslexia"). The federal court of appeals considering the case found that the impairments covered under the statute include, in addition to physiological disorders, "any mental or psychological disorder, such as mental retardation, organic brain syndrome, emotional or mental illness, and specific learning disabilities" (*Wynne v. Tufts University School of Medicine* (Wynne I), p. 23*)*. In another case, involving a private high school student who had idiopathic thrombocytopenic purpura (ITP), a serious autoimmune disease in which any bleeding could be life-threatening,[6] the trial court defined a "physical impairment" according to the regulations issued by the federal government as "any physiological disorder or condition which affects any one of the several body systems, including the hemic, or blood, system" (*Thomas v. Davidson Academy*, 1994, citing regulations at 28 C.F.R. § 36.104).

The regulatory listing of diagnostic categories is reasonably straightforward for judges and others to utilize. The disability classification becomes more complicated, however, as the courts have focused less on the diagnostic category, turning an increasing amount of attention to the statutory language limiting protections to individuals who are (1) "substantially limited" in a (2) "major life activity." In recent years, under the leadership of the US Supreme Court, judges have used these two provisions to narrow further and further the individuals entitled to statutory protection. At the same time, US courts have also paid increasing attention to whether reasonable accommodations could be offered to allow an individual with a disability to qualify to participate in a program or activity. Each of these types of determinations relative to the protections of US civil rights statutes for individuals with disabilities will be discussed below.

Major Life Activities

Thus far, US courts have recognized as "major life activities" such things as caring for one's self, performing manual tasks, walking, seeing, reading, hearing, speaking, breathing, learning, and working. There were also cases determining that "major life activities" did not include gardening, golfing, or shopping. It is the more ambiguous activities that have been the focus of litigation. The US Supreme Court has clarified the meaning of major life activity, finding that an activity may qualify even if it is not one specifically contemplated by a disability statute, as long as the activity is of central importance to most people's daily lives and the impairment's impact is permanent or long term (*Toyota Manufacturing v. Williams*, 2002). This determination, the Court has ruled, must be made on an individualized basis (*Sutton v. United Air Lines*, 1999). Determination that a disability impacts a major life activity is only one consideration a court must weigh under these statutes. Courts must also assess whether the disability "substantially limits" that major life activity, and whether reasonable accommodations would enable an individual to participate in the activity.

Comparison Groups

Recently, increasing judicial attention has been paid to whether an individual claiming disability-based civil rights protections was "substantially limited" in a major life activity. These court determinations are highly individualized and context-specific, but once the US Supreme Court decided a case calling for the determination of "substantial limitation" on the basis of using a comparison group approach, the trend in the litigation sharply turned. No bright line test was established here, but the considerations judges could take into account began to be articulated.

The consideration of whether an individual with a disability has a "substantial limitation" takes two factors into account, according to recent court decisions. The limitation on a major life activity must be substantial, not merely minor, and the limitation must require more than some difficulty as compared to most people. The issue of the appropriate comparison group to use in assessing limitations is a current focus of debate over whether to compare the individual claiming a violation of disability law with a close peer group (e.g., others in undergraduate or graduate school) or with the general population. Increasingly, courts are relying on the latter standard and comparing individuals with disabilities with the general population, thus making it harder to prove that one is both disabled and eligible for protection under the law. This classification trend began in 2002 with the US Supreme Court's decision in an employment case (*Toyota Manufacturing v. Williams*, 2002). In *Toyota*, a female employee with carpal tunnel syndrome who had difficulty with lifting heavy weights and engaging in repetitive arm movements sued her former employer for violation of ADA for failure to accommodate her disability, alleging substantial impairment with performing manual tasks (a major life activity). The Court held that major life activity of performing manual tasks refers to manual tasks in the daily life of most people, not manual tasks necessary for a person's job. As a result, to the Supreme Court, manual tasks did not mean lifting heavy objects as part of employment activities, but instead a person's ability to perform daily living tasks such as household chores, bathing, or brushing one's teeth.

Because much of the litigation subsequent to *Toyota* about comparison groups in education cases has arisen among members of professions or competitive graduate or professional programs, the outcomes are a little daunting for any consideration of US classification policy.[7] For example, in cases involving law students or medical students who claim a disability, if someone has difficulty reading or studying in school but, nonetheless, has achieved at least average success *as compared to most people*, the individual will likely not be considered eligible for protection under the statutes. In medical and law school cases, where students have been relatively successful throughout their educational history (as compared to the general population, as some judges have pointed out, or they probably never would have been accepted to a professional school in the first place), the application of this standard results in determinations that individuals who might have spent their entire lives, or at least a significant portion of their educational careers, with disability status, may no longer be regarded, at least under law, as being eligible for a disability classification entitled to the nondiscrimination provisions of federal civil rights laws.[8]

The *Toyota* line of cases represents a substantial diminishing of the number of individuals who are eligible for disability status and civil rights protections under the law. But these comparison group cases are not the only ones resulting in a limitation in the size of the population of individuals with disabilities protected by federal civil rights law.

The Mitigation Doctrine

The next set of significant cases concerning disabilities and eligibility for protection under the US civil rights laws focus on consideration of the issue of "substantial impairment" from another perspective, that is, whether corrective measures have or could be taken to mitigate the impact of a disabling condition. Before 1999, the US Supreme Court did not consider corrective devices or "mitigating measures" when determining whether one had a disability covered and protected under ADA. Therefore, if an individual had an impairment that substantially limited a major life activity, he or she was protected under the statutes regardless of whether corrective devices or medication were available to help cope with the disability. In 1999, however, the Supreme Court began to consider the effect of such measures on the impairment (*Sutton v. United Airlines*, 1999). These cases[9] assess whether corrective devices or measures exist that sufficiently mitigate an impairment so that it does not substantially limit a major life activity. Thus, a person with substantial vision impairment who could use glasses (or contact lenses) or a person with hearing impairment who could effectively use a hearing aid or a diabetic who could take medication that can significantly mitigate the challenges associated with a disability may lose eligibility for protection under the US civil rights laws barring discrimination on the basis of disability. The critical factor is that in order to be eligible for protection under these disability statutes, an individual must demonstrate that, notwithstanding the use of a corrective or mitigating device, that individual is substantially limited in a major life activity.

These fairly recent mitigation and comparison group cases open up the prospect of a potential "slippery slope" of legalistic distinctions further narrowing the number of persons with physical or mental impairments who are eligible for US civil rights statutory protections. Many disabilities are immutable and unmitigatible. But others are not, or are not in certain situations. So, would a person permanently in a wheelchair that considerably ameliorates disability in some circumstances, but not all, be protected under the statutes and in which circumstances? What about a child on Ritalin for attention deficit disorder (ADD)? In these cases, judges will look to the individual facts in a dispute to see if the use of corrective or mitigating approaches actually improves the situation in the particular context in which disability-based discrimination is being alleged. Use of medication or corrective measures by themselves, even if they have some beneficial effect, may not eliminate substantial limitations associated with the disability.[10]

The United States Congress generally has the power to amend the federal civil rights statutes to blunt the effect of the Supreme Court's bold limitations on the numbers of individuals entitled to civil rights protections, but it has not done so. And, in another contest with the Supreme Court over Congress' power to regulate state officials and agencies treatment of their own employees under the provisions of the ADA, Congress has been resoundingly defeated by the Court on grounds that it has overstepped the limits of its powers to intrude on the state's autonomy in efforts to regulate against disability-based discrimination against state employees (*Board of Trustees of University of Alabama v. Garrett*, 2001). The result is that employees of state governments have fewer legal rights than employees of other public or private employers.

It is worth noting that some states have refused to follow the US Supreme Court interpretations when it comes to determine the meaning of state laws, even if the language of those state laws is identical to the federal statutes. Under the US system of federalism, it is always within the power of a state to grant more protections to individuals than the federal law would grant, but never less. For example, Massachusetts judges interpret their state disability laws differently than federal courts, declaring that mitigative measures do not extinguish eligibility for protection by state antidiscrimination law (*Dahill v. Police Dep't of Boston*, 2001). Thus, a disability that can be mitigated or corrected does not disqualify an individual for protection under some state statutes and, as a result, state statutes may protect more individuals with disabilities than federal statutes.

Reasoning Around Accommodations

Another key provision in US civil rights statutes is the requirement that "reasonable accommodations" be provided to individuals with disabilities. Judicial determinations about what constitutes a "reasonable" accommodation are also worth considering here because they too impact classification determinations and the number of persons with disabilities protected by federal civil rights laws. An individual with a disability is eligible for protection under the federal statutes only if he or she is "qualified" and part of the consideration of qualification includes consideration of whether a reasonable accommodation can be made that would allow an individual with a disability to be eligible to be qualified to participate in an educational program or perform a particular job. The issue of qualification in essence asks: "But for the disability, would the individual be able to perform necessary functions or duties of the position or satisfy the necessary requirements of the program (or job)?" In the elementary and secondary education context, although the Supreme Court has not addressed the issue, where there is compulsory attendance, it is appropriate to assume that any student of school age is "qualified," although it is worth noting that prior to the passage of Public Law 94-142, the precursor to the Individuals with Disabilities Education Act (IDEA), many state statutes allowed local schools to exempt students with disabilities from compulsory attendance requirements (Lazerson, 1983).

If it is indeed true that every student of the age of compulsory atten-dance is deemed "qualified" to be in school, then the issue of qualification applies only to higher education. Here, there has been some litigation, which when read with similar litigation concerning employment is helpful in highlighting recent approaches to disability classification under federal civil rights laws. The matter of qualification is inextricably linked to the issue of accommodation. An accommodation is generally any change in the work or educational environment or the way things are customarily done that enables an individual with a disability to enjoy equal opportu-nities (see, e.g., *Thomas v. Davidson Academy*, 1994). Accommodations are those that satisfy the legitimate needs of the student without unduly com-promising the legitimate interests of the school. So, for example, in the medical school case cited earlier, when a student with learning disabilities is provided accommodations, but still cannot pass his medical school courses, he is no longer qualified, even if he was duly admitted and suc-cessful for the first phases of his studies (Wynne II, 1992).[11] But considera-tion of accommodations only occurs in the context of considering the "reasonableness" of an accommodation in a particular context. In deter-mining the "reasonableness" of accommodations, the courts have stated that it is important to take technological advances into account in deciding what is reasonable (see Wynne I, 1991). So, for example, recent develop-ments in assisted technology make it possible for students with visual or physical impairments to participate in law school who wouldn't have been able to do so even ten years ago. Courts have also found that inordinate costs associated with an accommodation might render it unreasonable, given the total budget available to an entity covered by the law.[12]

In general, an accommodation is not reasonable if it will compromise the legitimate interests of the school. In elementary and secondary educa-tion, issues of reasonable accommodation are assessed in a context in which all students are deemed to be eligible to be there, that is, otherwise quali-fied to be in school, and in which schools regularly provide a broad range of services to students for either pedagogic reasons or to meet obligations under special education laws, as will be discussed in the next chapter.

CONCLUSION

It may well be that the recent cases in higher education and employment limiting the numbers of individuals covered and the protections they should receive under federal statues barring discrimination on the basis of disability are simply sensible judicial interpretations of Congress' intent as expressed in the language of the statutes. Or, these decisions may reflect a shift in perspective about disability status as a social and political construct. An analogy to what is potentially a similar shift in social, political, and legal policy is useful for comparison. For a period of several decades, there was widespread government use of racial integration mandates and affirmative action practices to advance the interests of African Americans and other traditionally disadvantaged minorities. Then, a series of US Supreme Court decisions were made in cases challenging affirmative action under the Equal Protection Clause of the US Constitution. These cases did not ban affirmative action entirely, but placed such substantial limits on it as to considerably reduce the number of instances in which it could be lawfully utilized, based upon the Court's increasing reluctance about *any* type of race-based classification. Social, political, and economic circumstances related to race changed and the application and interpretation of constitutional and civil rights provisions shifted. One might wonder whether judges' views of the relationship between law and disability status in our society might change also. Recent trends in the application of special education and educational accountability statutes, as discussed in the next chapter, provide further insight into the growing complexity of classifications related to disability in the US context.

NOTES

The author expresses her appreciation to Julie Margetta, J.D., and Sal Ricciardone, J.D., doctoral students in the Lynch School of Education at Boston College, for their assistance in the preparation of this chapter.

1. See *City of Cleburne v. Cleburne Living Ctr.,* 473 U.S. 432, 446 (1985): Classifications based on mental disability are subject to rational basis review, not to any form of heightened scrutiny. "To withstand equal protection review," the Court concluded, "legislation that distinguishes between the mentally retarded and others must be rationally related to a legitimate governmental purpose."

2. Note that this includes all public schools and almost every public and private higher education institution in the United States. Private elementary and secondary schools may or may not choose to receive federal financial assistance and most, in the past, have not, although that number is shrinking as more incentives are created for receiving federal funds under the No Child Left Behind Act of 2001.

3. This is similar to the requirements for students covered by IDEA, as will be discussed in the next chapter. IDEA-eligible students are a subcategory of Section 504 students, who are all students with disabilities; the smaller category of IDEA students consists of those with disabilities who also require special education. Although the US Department of Education publishes data on the number of IDEA students, there are few statistics available on the total number of Section 504 students in the United States.

4. The ADA drops the term "otherwise" in describing the qualified individuals with disabilities protected by the statute.

5. Title I (42 U.S.C. § 12112 et seq.) applies to the employment context, regulating public and private employers, employment agencies, and unions, and prohibiting employment discrimination against individuals with disabilities. By recent US Supreme Court interpretation, it does not apply to employees of states. Title II (42 U.S.C. § 12132 et seq.) is applicable to public, government entities, including public schools, and colleges and universities. Title III applies to public accommodations, like hotels or shops, and private schools and universities.

6. The condition resulted in overly emotional reactions to any physical trauma and an inability to follow all of the school's disciplinary rules, which became the focus of an accommodations dispute under Section 504.

7. Indeed, some long-term disability advocates were so upset by the outcome of this case and two others decided contemporaneously by the Supreme Court that one of them referred to it as a return to the Dark Ages for individuals with disabilities. See Tucker, 2000.

8. Note that they could still be subject to the stigmas associated with disability and might, in fact, be eligible for protection under the separate "regarded as" or "having a record as" categories protected under the federal laws.

9. The cases discussed in this section of the paper have all come up under the ADA, but seem equally applicable to Section 504 claims.

10. See *Garcia v. State University of New York Health Science Center at Brooklyn*, 2000 U.S. Dist. Lexis 13562, E.D.N.Y. 2000.

11. This case was decided prior to the US Supreme Court cases limiting the categories of individuals with disabilities protected by federal laws, as discussed above.

12. It is not clear that cost prohibitions would apply as an appropriate analysis in the elementary and secondary education context, given the fact that the IDEA places no cost limit on the types of services required for students eligible under that statute.

REFERENCES

Americans with Disabilities Act, 42 U.S.C. §§ 12101 et seq. (1990).

Benveniste, G. (1986). Implementation strategies: The case of 94–142. In D. Kirp & D. Jensen (Eds.), *School days, rule days: The legislation and regulation of education* (pp. 146–163). Philadelphia: Falmer Press.

Board of Trustees of University of Alabama v. Garrett, 531 U.S. 356 (2001).

Butts, F., & Cremin, L. (1953). *A history of education in American culture.* New York: Basic Books.

Chambers, J., & Hartman, W. (Eds.). (1983). *Special education policies: Their history, implementation, and finance.* Philadelphia: Temple University Press.

Cremin, L. (1951). *The American common school: An historic conception.* New York: Teachers College Press.

Dahill v. Police Dep't of Boston, 434 Mass. 233 (2001).

Gratz v. Bollinger, 539 U.S. 244 (2003).

Grutter v. Bollinger, 539 U.S. 306 (2003).

Hehir, T., & Latus, T. (Eds.). (1992). *Special education at the century's end: Evolution of theory and practice since 1970.* Cambridge, MA: Harvard University Press.

Huefner, D. (2000). *Getting comfortable with special education law: A framework for working with children with disabilities.* Norwood, MA: Christopher-Gordon Publishers.

Lazerson, M. (1983). The origins of special education. In J. Chambers & W. Hartman (Eds.), *Special education policies: Their history, implementation, and finance* (pp. 15–47). Philadelphia: Temple University Press.

Minow, M. (1990). *Making all the difference: Inclusion, exclusion, and American law.* Ithaca, NY: Cornell University Press.

Pullin, D. (1999). Whose schools are these and what are they for? The role of the rule of law in defining educational opportunity in American public education. In G. Cizek (Ed.), *Handbook of educational policy* (pp. 3–29). San Diego, CA: Academic Press.

Section 504 of the Rehabilitation Act , 29 U.S.C. § 794 (1973).

Sutton v. United Airlines, 527 U.S. 471 (1999).

Thomas v. Davidson Academy, 846 F. Supp. 611 (M.D. Tenn. 1994).

Toyota Manufacturing v. Williams, 122 S.Ct. 681 (2002).

Tribe, L. (2000). *American constitutional law* (3rd ed.). New York: Foundation Press.

Tucker, B. P. (2000). The definition of disability under the ADA: A return to the Dark Ages. *Alabama Law Review, 52,* 321.

U.S. v. Virginia, 518 U.S. 515 (1996).

Weber, M., Mawdsley, R., & Redfield, S. (2004). *Special education law: Cases and materials.* Newark, NJ: Matthew Bender & Co.

Wynne v. Tufts University School of Medicine, 932 F.2d 19 (1st Cir. 1991) (Wynne I).

Wynne v. Tufts University School of Medicine, 976 F.2d 791 (1st Cir. 1992) (Wynne II).

7 Implications for Human and Civil Rights Entitlements

Disability Classification Systems and the Law of Special Education

Diana C. Pullin

The most significant financial support to states and local schools for the education of students in the United States in need of special education comes through the Individuals with Disabilities Education Act (IDEA; 2004). Associated with this funding are provisions regulating how special education is provided and criteria for determining classification for eligibility to participate in IDEA programs and services. The initial goal of the statute in 1975 (then known as Public Law 94-142, or the Education for All Handicapped Children Act), when the present schema for IDEA was first prescribed, was to address the fact that more than half the children with disabilities in the nation were not receiving full equality of educational opportunity, with over a million of these children excluded from school entirely (Public Law 94-142 Sec. 3(b)). The 1975 version of the statute reflected many then-current understandings of disability status and the stigmatizing effects of particular disability labels. So, for example, the term "crippled" was removed from the previous version of the statute and replaced by the term "orthopedically impaired," and children with "specific learning disabilities" (SLD) were added to the eligibility group (Sec. 4(a)). At the same time, the statute placed some statistical limitations on the proportion of all students who could be eligible for IDEA services (12%) and limited the SLD label to one sixth of the total of all IDEA students (Sec. 611).

The statute was reviewed and reauthorized again in 1986 and 1991, when it became IDEA, and then again in 1997 and 2004 (when it was named the Individuals with Disabilities Education Improvement Act). Each time, either through the statute itself or through the implementing regulations written by the US Department of Education, there were slight changes made in the definitions of the disability conditions covered by the law. At each review and revision of the federal special education statute, determinations on revisions have been a response to a variety of factors, including pressures from special interest groups, developments in medical and social science, and implementation evidence from the field. In addition to changes in the diagnostic categories covered by IDEA, each time the statute was revised, there were other modifications, either through statute or regulation, which impacted other classification-related practices that governed eligibility for IDEA protections. Finally, the changes made pursuant to the 1997 and 2004 revisions of IDEA impacted students with disabilities by embracing a policy choice to promote participation of these students in education reform and accountability initiatives throughout the nation for all types of students, as will be discussed below.

The provisions of IDEA contain, first, a classification scheme to determine children's eligibility to be covered by the statute. This classification requires being in the age group covered by the statute, having a disability listed in the statute, and having need for special education services.[1] The age eligibility provisions of IDEA extend primarily from age five through the student's graduation from high school or age twenty-one, although there are also some provisions (Parts B and C of the law) that apply to children under five.

The second IDEA eligibility provisions define the disability conditions covered by the law. At present, the statute applies to the following conditions:

Mental retardation, hearing impairments (including deafness), speech or language impairments, visual impairments (including blindness), serious emotional disturbance (referred to in this title as "emotional disturbance"), orthopedic impairments, autism, traumatic brain injury, other health impairments, or specific learning disabilities. (20 U.S.C. 1401(3)(A))

In addition, for children ages three through nine, an additional group of children with "developmental delays" is eligible under IDEA at the discretion of individual states. These students are those

> Experiencing developmental delays, as defined by the State and as measured by appropriate diagnostic instruments and procedures, in one or more of the following areas: physical development; cognitive development; communication development; social or emotional development; or adaptive development. (20 U.S.C. 1401(3)(B))

The implementing regulations written by the US Department of Education define specific criteria for each of these disability conditions. The accompanying regulations, however, have been a source of controversy over the years of IDEA implementation based upon political, educational, and scientific disputes on how to diagnose or categorize a condition, particularly in regard to the large and largely subjectively defined categories such as "specific learning disabilities" (see Speece, Chapter 14) or "seriously emotionally disturbed." Recently recognized and increasingly popular diagnostic classifications like "attention deficit disorder" and "attention deficit hyperactivity disorder" have also stirred controversy and resulted in regulatory provisions designating them as falling within the category of "other health impairment," although the Department of Education noted at the same time that these conditions could also be classified under "emotional disturbance" or "specific learning disability" (64 Federal Register 12406, 12542–43, 2006). The elasticity of some of these classification decisions illustrates the difficulties associated with IDEA classifications and with disability classification in general.

Case law has developed over the parameters of these disability classifications. So, for example, case law has established that children covered by the statute are not excluded even if their disability is profound (*Timothy W. v. Rochester, N.H. School District*, 1989). Other cases have delved into controversies[2] over the meaning of the "serious emotional disturbance" classification, with some judges sorting through the distinctions between "serious emotional disturbance" and "social maladjustment," which is specifically excluded by regulatory definition from IDEA eligibility (*Springer v. Fairfax County School Board*, 1998), and other judges sorting through such matters as whether a child's difficulties were attributable to a disability condition or bad parenting (*Johnson v. Metro Davidson County School System*, 2000). It is only a matter of time before courts and administrative hearing officers will, if they have not already, have to sort their way through the new use of brain imaging techniques to diagnose specific learning disabilities (see Shaywitz, 2003).

The third eligibility condition under IDEA is the requirement that, as a result of the disability, the student must *need* "special education and related services" or have a disability that causes "an adverse effect on educational performance" (20 U.S.C. 1401(a)). The federal regulations provide limited guidance on the meaning of these provisions. The cases that have arisen concerning these provisions, though few in number, present an interesting window into IDEA classification controversies. For example, in one case, *J.D. v. Pawlet School District* (2000), a high school student had emotional and behavioral problems but he was also academically gifted and attained scores in the top two percentile on an intelligence test and high scores in norm-referenced achievement tests, also skipping grades and courses in the regular curriculum. Here, in the absence of federal regulations applicable to the situation, the federal appellate court looked to state regulations. The state regulations applied a discrepancy model for determining an adverse effect on educational performance, but gauged performance only in the basic skills. If basic skills achievement is the metric for performance, a high-functioning student with disabilities will almost always be ineligible for IDEA coverage and this was the determination in *J.D.*[3]

APPLYING IDEA CLASSIFICATIONS

There have been several other types of particular problems associated with the disability classifications created by IDEA. Issues of over- and underrepresentation of racial and ethnic minorities in certain disability categories and the overrepresentation of boys persist. Also, the issue of classification cannot be disentangled from determinations about the meaning of the appropriateness requirement of the federal law. School discipline issues have also pressed against classification determinations. And finally, the new accountability requirements and the inclusion of students with disabilities in accountability mandates also present new classification issues.

Race, Ethnicity, Gender, and Misclassification

Application of the IDEA classification rules has presented a particular challenge when classification for IDEA eligibility intersects with other social and pedagogic issues. The impact of race, ethnicity, gender, and socioeconomic status on IDEA classifications has been profound. In both 1997 and in 2004, Congress declared its commitment in revising IDEA to the resolution of problems arising from misclassifications that are attributable to factors other than disability. Although the statistical patterns of possible misrepresentation have shifted slightly, there is still a widespread problem of misclassification into special education associated with race, ethnicity, gender, and socioeconomic status (Dyson & Kozleski, Chapter 11; Ferri & Connor, 2006; Ladner & Hammons, 2001; Losen & Orfield, 2002; National Research Council, 2002; Ware, 2004).

The Interaction Between Classification and "Appropriateness" Determinations

In addition to diagnostic choices, there are inherent classification choices also embedded in determinations about the programs and services that would be appropriate for an IDEA student. The cornerstone of IDEA is its provision that every eligible child will receive a free and appropriate education (FAPE) specifically tailored to the child's individual needs as determined by a cooperative school-parent team writing an individualized education program (IEP). The landmark case *Board of Education v. Rowley* (1982), the very first US Supreme Court case to consider IDEA and its provisions, established the precedent that the statute was not intended to maximize the potential of an IDEA student, but instead that the statute was intended to provide access to education that would allow the student to "benefit" from educational programs and services.[4] The case was perhaps an unfortunate one to create the first Supreme Court case law given the facts in the dispute, as Amy Rowley was a high-functioning student with a severe hearing loss who was able to progress successfully through general education with her age peers.

Later Supreme Court decisions clarified that related services had to be provided if necessary to allow a student to access education and if they did not have to be provided by a physician (*Irving Independent School District v. Tatro*, 1984; *Cedar Rapids Community School District v. Garret F.*, 1999). Subsequent lower court cases concerning students with severe disabilities have established that the benefit due these students is "more than trivial" (*Polk v. Central Susquehanna Intermediate Unit 16*, 1988). But a note of caution is called for in light of appellate level court cases in which courts have considered such factors as the cost of placements and the impact on other students that might result from the inclusion of a student with significant disabilities in a general education classroom setting (see, e.g., *Sacramento City Unified School Dist., Bd. of Educ. v. Rachel H.*, 1994).

Even if a student has a disability classified as appropriate for IDEA coverage, the evolving case law is beginning to take into account more complex classifications and eligibilities in the course of resolving appropriateness disputes. School discipline disputes present an example here.

The Trouble With Troubled Teens

Another set of classification choices concerning students with disabilities that has caused substantial controversy, particularly among general educators and school administrators and politicians, is school discipline, particularly disciplinary exclusion. Because IDEA provides both substantive protections (appropriate education for IDEA students) and procedural protections (due process mechanisms for administrative and judicial hearings over IDEA disputes), the imposition of disciplinary sanctions on IDEA students can sometimes differ from the approach taken with students who do not have disability classifications. In a landmark federal appellate court case, judges determined that IDEA students should not be penalized for conduct related to their disabilities (*S-1 v. Turlington*, 1981). The result was a series of significant issues on how to impose disciplinary sanctions without punishing IDEA students for misconduct related to their disability and how to impose sanctions without impinging on the right to appropriate education.

The US Supreme Court eventually resolved some of the disciplinary exclusion issues in one of the earliest IDEA cases it decided. The Court recognized that there were some situations in which imposing a school's regular school discipline rules on IDEA students could result in denying those students access to the appropriate education defined in their IEPs. Here, the Court stated, Congress clearly intended to restrict local schools in favor of ensuring that IDEA goals were met. Thus, a disciplinary suspension or expulsion for more than ten days was regarded as a change in placement, requiring a due process hearing, unless school officials could demonstrate that continuation of the placement was substantially likely to result in injury either to the student or to others (*Honig v. Doe*, 1988).

The reaction to Honig was a firestorm of complaints from local educators and some parents of students without disabilities that the interpretation of IDEA resulted in the creation of a new privileged disability classification: students who would not have to obey school rules. This overreaction to the Honig decision became a major factor in negotiations to reauthorize IDEA in both 1997 and in 2004. The provisions of IDEA were revised as a result. Schools are now required to follow the same general education procedures for IDEA students possessing drugs and weapons or for students who are dangerous to themselves or others. If as a result, however, a suspension or expulsion of an IDEA student would occur, schools must ensure continuation of services in the least restrictive appropriate environment, consistent with the student's IEP. Thus, schools can use "appropriate interim alternative educational settings" for IDEA students during disciplinary sanctions (20 U.S.C. 1415(k)).

In conjunction with the availability of these disciplinary sanctions, however, is a requirement that creates a new set of classification and eligibility issues under IDEA. Now, under the more recent statutory and regulatory provisions, one component of the IDEA system is a "manifestation review" in situations in which an IDEA student faces a disciplinary change in placement that exceeds ten school days. The review is required when the IDEA student might have engaged in misconduct as a direct result of the disability[5] or as a result of the school's failure to implement the student's IEP (20 U.S.C. 1415(k)). If a manifestation is found, then relevant IEP team members and the parent must conduct a functional behavioral assessment and implement a behavioral intervention plan.

In some respects, the issues related to disciplinary exclusions for IDEA students represent a delicate balance between maintaining the policy goals ensuring an appropriate education for IDEA students while at the same time addressing the "law and order" mentality of judges and legislators who seem increasingly convinced that US public schools are frightening places populated by many, many very unruly children. On the other hand, these approaches lose sight of the fact that one important role of public elementary and secondary education for all children is teaching good conduct, good citizenship, and effective and thoughtful self-regulation, a goal for *all* students, whether they have an IEP or not.

IDEA AND THE NO CHILD LEFT BEHIND ACT

One area in which legislators have articulated at least an aspirational commitment to *all* students is in current approaches to education reform. After the United States and many of its states began to adopt standards-based, test-driven education reform and accountability programs, policymakers began to understand the importance of the participation of students with disabilities in these initiatives (National Research Council, 1997). In 1997 and then again in the 2004 reauthorization of IDEA, Congress set out the importance of increasing the participation of IDEA students in local and statewide educational assessments. And, in 2001, when Congress passed the No Child Left Behind Act (NCLB; 20 U.S.C. 6301 et seq.), the importance of this participation was further articulated (Pullin, 2005). The NCLB is the latest version of the federal Elementary and Secondary Education

Act (2001), the largest source of general federal financial support for state and local education programs. This statute provides support for a broad range of educationally disadvantaged students, including those from low-income families and those who are English language learners. Unlike the IDEA, this law does not constitute an entitlement to additional services or resources for eligible students. The statute, however, provides the largest amount of federal funds to elementary and secondary schools and is a major driver of current educational policies across the states.

The NCLB provisions include not only requirements that students with disabilities[6] participate in state accountability testing and assessments, but also requirements that reasonable modifications and accommodations be provided for them. The law also requires that the score results for these students be both aggregated with the scores reported for all students and disaggregated so that the particular performance of students with disabilities can be assessed for school accountability purposes (20 U.S.C. 6311(b)). Because of the importance in the NCLB design of the use of measures of "adequate yearly progress" (AYP) in improving academic performance in schools, districts, and states, the inclusion of students with disabilities is vitally important, since it may be these students alone whose performance determines whether a school meets its AYP goals (Pullin, 2005).

The values associated with the public policy determination to include students with disabilities in recent education reform and accountability mandates that began in the mid-1990s marked an important turn in the full inclusion of these students in general education. However, an increasing number of exceptions to full inclusion are being created. First, in the 2004 reauthorization of IDEA, Congress allowed some students with disabilities to be exempted from taking the assessments taken by most students. Then, the US Department of Education began a series of steps, in the formulation of regulations and in other policy determinations, allowing more and more variations in the types of participation of students with disabilities in assessments and the calculation of AYP (United States Department of Education, 2003, 2007). First, the department recognized the use of alternate assessment approaches for students with severe cognitive disabilities. Then, later, the department announced a new categorization of students who would participate in modified achievement standards and modified achievement assessments with appropriate accommodations directly aligned with age appropriate grade level content standards and testing. This policy was adopted to give states "more flexibility" and to allow special treatment for students struggling in the assessment process but not eligible for alternate assessments. The result of this series of policy changes allows some students with disabilities in a school to be subject to special treatment in the assessment system without causing an AYP penalty for local schools whose students with disabilities are not meeting overall achievement performance goals.

To the already many, many layers of classification and eligibility determinations associated with educating students with disabilities, accountability assessment creates the occasion for still more types of classifications and eligibility determinations. And the continually evolving federal requirements concerning accountability assessment again reflect our social and political ambivalence about the meaning of disability and the extent to which individuals with disabilities will be fully included in both education reform and accountability and in social, political, and economic life in the community. In effect, assessment for accountability has created new classifications, such as the one likely to result now that we can deem students "modified achievers" or "modified achievement standards students," drawing finer and finer distinctions among individuals with disabilities and how they are treated in the educational system. Further, to the extent accountability participation impacts life events such as the receipt of a credential at the end of high school (diploma, certificate of completion, alternate diploma, GED), life chances are also impacted when access to further education or the workplace include scrutiny of the type of credential awarded (which is, of course, another classification opportunity).

NEW CONTEXTS FOR CLASSIFICATION

The discussion above, as well as the one in the previous chapter, illuminates the role of law in the evolving history of the classification of disabilities in the United States and the recent narrowing of the eligibility of individuals with disabilities for participation in the protections of IDEA or federal civil rights statutes. It is also important to highlight some additional recent changes in contexts and classifications in addition to those discussed above. The role of disability classifications is only one aspect of what has become an expanding view of education as an individual rather than a public good. As a result, part of the role of classification also requires consideration of the possible manipulation of classification and eligibility determinations, the economic and efficiency pressure for government to decrease the number of students with disabilities and the costs of special education services, and the significance of classification on access to educational opportunity for all students, each of which will be briefly enumerated here.

Commentators have noted the increasing trend in US education to turn from a perspective of education as serving the common good to a perception that education is really a private good, a commodity used to obtain credentials to facilitate access to social, economic, and political capital (Labaree, 1997). To the extent this is true, individuals have incentives to leverage disability status, or to seek to obtain disability status, if it can be of individual benefit and if the benefit outweighs any potential costs associated with stigmatization. Some pursuit of disability status is legitimate; some might be regarded as a form of gaming the system.

Games and Gaming in the Classification System

Potential abuses of the disability classification system have been noted in several different contexts. A set of lawyers assessing the implementation of one state's special education law concluded that the learning disabilities classification awarded some students provided them with access to programs and services from which other students without disability labels might benefit as well (Kelman & Lester, 1997). One political scientist likened special education under IDEA to a form of welfare or the dole, subject to the politics, abuses, and idiosyncrasies of both those claiming eligibility and the bureaucrats administering the system as well as the judges resolving special education disputes (Melnick, 1994). As the implementation of disability statutes moves into the twenty-first century, perspectives like these can be expected to continue to arise, particularly given the shrinking public budgets to pay for special services. Several recent examples are useful for the consideration of classification and its implications.

Testing Accommodations

There are some circumstances in which individuals may seek disability status even if their eligibility for a disability classification is tenuous at best. So, for example, high school students taking college admissions exams, older individuals participating in graduate or professional school admissions testing programs, or persons taking licensure or certification tests might seek disability status to obtain accommodations like extended time or private testing sites in order to enhance their scores. For some, this was simply a wise strategy in the quest for more impressive credentials. For some exams, individuals were perhaps not aware that these accommodated administrations could result in scores accompanied by a notation signifying that accommodations in testing were received[7] or that a different credential could be awarded as a result of an accommodation or an alternate assessment. Similar practices to these may occur in some high-stakes accountability testing programs.

Economy and Efficiency

In response to the increasing desirability of disability status among some parents seeking additional services for their students, some policy-makers have resorted to what might be termed "gaming the gamers." So, for example, in Massachusetts, there was a perception that the state had achieved an excessively high level of classifications into special education in the twenty-five years after the state passed its special education law, which preceded the federal law.[8] At one point, the proportion of students with disabilities in Massachusetts noticeably exceeded the national rate. In 1993, when the state legislature was implementing a new school finance formula in conjunction with a massive education reform initiative, a choice was made to build into the school finance formula some fiscal disincentives to discourage local schools from admitting students into special education by forcing the local districts to pick up more of the costs of special education, shifting the expenses from the state. This did have some impact, but in the face of arguments that the number of students with disabilities was naturally increasing due in part to medical advances (see Berman, Davis, Koufman-Frederick, & Urion, 2001), the state eventually adopted a "circuit breaker," channeling additional funds for the excess costs of special education to alleviate some of the budget burden on local schools.

The ongoing struggle to balance competing interests concerning education should not be dismissed so blithely by describing it as a game, yet in some respects the effort to balance the tensions between the perceived benefits of disability classifications against the costs associated with education has been a political game. Most recently, the quest for economy and efficiency, coupled with the interest in trying to reduce the growth of disability classifications, has also led to a new federal mandate, in the 2004 version of the IDEA, to attempt to avoid special education classifications altogether for some students. The Response to Intervention (RTI) initiative (see Speece, Chapter 14) attempts to target specific and short-term teaching interventions to students who fail to progress in education well before disability status is even considered as a possibility. To the extent that disability classification might have become a fallback position in the face of inadequate teaching, funding or other resources, or limited familial opportunities, a meaningful and effective early intervention could be a useful way of avoiding disability classifications and enhancing learning opportunities.

Opportunity to Learn

When all is said and done, what is really important about the role of law in classification and eligibility determinations concerning students is whether or not schools provide full and meaningful opportunity to learn for each individual. In some respects, the operation of the disability rights and special education systems as defined by state and federal laws does obscure the fact that schools and educators often fall short in educating *all* sorts of students, some who receive particular legal protections, some of whom do not. For example, to the extent that a tool like an individualized education program (IEP) or a Section 504 plan (which is prepared in some schools for students who have disabilities but are not in need of special education and fall under the protections of Section 504 of the Rehabilitation Act, as discussed in the previous chapter) is useful, it could also be useful in enhancing opportunities to learn for all sorts of students, not just eligible students with disabilities. Indeed, in Massachusetts, students who do not qualify as having a disability or being in need of special education but who are educationally at risk of failing a state accountability test (which has the ultimate high stakes for individual students—the denial of the high school diploma) can receive an individual Student Support Plan. The document looks in some respects like an IEP. While it is too early yet to have evidence of the impact of this plan, it may usefully transfer some of the provisions of special education and reasonable accommodations to high-risk students without disabilities.

CONCLUSION

As judges, legislators, and educators struggle to understand the construct "disability" and continue to struggle with the dilemmas of difference, the law has developed and its application to educational practices has changed. The meaning of disability and how disability differentiates one individual from another has also changed in society and in schools. The extent to which disability status is a protected status has also changed. As the law and society have evolved, the diagnosis of disability status is only one of many classification decisions impacting access to full and meaningful educational opportunity for individuals with disabilities. In addition to a disability diagnosis, the law increasingly takes into account eligibility factors such as the reasonableness of accommodations or the capacity to benefit from special education services.

Issues associated with disability classification in education are significant and substantial. Judges, legislatures, public officials, and educators have struggled to determine appropriate classification practices and eligibility determinations in the context of social, political, pedagogic, and scientific changes. Issues of disability classification, however, are nested within a broader set of considerations of how society defines and ensures fair and meaningful opportunity to learn for *all* children.

NOTES

The author expresses her appreciation to Julie Margetta, J.D., and Sal Ricciardone, J.D., doctoral students in the Lynch School of Education at Boston College, for their assistance in the preparation of this chapter.

1. Each state has its own state law covering special education and most of these parallel almost exactly the eligibility (and other) provisions of the federal law. Some states, however, have additional eligibility categories. So, for example, Massachusetts extends coverage up to age twenty-two and Louisiana includes in its list of conditions covered "gifted and talented" (see Weber, Mawdsley, & Redfield, 2004).

2. There is a long tradition of judicial deference to educators in all types of education law litigation and this tradition has been consistently adhered to in the IDEA litigation. See, for example, *Springer v. Fairfax County School Board* (1998): "in interpreting [the state's IDEA eligibility regulations] courts are required to give deference to the state and local education agencies whose primary duty is to administer IDEA" (134 F.3d 659 at 663). It is also clear that many IDEA classification disputes revolve heavily around conflicting and often highly technical expert testimony over classification. See Weber et al. (2004).

3. This interpretation parallels in many ways recent case law concerning eligibility under Section 504 and the Americans with Disabilities Act (see the discussion in the previous chapter).

4. States are allowed to adopt higher standards and four (Michigan, New Jersey, North Carolina, Tennessee) retain a higher standard for services than that articulated in *Rowley*. Two other states with a higher standard (Missouri and Massachusetts) lowered their standards after *Rowley* was decided (Weber et al., 2004).

5. The statute incorporates a recognition that serious disciplinary misconduct may be a manifestation of an undiagnosed disability covered by IDEA and requires a manifestation hearing also if there were any prior indicators that a student should have been evaluated for potential IDEA eligibility (20 U.S.C. 1415(k)).

6. This would include both IDEA students and Section 504 students.

7. These flags could lead to a conclusion that an individual had a disability, even if they did not since the reasons for a score coming from a test that did not receive a standardized administration could be variable. See, for example, Pullin and Heaney, 1998. Although some testing companies have voluntarily agreed to remove signals of accommodations in testing, particularly for college admissions testing, such practices continue in other testing contexts.

8. This phenomenon could have been exacerbated by the fact that students in the state came to be labeled not by a disability category, but by the type of placement they received. As a result, students would be referred to by the section number of the regulation describing the type of placement they received. This classification meant a good deal to educators and some parents but unlike traditional disability labels probably had little meaning, or stigmatizing effect, outside of school.

REFERENCES

Americans with Disabilities Act, 42 U.S.C. §§ 12101 et seq. (1990).

Berman, S., Davis, P., Koufman-Frederick, A., & Urion, D. (2001, May). The rising costs of special education in Massachusetts: Causes and effects. In C. E. Finn, Jr., A. J. Rotherham, & C. R. Hokanson, Jr. (Eds.), *Rethinking special education for a new century*. Washington, DC: Thomas B. Fordham Foundation and Progressive Policy Institute. Retrieved May 10, 2001, from http://www.edexcellence.net/library/special_ed/index.html

Board of Education v. Rowley, 458 U.S. 176 (1982).

Cedar Rapids Community School District v. Garret F., 526 U.S. 66 (1999).

Elementary and Secondary Education Act, 20 U.S.C. 6301 et seq. (2001).

Ferri, B., & Connor, D. (2006). *Reading resistance: Discourses of exclusion in desegregation and inclusion debates.* New York: Peter Lang.

Honig v. Doe, 484 U.S. 305 (1988).

Individuals with Disabilities Education Improvement Act, 20 U.S.C. §§ 1401 et seq. (2004).

Irving Independent School District v. Tatro, 468 U.S. 883 (1984).

J.D. v. Pawlet School District, 224 F.3d 60 (2nd Cir. 2000).

Johnson v. Metro Davidson County School System, 108 F. Supp. 2d 906 (M.D. Tenn. 2000).

Kelman, M., & Lester, G. (1997). *Jumping the queue: An inquiry into the legal treatment of students with learning disabilities.* Cambridge, MA: Harvard University Press.

Labaree, D. (1997). *How to succeed in school without really trying: The credentials race in American education.* New Haven: Yale University Press.

Ladner, M., & Hammons, C. (2001). Special but unequal: Race and special education. In C. E. Finn, A. J. Rotherham, & C. R. Hokanson (Eds.), *Rethinking special education for a new century* (pp. 85–110). Washington, DC: Thomas B. Fordham Foundation and Progressive Policy Institute.

Losen, D., & Orfield, G. (2002). *Racial inequity in special education.* Cambridge, MA: Harvard Education Press.

Melnick, R. S. (1994). *Between the lines: Interpreting welfare rights.* Washington, DC: The Brookings Institution.

National Research Council. (1997). *Educating one and all: Students with disabilities and standards-based reform* (L. McDonnell, M. McLaughlin, & P. Morison, Eds.). Washington, DC: National Academy Press.

National Research Council. (2002). *Minority students in special and gifted education* (S. Donovan & C. Cross, Eds.). Washington, DC: National Academy Press.

No Child Left Behind Act, 20 U.S.C. 6301 et seq. (2001).

Polk v. Central Susquehanna Intermediate Unit 16, 853 F.2d 171 (3rd Cir. 1988), cert. den., 488 U.S. 1030 (1989).

Pullin, D. (2005). When one size does not fit all: The special challenges of accountability testing for students with disabilities. *Annual Yearbook of the National Society for the Study of Education, 104*(2), 199–222.

Pullin, D., & Heaney, K. (1998). Accommodations, flags, and other dilemmas: Disability rights and admissions testing. *Educational Assessment, 5*(2), 71–93.

S-1 v. Turlington, 635 F.2d 342 (5th Cir. 1981).

Sacramento City Unified School Dist., Bd. of Educ. v. Rachel H., 14 F.3d 1398 (9th Cir. 1994).

Section 504 of the Rehabilitation Act, 29 U.S.C. § 794 (1973).

Shaywitz, S. (2003). *Overcoming dyslexia: A new and complete science-based program for reading problems at any level.* New York: Knopf.

Springer v. Fairfax County School Board, 134 F.2d 659 (4th Cir. 1998).

Timothy W. v. Rochester, N.H. School District, 875 F.2d. 954 (1st Cir. 1989).

United States Department of Education. (2003, December 9). Title I–Improving the Academic Achievement of the Disadvantaged; IDEA (Proposed regulations), 68 Fed. Reg. 68699.

United States Department of Education. (2007, April 9). Title I–Improving the Academic Achievement of the Disadvantaged; IDEA (Final rule), 72 Fed. Reg. 17748–01 (to be codified at 34 C.F.R. Parts 200 and 300).

Ware, L. (Ed.). (2004). *Ideology and the politics of (in)exclusion.* New York: Peter Lang.

Weber, M., Mawdsley, R., & Redfield, S. (2004). *Special education law: Cases and materials.* Newark, NJ: Matthew Bender & Co.

8 The Classification of Pupils at the Educational Margins in Scotland

Shifting Categories and Frameworks

Sheila Riddell

INTRODUCTION

In the field of special needs education, understanding classification systems is extremely important because they reveal a great deal about dominant discourses and underlying relationships of knowledge and power. From a social policy perspective, Kirp (1982) and others have noted that *the way* in which a social problem is described says a great deal about *how* it will be resolved. For children who are the recipients of special education, systems of classification have material consequences in terms of where they are educated, which professionals they encounter, and what life courses are mapped out. This chapter begins by presenting a theoretical framework developed in the course of a project entitled Justice Inherent in the Assessment of Special Educational Needs in England and Scotland, which was funded by the UK Economic and Social Research Council (ESRC) and conducted by researchers at the Universities of Edinburgh and Glasgow between 1997 and 2000 (Riddell, Wilson, Adler, & Mordaunt, 2002). It then explores the outcomes of dominant policy frameworks in terms of identification and placement patterns of children with additional support needs in Scotland. Finally, it considers recent legislative and policy developments, particularly the passage of the Education (Additional Support for Learning) (Scotland) Act 2004, which is likely to have a major impact on provision for children with difficulties, disabilities, and disadvantages in the future.

SPECIAL EDUCATION NEEDS (SEN) POLICY FRAMEWORKS

Table 7.1   Policy Frameworks Adapted From Mashaw's Study of Disability Insurance in the United States

Policy Framework	Decision-Making Mode	Legitimating Goal	Nature of Accountability	Characteristic Remedy
Bureaucracy	Applying rules	Accuracy	Hierarchical	Administrative review
Profession	Applying knowledge	Service	Interpersonal	Complaint to a professional body
Legal System	Weighing-up arguments	Fairness	Independent	Appeal to a court or tribunal

SOURCE: Adapted from Mashaw, 1983.

The starting point of the ESRC study referred to above was Mashaw's (1983) analysis of the operation of the disability insurance system in the United States in the 1970s, which identified three models of procedural justice (see Table 7.1). Kirp (1982), drawing on Mashaw's typology, argued that policy frameworks tend to coexist with one another in a state of dynamic tension:

> They are pursued by different policy actors for different reasons. They have distinctive potentialities and equally distinctive pathologies, and tend to fall in and out of favor with policy makers over time. Choosing among these policy frameworks affects the policy system and, vitally, the supposed beneficiaries. (Kirp, 1982, p. 138)

Methods used in the ESRC project included a detailed analysis of Scottish and English policy and statistics, a questionnaire survey of Scottish and English local authorities, in-depth case studies of four contrasting local authorities, and fifty-nine case studies of families going through the statutory assessment process. We began the project with the intention of assessing the adequacy of the Mashaw/Kirp framework to encompass the range of policies in play at the time of the research. We found that, while SEN policy context in Scotland had been relatively stable for almost two decades, in England there had been rapid changes during the 1990s, in response to the Conservative government's neoliberal reforms. Reflecting the growing complexity of the field, three additional policy frameworks were added to the typology (consumerism, managerialism, and marketization). As illustrated in Table 7.2, each policy framework is characterized by specific forms of decision making, legitimating goal, nature of accountability, and characteristic remedy. Each framework also has a typical approach to the classification of pupils deemed to require some sort of special education.

The first three policy frameworks in Table 7.2 dominated the field of SEN until very recently. Bureaucracy was characterized as using hierarchical rules for decision making, promising accuracy and consistency, and having administrative review as the appropriate remedy. The professional policy framework was based on the application of professional judgment, sought legitimacy through placing the client's interests above those of the practitioner, was accountable to clients and other professionals, and used complaint to a professional body as the form of redress. A policy framework based on legal principles was characterized as weighing-up arguments to determine fair outcomes. It claimed to be independent and appeal was to a court or a tribunal.

Let us now consider the characteristics of the new policy frameworks (managerialism, consumerism, and marketization), which became increasingly important during the 1990s, particularly in England. New Public Management promoted the regulation and measurement of public services, with a view to increasing efficiency, effectiveness, and value for money (Newman, 2001). To achieve efficiency gains, performance measures were used to assess whether individuals and services had attained prespecified outcomes. If targets were not met, management sanctions might be applied, involving financial penalties or the loss of contracts. Dissatisfied users might complain to the ombudsman. Consumerism, which flourished in the 1990s, was based on the view that service users should have the major say in the nature and delivery of public services. In the field of education, parents were regarded as proxy consumers of services on behalf of their children. The underlying assumption was that consumer choice

Table 7.2 Six Normative Models of Procedural Justice

Model	Mode of Decision Making	Legitimating Goal	Mode of Accountability	Characteristic Remedy for User	Classification System
Bureaucracy	Applying rules	Accuracy	Hierarchical	Administrative review	Postwar medical categories
Professionalism	Applying knowledge	Public service	Interpersonal	Second opinion: Complaint to a professional body	Broad: Special educational needs/additional support needs
Legality	Weighing-up arguments	Fairness	Independent	Appeal to a court or tribunal (public law)	DDA definition underpinned by medical categories
Managerialism	Managerial autonomy	Efficiency gains	Performance measures	Management sanctions/complaint to ombudsman	SEN/ASN-broad categories
Consumerism	Active participation	Consumer satisfaction	Consumer charters	"Voice" and/or compensation through charter	Variety, including "new disabilities"
Marketization	Price mechanism	Private sector-profit/ Public sector-efficiency	Commercial viability	"Exit" and/or court action (private law)	Variety, including "new disabilities"

and voice were the essential mechanisms driving the market. Using the information provided under the New Public Management regime, consumers could actively engage in the governance of services. Consumer charters were intended to provide information on the nature and quality of services people had a right to expect, and were expected to include complaint procedures indicating rights to redress if services failed to meet specification. Finally, markets were seen by the New Right as the ultimate means of raising standards and achieving better value for money. People were increasingly given the power to choose between existing services. Those that were more popular were expected to expand and flourish, while unpopular services were intended to wither and die. The mode of accountability within this version of procedural justice is commercial viability and the characteristic remedy for those dissatisfied with services is to exercise their power of exit by choosing a different service.

Clearly, there are interconnections between these frameworks, for example, within the public sector marketization has been driven in part by consumer choice, but also by the operation of internal markets controlled by service commissioners. It is also conceivable that a system based on consumerism might be driven by principles of individual or group empowerment rather than consumer choice being seen merely as the engine of the market. Policy issues are not usually expressed in terms of a single policy framework, indeed, they are more commonly described in terms of composite policy frameworks. Interest groups may suggest that their perspective reflects superior values to those of other contenders, but in practice policy frameworks have different strengths and weaknesses and trade-offs are made between them. Thus, for example, the professional policy framework emphasizes service and the need to provide individual solutions to particular problems, but provides few opportunities for legal recourse if the service user disagrees with professional judgment. A policy framework based on legality promises to judge individual claims for resources fairly, but the negative trade-off might be that parents who are poor and inarticulate may not be in a position to claim their rights. Such a policy framework has no concern for systemic equity and collective justice, but is simply concerned with making judgments relating to individual cases, which may have perverse consequences for the system as a whole. A bureaucratic policy framework might score highly on sticking to agreed procedures, but may be inflexible and unable to meet individual needs. Establishing the dominance of a policy framework is thus a highly political activity, because proponents of different frameworks are in competition with one another.

It is not my intention to suggest that the policy framework outlined here is the only one that might be possible. Indeed, Wedell (Chapter 4) and Norwich (Chapter 9) suggest slightly different ways in which administrative systems might be characterized, although their systems appear to be consistent with the conceptualization developed by me and my colleagues.

POLICY FRAMEWORKS AND CLASSIFICATION SYSTEMS

Each policy framework has an associated classification system, which acts to legitimate the underlying discourse. Thus the postwar bureaucratic framework operated on the basis of assigning children to one of a number of fixed medical categories. The Education (Scotland) Act 1945 put in place a general duty on education authorities to provide education to meet children's "age, aptitude, and ability." As part of the general duty, education authorities were obliged to "ascertain" which children over the age of five in their area had a disability of "mind or body" requiring "special educational treatment" at school (including occupational centers) and which were too handicapped to be suitable for education or training at school at all. The Special Educational Treatment (Scotland) Regulations 1954 established nine legal categories of handicap, for which "special educational treatment" should be made. These were deafness, partial deafness, blindness, partial sightedness, mental handicap, epilepsy, speech defects, maladjustment, and physical handicap.

The Education (Scotland) Act 1980 (as amended) abolished these categories of handicap and replaced them with an overarching category of "special educational needs." Professionals, principally educational psychologists, were given the power to determine which children fell under this umbrella category and the extent to which subclassifications should be used. The adoption of the broad category of special educational needs was thus linked with an increase in professional power, which could sometimes lead to conflict with local authority officers. For example, the local authority might insist on the use of particular terminology such as "specific learning difficulties" rather than "dyslexia" against the professional judgment of some psychologists (see Riddell, Brown, & Duffield, 1994, for an account of local authorities' efforts at professional co-option). In addition, the local authority might object to resources being specified as part of a needs assessment, which again might run counter to professional judgment.

The policy framework of legality or rights has promoted the idea that if a child's difficulties are classified in a certain way, then a right to a particular sort of provision may arise. As parents and voluntary organizations grew in strength in the 1990s, parents who wanted a particular diagnosis of their child's difficulties (e.g., autism or attention deficit disorder) were increasingly likely to seek the backing of the legal system, in England appealing to the Special Educational Needs Tribunal. Although appeal to a tribunal was not possible in Scotland, parents might threaten proceeding toward appeal to Scottish ministers in order to reach agreement with the local authority. Parents who obtained an independent psychological assessment and clinical diagnosis were particularly likely to obtain the local authority's support. However, in the absence of a tribunal system and an equivalent of the English Code of Practice (Department for Education, 1994), parents were in a much weaker position than their English counterparts. The Special Educational Needs and Disability Act 2001, which amended the Disability Discrimination Act 1995, offered further opportunities for the legal enforcement of rights. The act established the new legal category of disability, which overlapped with that of SEN, so that some children were included in both classifications, but others were only included in one (see below for further discussion).

The more recent policy frameworks of consumerism and marketization have been reinforced by the framework of legality, further promoting medical classification in order to secure a particular placement or level of resourcing. The final category, managerialism, has its focus on regulating the delivery of public sector services, and is therefore less concerned with establishing a classification system that meets with the approval of parents and voluntary organizations. Professional performance has been measured in terms of the time taken to open a Record of Needs and the cost of delivering special education services in different settings. The blanket term "special educational needs" (or "additional support needs") has therefore been adopted.

To summarize, the policy frameworks operating within the Scottish special education context described in Table 7.2 are underpinned by discourses that describe and legitimate a particular view of the world. They also promote the interests of particular groups, and the classification systems with which they are associated play a critical role here. The development of special education in the postwar period was characterized by the use of rigid and bureaucratized medical categories. Subsequently, the postwar settlement replaced doctors with psychologists as the dominant group, and introduced a system of classification that was based on the legitimacy of professional judgment and benign paternalism. Subsequently, the diverse policy frameworks that have appeared on the scene have seen a partial return to previously rejected medical classification systems. The introduction of the new category of "additional support needs" may be seen as an attempt to revert, once again, to a unitary category embracing all children with disabilities, disadvantages, and difficulties. As I argue in the following sections, subcategories of impairment are likely to persist in the gathering of official statistics. The most salient distinction in the future, however, is likely to be between children who qualify for a Co-ordinated Support Plan, who will be relatively generously supported, and others with additional support needs, who do not meet the tight qualification criteria and are dependent on the vagaries of local decision making.

POLICY OUTCOMES: SPECIAL EDUCATION AND THE CLASSIFICATION OF CHILDREN IN SCOTLAND

As noted earlier, policy frameworks have material consequences for children in terms of the classification systems adopted. In this section, we explore the consequences of the post-Warnock (Department of Education and Science, 1978) settlement in Scotland in terms of how children were categorized and the settings in which they received their education. As noted earlier, the nine statutory categories were replaced in the 1980 Education (Scotland) Act by the overarching concept of "special educational needs." The Scottish Executive, however, continued to gather information in the schools census in relation to the child's principal difficulty and these data have been published on an annual basis. Since 2003, the Scottish Executive has published data on pupils with either a Record of Needs and/or an Individualised Educational Programme (IEP), signaling the demise of the official system of recording (Scottish Executive, 2006b). Table 7.3 shows the main difficulty in learning of pupils with a Record of Needs and/or an Individualised Educational Programme by gender in 2005. About 4.8% of pupils are now identified as having additional support needs.

The number of categories has continued to expand, so that language and speech disorders and autistic spectrum disorders are now reported separately. Furthermore, complex and multiple difficulties are now subdivided into a number of different categories. This is in marked contrast to the Warnock ambition of replacing multiple categories with one overarching category. Despite this expansion of the classification system, a number of established patterns remain. For example, boys make up about two thirds of pupils identified as in need of additional support, and the gender gap is particularly marked in the fields of autistic spectrum disorder and social, emotional, and behavioral difficulties. There is also a strong association between being looked after by the local authority, being entitled to free school meals, and being identified as having additional support needs (see Figure 7.1).

Table 7.3   Main Difficulty in Learning of Pupils With a Record of Needs and/or an Individualised Educational Programme in Primary, Secondary, and Special Schools by Gender, 2005

	Female	Male	Total	Rate Per 1,000 Pupils		
				Female	Male	Average
Total	10,445	24,132	34,577	29.8	66.6	48.5
Significant hearing impairment	261	363	624	0.7	1.0	0.9
Significant visual impairment	218	286	504	0.6	0.8	0.7
Significant physical or motor impairments	506	792	1,298	1.4	2.2	1.8
Significant language and speech disorder	428	1,251	1,679	1.2	3.5	2.4
Autistic spectrum disorder	486	2,998	3,484	1.4	8.3	4.9
Social, emotional, and behavioral difficulties	803	3,642	4,445	2.3	10.0	6.2
Learning Difficulties:						
Moderate	2,728	4,649	7,377	7.8	12.8	10.3
Severe	462	729	1,191	1.3	2.0	1.7
Profound	68	78	146	0.2	0.2	0.2
Specific: In language and/or mathematics (including dyslexia)	2,135	5,097	7,232	6.1	14.1	10.1
Complex or Multiple Impairments:						
Dual sensory impairment	32	40	72	0.1	0.1	0.1
Moderate learning difficulties and significant additional impairments or disorders	627	1,197	1,824	1.8	3.3	2.6
Severe learning difficulties and significant additional impairments or disorders	412	679	1,091	1.2	1.9	1.5
Profound learning difficulties and significant additional impairments or disorders	253	295	548	0.7	0.8	0.8
Other	1,008	1,993	3,001	2.9	5.5	4.2
Not known/Not disclosed	18	43	61	0.1	0.1	0.1

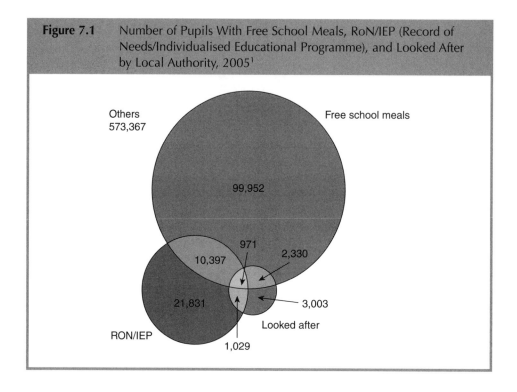

Figure 7.1 Number of Pupils With Free School Meals, RoN/IEP (Record of Needs/Individualised Educational Programme), and Looked After by Local Authority, 2005[1]

The question arises as to why a system dominated by managerialism and professionalism is classifying a growing number of pupils as having social, emotional, and behavioral difficulties. Armstrong (in Armstrong & Galloway, 1994) reported on the tendency of teachers to label boys as "disturbed" rather than "disruptive," the former denoting a deficit located within the pupil whereas the former might indicate a problem with the learning environment. He suggested that the tendency to pathologize the pupil might reflect pressures of performativity on professionals within education. Osler and Vincent (2003) have drawn attention to the ways in which schools fail to identify exclusion as an issue for girls because of their generally quiet withdrawal. Girls often self-exclude from school as a result of pregnancy, truancy, or long-term absence, whereas boys are formally excluded as a result of persistent disobedience or violence against other pupils or staff members. Girls' self-exclusion is not seen as problematic, because it neither inconveniences teachers nor is seen as threatening the education of others and the overall performance of the school in league tables. The greater likelihood of boys becoming entangled in school disciplinary systems is borne out in the statistics on discipline and exclusion. The statistical bulletin on *Incidents of Violence and Anti-Social Behaviour Against Local Authority School Staff in 2002/03* (Scottish Executive, 2004) shows that 83% of incidents against education authority school staff were carried out by boys. During the 2004–2005 school year, there were 41,974 exclusions from local authority schools in Scotland, an increase of 8% from 2003–2004. In total, 22,000 children were excluded (3% of the total school population) and 79% of these were boys. There is also a strong social class dimension here; pupils entitled to free school meals, pupils with a Record of Needs and/or Individualised Educational Programmes, and those looked after by the local authority were particularly likely to be excluded (Scottish Executive, 2006a).

Of course, some categories may bring with them certain advantages. For example, pupils categorized as having specific learning difficulties, the majority of whom are middle-class boys, may qualify for allowances in the form of extra time in examinations, the assistance of scribes or readers, and (possibly) lower university entrance level requirements (Riddell et al., 1994). Despite the possibility that some labels may confer certain advantages, the obvious example being dyslexia, the majority of SEN labels have stigmatizing and excluding consequences. Pressured by growing expectations of performance, it appears that professionals have used their powers of classification to pathologize and exclude certain groups of children, in particular socially disadvantaged boys, from the classroom. These children are likely to be classified as not in education or training when they leave school, and subsequently move into the category of economically inactive.

THE IMPACT OF DISABILITY LEGISLATION IN SCOTLAND

Having examined the classification systems in use in Scottish special education at the moment, let us now consider the implications of two new forms of classification, embodied in antidiscrimination legislation and additional support for learning legislation. As noted earlier, the Special Education Needs and Disability Act (SENDA) was passed in 2001 and covers the whole of Great Britain (Northern Ireland has separate equalities legislation). Under the act, disability is defined as "a physical or mental impairment which has a substantial and long-term adverse effect on an individual's ability to carry out normal day-to-day activities." In order to claim protection under the act, an individual has first to prove to a court that his or her impairment is covered by the official definition of disability, and this has led to many cases being dismissed particularly in the field of employment (Gooding, 2000).

The definition of disability within the act is based on the notion that it is possible to draw a boundary between the disabled and the nondisabled population and that impairment is a normative construct. This is in contrast with much disability movement writing, which emphasises the socially relative nature of disability (Thomas, 1999). Corker and Shakespeare (2002) have argued that disability should be seen entirely in cultural rather than biological terms:

> Considering the range of impairments under the disability umbrella; considering the different ways in which they impact on individuals and groups over their lifetime; considering the intersection of disabilities with other axes of inequality; and considering the challenges which impairment issues to notions of embodiment, we believe it could be argued that disability is the ultimate postmodern concept. (Corker & Shakespeare, 2002, p. 14)

The modernist reading of disability implicit in the Disability Discrimination Act (DDA) reflects the view that social justice goals may be achieved through adopting categorical approaches to measuring difference and monitoring change over time. The act stipulated that those classified as disabled should be subject to additional protection to counteract the disadvantage arising as a result of impairment. Duties are placed on responsible bodies for school education to avoid discriminating against a disabled pupil or prospective pupil. Within the act, disability is defined very precisely as treating a disabled person less favorably than a nondisabled person for a reason relating to their disability, or failing to make reasonable adjustments, without justification. Unfortunately, the reasonable adjustment measures were weakened by the fact that auxiliary aids and services and adjustments to physical features were exempt. It was assumed that these would be covered by the SEN framework, but this was a particularly serious omission in Scotland because, as discussed earlier, the lack of regulation and the continued power of professionalism meant that Records of Needs were generally drafted with no reference to resource allocation.

Research on the impact of Part 4 of the DDA in Scotland was commissioned by the Disability Rights Commission in 2002 (Cogan, Riddell, & Tisdall, 2003). A questionnaire survey was administered to local authority and school representatives and a sample of parents. A key finding was that local authorities reported a generally high level of understanding, followed by schools. Parents generally reported that they had little knowledge and understanding of the legislation (see Figure 7.2). Local authorities reported that they had policies in place, but had generally failed to convert these into practical actions. It was evidence that their knowledge often took the form of a risk assessment, designed to provide information about what was required to avoid court action, rather than to comply with

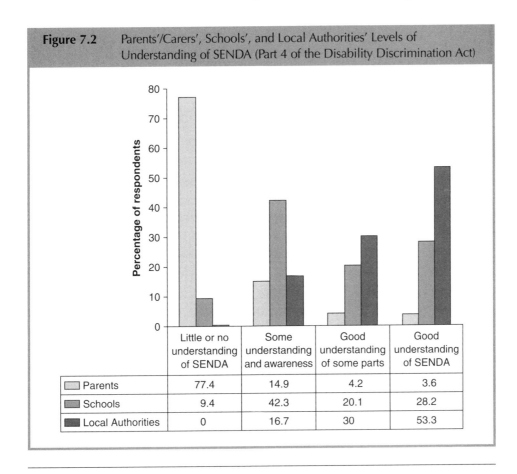

Figure 7.2 Parents'/Carers', Schools', and Local Authorities' Levels of Understanding of SENDA (Part 4 of the Disability Discrimination Act)

	Little or no understanding of SENDA	Some understanding and awareness	Good understanding of some parts	Good understanding of SENDA
Parents	77.4	14.9	4.2	3.6
Schools	9.4	42.3	20.1	28.2
Local Authorities	0	16.7	30	53.3

SOURCE: Cogan et al., 2003.

the spirit of the legislation. Although the legislation was intended to boost the framework of legality, strengthening the political rights of disabled children and their parents, the power imbalance between local authorities and parents suggested that this change was unlikely to be very significant.

THE EDUCATION (ADDITIONAL SUPPORT FOR LEARNING) (SCOTLAND) ACT 2004

Potentially far more significant is the Education (Additional Support for Learning) (Scotland) Act 2004, implemented in November 2005. Earlier legislation defined children as having special educational needs if they had much greater difficulty in learning than most other children of their own age, or suffered from a disability or handicap that prevented them from being educated with their own peer group, or were under five years old and belonged to either of these groups. The law, however, did not cover children or young people who had difficulties arising from other factors, such as being taught in a language they did not speak at home.

The new definition of additional support needs (ASN), as specified in Section 1 of the Education (Additional Support for Learning) (Scotland) Act 2004, is much broader:

> A child or young person has additional support needs for the purposes of this Act where, for whatever reason, the child or young person is, or is likely to be, unable without the provision of additional support to benefit from school education provided or to be provided for the child or young person.

Other agencies include any other local education authority, any local authority department other than education (e.g. social work) and any health board or National Health Service Trust. The definition thus covers disabled children as well as those who are looked after by local authorities, Gypsy, and Traveller children, those with English as a second language, and children of refugees and asylum seekers. The report accompanying the draft bill noted that children in particular groups should not be seen in isolation from one another (e.g., a looked-after child may have learning difficulties), but it should also be recognized that the barriers facing particular groups of children are the same. In the future, it will be important to monitor which children come to be defined as having additional support needs, and whether the definition of additional support needs works equally well for all. The act abolishes the Record of Needs and establishes a new document, the Co-ordinated Support Plan, for recording children's difficulties in learning and specifying the support to be given.

Qualification criteria for a Co-ordinated Support Plan are tightly specified. According to the Code of Practice, *Supporting Children's Learning* (Scottish Executive, 2005), a child will qualify for a Co-ordinated Support Plan if he or she has additional support needs arising from one or more complex factors or multiple factors, and if they require additional support to be provided by the education authority and by one or more appropriate agencies. Under the definition, a child who was blind and had additional learning difficulties would not qualify for a Co-ordinated Support Plan unless another agency (e.g., health or social work) was also making a significant contribution to their support. A child who is only receiving services from education, no matter how significant his or her impairment, will have his or her needs assessed and recorded in some other document, such as an Individualised Educational Programme. Unlike the US Individualized

Education Program (Florian & Pullin, 2000), however, Scottish IEPs do not have to specify additional resources, are not legally binding on the school or the local authority, and do not have a route to legal redress. They are also unlikely to involve multidisciplinary teams (Kane et al., 2003).

IDENTIFYING CHILDREN WITH ADDITIONAL SUPPORT NEEDS

Under existing legislation, local authorities have a duty to identify which children have special educational needs as defined above. The new legislation is somewhat vague about the local authorities' duties vis-à-vis the assessment of additional support needs and, according to the Code of Practice, "The Act does not prescribe any particular model of assessment or intervention" (Scottish Executive, 2005, p. 26). Appropriate agencies (e.g., health or social work) have a duty to assist an education authority in assessment, intervention, planning, provision, and review, unless this is prejudicial to the agency's other functions. Overall, it appears that multi-professional assessments, which happened automatically in the context of assessment and recording, are less likely to take place under the terms of the new legislation, and drawn-out legal wrangles appear inevitable if another agency declines to provide the support that might be deemed necessary. For most children, assessment is likely to be much less formal and will depend on the discretion of the local authority and the school. In most cases, the responsibility for assessment is likely to lie with the learning support teacher, but in the absence of mandatory specialist qualifications, knowledge of diagnostic assessment is likely to vary greatly between schools.

RIGHTS OF APPEAL, ADJUDICATION, AND MEDIATION

Research on assessment and provision for children with SEN indicated that parents had weaker rights of appeal in Scotland than in other jurisdictions, and that the appeals process was inaccessible and time-consuming (Riddell, 2002). The establishment of an Additional Support Needs Tribunal is a major new development. Parents can appeal all aspects of the Co-ordinated Support Plan, including provision, decisions to draw up or not to draw up a Co-ordinated Support Plan, to discontinue or not to review a Co-ordinated Support Plan, and delays in drawing up or not drawing up a Co-ordinated Support Plan. The qualification criteria, however, for accessing additional support needs are very high. Only those who already have a Co-ordinated Support Plan, or who can show that they have a reasonable case for arguing that they meet the criteria for such a plan, are eligible to make a reference to the tribunal. This automatically rules out parents whose children have very significant disabilities, but are receiving all their services from education. The Scottish Executive may thus have created a catch-22 situation: Only those who qualify, or believe they qualify, for a Co-ordinated Support Plan may make a reference to the tribunal, but the requirements for a Co-ordinated Support Plan have been set so high that less than 0.5% of children are likely to qualify. Unlike England and Wales, where the Special Educational Needs and Disability Tribunal now hears disability discrimination cases, in Scotland these are still heard by the Sheriff Court. In England, when the Special Educational Needs and Disability Tribunal was introduced in 1994, cases in the first year were threefold greater than expected. In Scotland at the time of writing (June 2006), even though the tribunal had been operational for six months, not a single reference had gone forward to a hearing.

Parents whose children have additional support needs but who do not meet the criteria for a Co-ordinated Support Plan may request independent adjudication if there is a dispute with the local authority. Adjudicators are appointed by the Scottish Executive and make decisions on the basis of written documents submitted by the local authority and the parents. There is no hearing and the process appears to lack transparency and independence. Potentially, however, there could be far more cases requiring adjudication compared with the number that are likely to be heard by the Additional Support Needs Tribunal.

Another important measure in the legislation is the requirement for local authorities to have independent mediation schemes in place to provide advice and support to parents and to help resolve disputes between parents and local authorities. Although mediation schemes may empower parents, there is no requirement on local authorities to provide access to advocacy services. As a result, some people may be prevented from using mediation services effectively because of their own disadvantage or disability. The success of mediation schemes, particularly in reaching socially disadvantaged and excluded parents, therefore, needs to be monitored.

INCLUSION AND ADDITIONAL SUPPORT FOR LEARNING

There is a commitment in Scotland to increase the proportion of pupils with SEN being included in mainstream schools (see, for example, *For*

Scotland's Children [Scottish Executive, 2001]) and the Scottish Executive's learning disabilities review *The Same As You?* [Scottish Executive, 2000]. The new legislation is intended to extend support to a much wider group of children, with the implicit understanding that needs should be met irrespective of whether they arise from disability, difficulty, or disadvantage. It is evident, however, that the implementation of the legislation coincides with a backlash against inclusion, with teachers' unions calling for a fundamental review of the presumption of mainstreaming. Interestingly, teachers appear to be most severely exercised by the presence of disadvantaged children with behavioral difficulties in mainstream classes, although their objections are broadly grouped under opposition to inclusion. As I have argued above, the new legislation widens the qualification criteria for general support to all children with additional support needs, but simultaneously restricts access to specifically targeted support from a range of agencies to those qualifying for a Co-ordinated Support Plan. There may, therefore, be pressure in the future from schools and parents for more placement in special settings for disabled children with significant needs who do not qualify for a Co-ordinated Support Plan. It will be recognized that in mainstream settings they will have to compete for resources with many other groups, including the children of refugees and asylum seekers, Travellers, and looked-after children. In special settings, on the other hand, resources may be seen as guaranteed. Clearly, much will depend on the local decisions made by managers in schools and local authorities. There is, however, a precedent in Sweden, where Persson (2004) reports an increase in the special school population as a result of the delegation of resources for special educational needs to municipalities, with much less control from the center.

CONCLUSION

In this chapter, we began by proposing a policy typology to be used in understanding the classification systems used in Scotland since the SEN reforms of the early 1980s. Following the Warnock Report, the postwar bureaucratic categorization framework was replaced with an emphasis on the professionals' right to determine which children should be identified as having SEN. During the 1990s, the SEN policy frameworks in Scotland became more diverse, with growing emphasis on legality, managerialism, consumerism, and marketization, although the diversity was more apparent south of the border. Each policy framework tends to have a particular group of protagonists, who play a major role in managing the boundaries of the classification systems associated with it. For example, pre-Warnock systems used doctors as arbiters of medical classification frameworks, whereas post-Warnock systems gave greatest power to educational psychologists acting in consort with local authority officers. Subsequent policy frameworks have given greater power to parents through the enhancement of legal rights, and the new additional support for learning frameworks seems to invest most power in local authority and school managers.

The outcome of existing classification systems was discussed in terms of the identification and placement of children with special educational needs/additional support needs and the availability of additional resources. I noted that, despite attempts to establish special educational needs, and, more recently, additional support needs, as unitary categories, there has actually been a proliferation of subcategories, with a marked increase in the number of pupils with certain classifications of impairment (in particular social, emotional, and behavioral difficulties and autistic spectrum disorders). The numerical predominance of boys is particularly evident in nonnormative areas, and there are clear associations between poverty and gender in the identification of special educational needs/additional support needs. This may be an ideological construction used to explain and justify working-class boys' greater likelihood of being excluded from the labor market (Armstrong, 2005). On the other hand, it may reflect the cultural and educational alienation of working-class boys in areas of industrial decline.

Finally, the chapter summarized some key features of the new Scottish additional support for learning legislation and considered its implications for pupils with difficulties, disabilities, and disadvantages. As in the post-Warnock era, it is unlikely that subcategories of impairment will disappear. In terms of additional resourcing arrangements, however, it seems that two broad classifications will be of great significance. Pupils with additional support needs qualifying for a Co-ordinated Support Plan, a numerically small group, are likely to receive relatively generous support backed up by a strong system of legal redress. Children who have additional support needs but who do not qualify for a Co-ordinated Support Plan will have much weaker rights to access additional resources and obtain redress, and provision will depend on possibly arbitrary school-level decisions. Those controlling access to additional resources in this case will be managers at school and local authority levels, suggesting that policy frameworks based on managerialism and professionalism are in the ascendancy. Despite the official endorsement of inclusion, this may result in greater pressure to use special settings, where additional resources may be guaranteed. The possibility of growing segregationist pressure is also indicated by the fact that disabled children who do not have Co-ordinated Support Plans will be in competition with other groups (e.g., looked-after children, children with

English as a second language) for scarce resources, and their parents may therefore seek placements where such competition will be minimized. The advent of disability discrimination legislation, which might have boosted the rights of disabled children and their parents, is likely to have far less impact than the additional support for learning legislation, the impact of which will undoubtedly be felt for many years.

NOTE

1. Data do not include grant-aided special schools.

REFERENCES

Armstrong, D. (2005). Reinventing inclusion: New Labour and the cultural politics of special education *Oxford Review of Education, 31*(1): 135–151.

Armstrong, D., & Galloway, D. (1994). Special educational needs and problem behaviour: Making policy in the classroom. In S. Riddell & S. Brown (Eds.), *Special educational needs policy in the 1990s: Warnock in the market place* (pp. 175–196). London: Routledge.

Cogan, N., Riddell, S., & Tisdall, K. (2003). *Knowledge and awareness of Part 4 of the Disability Discrimination Act 1995 (as amended) in Scotland.* Edinburgh, Scotland: Disability Rights Commission.

Corker, M., & Shakespeare, T. (2002). *Disability/postmodernity: Embodying disability theory.* London: Continuum.

Department for Education. (1994). *Code of practice on the identification and assessment of special educational needs.* London: Author.

Department of Education and Science. (1978). *Special educational needs: Report of the Committee of Enquiry Into the Education of Handicapped Children and Young People* (Warnock Report). London: Her Majesty's Stationery Office.

Florian, L., & Pullin, D. (2000). Defining difference: A comparative perspective on legal and policy issues in education reform and special educational needs. In M. J. McLaughlin & M. Rouse (Eds.), *Special education and school reform in the United States and Britain* (pp. 11–38). London: Routledge.

Gooding, C. (2000). Disability Discrimination Act: From statute to practice. *Critical Social Policy, 20*(4), 533–551.

Kane, J., Riddell, S., Banks, P., Baynes, A., Dyson, A., Millward, A., & Wilson, A. (2003). Special educational needs and individualised educational programmes: Issues of parent and pupil participation. *Scottish Educational Review, 35*(1), 38–48.

Kirp, D. L. (1982). Professionalization as a policy choice: British special education in comparative perspective. *World Politics, 34*(2), 137–174.

Mashaw, J. L. (1983). *Bureaucratic justice: Managing Social Security disability claims.* New Haven and London: Yale University Press.

Newman, J. (2001). *Modernising governance: New Labour, policy and society.* London: Sage.

Osler, A., & Vincent, K. (2003). *Girls and exclusion: Rethinking the agenda.* London: Routledge Falmer.

Persson, B. (2004, September). *Policies and practices in special needs education. Discourses of inclusion and exclusion: Experiences from Sweden.* Paper presented at the Exceptional Child Education Resources Conference, Rhethymnon, Greece.

Riddell, S. (2002). *Policy and practice in special education: Special educational needs.* Edinburgh, Scotland: Dunedin Academic Press.

Riddell, S., Brown, S., & Duffield, J. (1994). Conflicts of policies and models: The case of specific learning difficulties. In S. Riddell & S. Brown (Eds.), *Special educational needs policy in the 1990s: Warnock in the market place* (pp. 113–140). London: Routledge.

Riddell, S., Wilson, A., Adler, M., & Mordaunt, E. (2002). Parents, professionals and special educational needs policy frameworks in England and Scotland. *Policy and Politics, 30*(3), 411–427.

Scottish Executive. (2000). *The same as you? A review of services for people with learning disabilities.* Edinburgh, Scotland: The Stationery Office.

Scottish Executive. (2001). *For Scotland's children.* Edinburgh, Scotland: The Stationery Office.

Scottish Executive. (2004). *Incidents of violence and anti-social behaviour against local authority school staff in 2002/03.* Available online at: www.scotland.gov.uk/

Scottish Executive. (2005). *Supporting children's learning: Code of practice.* Edinburgh, Scotland: The Stationery Office.

Scottish Executive (2006a). *Exclusions from schools 2004/05.* Retrieved June 2, 2006, from www.scotland.gov.uk/Resource/Doc/90946/0021841.pdf

Scottish Executive. (2006b). *Pupils in Scotland, 2005.* Retrieved June 2, 2006, from www.scotland.gov.uk/Publications/2006/02/28083923/9

Thomas, C. (1999). *Female forms: Experiencing and understanding disability.* Buckingham, UK: Open University Press.

Part II

Interaction and Impacts of Classification Policies on Educational Systems

9 Perspectives and Purposes of Disability Classification Systems

Implications for Teachers and Curriculum and Pedagogy

Brahm Norwich

INTRODUCTION

Do teachers, teacher educators, and program designers require a classification of childhood disabilities and difficulties? If so, what kind of classification would this be? What value would such a classification have in decisions about what and how to teach that would be different from decisions for children not identified as having disabilities and difficulties? The aim of this chapter is to examine some general issues about the nature of special education classification systems and the specialization of curriculum and teaching. The basis for this argument will be a summary of the key conclusions from a particular project undertaken in the United Kingdom over several years that aimed to conceptualize the relationship between special educational categories, specialization, and teaching. The chapter is organized in three sections. The first section is about different kinds of classification systems and their underlying rationales and assumptions. The second section is about whether categories of special education are relevant to teaching, and the third section is about the implications of a teaching and curriculum approach for how we think about special education needs (SEN) classification. This chapter is written from the perspective of someone working within a UK English context. The approach taken can be seen as an example of a national approach to classification. This means that the discussion has a UK perspective and is based initially on work from the current systems in this country. The examination of the issues from this perspective will raise issues of wider significance, and, as the argument progresses, it will be shown how the conclusions have international relevance.

DIFFERENT KINDS OF CLASSIFICATIONS

The Warnock Report (Department of Education and Science, 1978), which established the current conceptual and policy framework for the United Kingdom and led to the introduction of the Education Act 1981, had the effect of reducing the significance and use of categories. As discussed by Wedell in Chapter 4, the purpose behind introducing the term "special educational needs" was to reduce the negative impact of labeling and to focus on what was needed to promote learning, rather than focusing on children's difficulties and deficits. The key arguments against the current categories associated with the position in the Warnock Report were that they were focused on deficits and that this had the effect of reinforcing labeling and stigma. There were also uncertainties about thresholds or cutoffs for category use (at what point along a continuum of low performance on an ability or attainment scale a difficulty was to be identified). In addition, it was also argued that exclusive use of categories ignored the interactions of difficulties with personal strengths and contextual factors that affect personal functioning. Although the report recognized that categories could inform the planning of provision and highlight the additional needs of vulnerable minorities, the negative arguments, especially those pertaining to labeling and stigma, were seen as dominant.

Despite the "abandoning of categories," the Warnock position introduced a new general category of SEN, a term which even when introduced into the 1981 legislation was left without more specific definition. The 1981 legislation merely defined SEN in terms of "learning difficulties" that called for additional or different provision. "Learning difficulties" itself was only defined as "difficulties greater than the majority of the same age." The report also suggested that subareas concerned with degrees of cognitive impairment, referred to then as "educational subnormality," be replaced by the term "learning difficulties." The effect of the Warnock tradition, which has operated for almost thirty years and still has some influence, was to create a climate suspicious of categories, while supporting the use of vague general categories. The justification for this was that the focus should be on need, not deficit, and that need had to be identified in individual terms, leaving it mainly to professionals to decide on the criteria for when a child's educational needs became "special." It is interesting that, despite the use of categories to designate provision and areas of SEN (in the first national SEN Code of Practice [DfE, 1994]), the UK system was represented as noncategorical in an Organisation for Economic Cooperation and Development (OECD, 2000) study of international classification practices.

It took about twenty years for the government to reintroduce a classification, this time of areas of SEN (Department for Education and Skills [DfES], 2003). The weight given to the old points in favor of categorization now changed to become more dominant. But, sensitive to a professional climate that was critical of the negative effects of labeling, the government introduced the classification officially for pupil census/monitoring purposes, and not for use in describing types of provision, decision making about identifying children as having SEN, or planning provision for these children. All children with SEN at levels of "school action" and "school action plus" in ordinary schools receive additional or different provision in a range of ways and settings, as specified in their Individualised Educational Programmes (IEPs) from school resources, and sometimes with the support of outside support services. The 3% of children with statements are mostly placed in ordinary schools (about two thirds), and the rest are in special schools. The current SEN classification applies to children at the 2 highest levels of SEN in the English system (school action plus and statement levels). Table 8.1 shows the current special education classification, which involves four broad areas or dimensions of need covering a range of subareas or categories. This is an ad hoc system that has no clear theoretical rationale. The system does, however, enable some identification within more than one subarea or category.

Many of the problems with this classification were aired during the government's consultation process, but many of the issues remain unresolved. Key terms like "needs," "disorder," or "impairment" are used synonymously. The implication is that difficulties/disorders lead to having additional educational needs. But there is little said about what is "needed"—whether it is resources, staffing, equipment, learning setting, kind of curriculum, and/or teaching approach/pedagogy. Some of the

Table 8.1   SEN Classification

Dimensions	Categories
1. Cognition and Learning Needs	Specific learning difficulty (SpLD)
	Moderate learning difficulty (MLD)
	Severe learning difficulty (SLD)
	Profound and multiple learning difficulty (PMLD)
2. Behavioral, Emotional, and Social Development Needs	Emotional and behavioral difficulty (EBD)
3. Communication and Interaction Needs	Speech, language, and communication needs (SLCN)
	Autistic spectrum disorder (ASD)
4. Sensory and/or Physical Needs	Visual impairment (VI)
	Hearing impairment (HI)
	Multisensory impairment (MSI)
	Physical disability (PD)
5. Other	

SOURCE: Department for Education and Skills, 2003.

Table 8.2   Dimensions of a Possible Classification of Educational Disability

1. Educational Functional Difficulties	Covering range of functional areas
2. Health Conditions	Physical diseases and mental health disorders
3. Environmental Factors	Facilitators and barriers in current situations
4. Personal Factors	Abilities, skills, dispositions
5. Learning Activity Limitations	Activity limitations in range of curriculum areas
6. Learning Participation Restrictions	Learning participation restrictions in class, wider school, home, and community

SEN groups are identified in terms of medical terms (autism); others are in terms that are specific to the educational system (severe and moderate learning difficulties). The recent SEN classification, however, does set out that terms can only be applied if additional provision has already been tried; but there is no detail about what counts as additional provision that has already been tried. This vagueness reflects a silence about what is distinctive about a special educational classification system. This raises the question about what an educational classification of additional educational needs for those with disabilities would address. It is suggested that the following questions would be considered:

1. For whom is additional provision required in terms of educational processes (e.g., modes of communication) and outcomes (attainments and wider achievements)?

2. When is additional provision required, assuming that good enough provision has been tried (involving the setting of thresholds)?

3. In what terms is additional educational provision specified (such as general curriculum, learning context, and teaching approaches, facilities, and materials)?

4. Does special provision have differential benefits compared with good quality provision for those without disabilities?

5. What values underpin the classification and what is the assumed causal model of the child in her or his context?

Classification systems can be evaluated in terms of how well they deal with these questions, as what follows will demonstrate.

ARE CATEGORIES OF DISABILITIES AND DIFFICULTIES USED IN SPECIAL EDUCATION RELEVANT TO TEACHING?

Initial Study

In this section, I will address the question of the relevance of special education categories to decisions about curriculum and pedagogy. This discussion is based on work that was started seven years ago by Ann Lewis and myself into whether there is a distinctive or specialized teaching/ pedagogy for children with SEN (Norwich & Lewis, 2001). This involved an international literature review of research and theory, funded by the British Educational Research Association (BERA), related to these questions:

1. Can differences between learners (by particular special educational needs group) be identified *and* systematically linked with learners'

needs for differential teaching? Many studies have addressed only the first part of this question.

2. Second, what are the key criteria for identifying pedagogically useful learner groups?

The scope of the literature review is set out in Norwich and Lewis (2001). This included research evaluations, position pieces, and research reviews from the United States, the United Kingdom, and Europe that were published in English, using ERIC, PsycINFO, and the British Education Index. A national network was set up and a national conference held to identify a range of current views in the United Kingdom. Our initial focus was on teaching approaches, called pedagogy, which we took to refer to broad clusters of decisions and actions taken in classroom settings that aim to promote school learning. Our focus was not on curriculum, which we took as objectives to be learned. We used a three-dimensional model of educational need that distinguished between "unique," "distinct," and "common pedagogic needs" (Norwich, 1996). This model assumes that children's educational needs are identified in terms of three dimensions— what they share with all others (common needs, common to all those with and without SEN), what they share with some groups (distinct or specific group needs), and what they share with nobody (unique needs). In trying to develop some models of differentiation we made the further assumption that an acceptable model would include both unique and common pedagogic needs. This meant that there are two possible models of differentiation: the "unique differences" and "general differences" positions.

These positions represent distinct philosophical assumptions about how we make sense of difference. The key difference is about whether distinct specific group needs, associated with special education categories, lead to clear implications for pedagogy. These group needs that arise from different kinds of group membership are in a generalized form—they could involve a disability or difficulties category, but not necessarily. Though we were open to other kinds of classification, the review showed that there was little evidence to support the general differences position for various areas of learning difficulties, namely, profound and multiple learning difficulties (PMLD), severe learning difficulties (SLD), moderate learning difficulties (MLD), specific learning difficulties (SpLD), and pupils with low attainment.[1] Putting this in slightly different terms, we found a trend away from SEN-specific pedagogies, although we also concluded that there were few directly relevant studies. The result was that we presented evidence and arguments to accept the unique differences position for these areas of SEN. In this position, we rejected the view that general categories had distinctive pedagogic implications over and above common and unique pedagogic needs. The unique differences position, it needs to be recalled, does not deny the significance of differences, but conceptualizes them in individual terms.

From this we drew the implication that common pedagogic principles are relevant to differences between all pupils including those identified as having SEN. We stressed, however, the importance of recognizing the significance of more intense and focused teaching for those with SEN, partly in recognition of their unique needs. We introduced the term "continua of teaching approaches" to capture the appropriateness of more intensive and explicit teaching for pupils with learning difficulties. This intensification could be analyzed in terms of different facets or pedagogic strategies, with teaching that involved more intensive strategies, for example, more practice, or more examples of concepts. In this view, pedagogic strategies were not in principle qualitatively different for those with and those without learning difficulties. We concluded that the strategies sometimes look different in practice, but they still reflected the same principles applied differently, often more intensively. This difference in look can be seen to underpin the historic professional split between specialist and general teaching.

Collaborative Project

More recent work in the form of a collaborative project has built on this initial framework by including in the analysis of teaching the interaction between pedagogy-curriculum-knowledge (Lewis & Norwich, 2004).

In this expanded model of teaching, we provided reasons for assuming an interaction between the deployment of pedagogic strategies and teachers' knowledge within a curriculum context. The commonality-specialization question arises with each of these three elements. In the first element, teachers' knowledge, we included knowledge about the curriculum area, about learners, and about learning processes. In the second element, curriculum, we focused on *what* was worth learning, how worthwhile learning was organized, and programs designed to these ends. This included questions about the balance between different areas of learning and different design orientations, such as process *versus* product models. In a process model, the curriculum is cast as a process toward wider and general educational and developmental aims, with the content of learning (what to learn) and the teaching or instruction (how to learn) seen as strongly interlinked. Process models assume that teaching strategies and relationships embody the aims of education and what is to be learned.

In product models, curriculum content is defined in more specific and separable terms, which are distinct from the means or techniques of enabling the learning of the content. Product models are also known as objectives models and the design of the National Curriculum in the United Kingdom (as in curricula elsewhere) reflects this kind of model, with its primary focus on content in subject areas. This product orientation to curriculum design lends itself to setting standards of attainment and asking what are the optimal or more effective forms of teaching to achieve specified learning goals or outcomes. This approach has international currency in the moves to raise school standards of attainments.

This expanded model enabled us to ask questions about the commonality—and differentiation of the design at different levels—for instance, having common goals but different pathways to and objectives for these common goals. This made it possible to conceptualize the variety and complexity of curriculum goals, including specialized goals, where these may be judged to be effective and viable. In this way, the model can address the area where school-teaching interfaces with therapeutic interventions that are learning based.

The project involved fourteen colleagues who were recognized national specialists in different areas, many with international reputations for their work. Each participant focused on their specialist area, ranging from profound and multiple learning difficulties (PMLD), through to specific learning difficulties (SpLD, e.g., dyslexia, dyspraxia), emotional and behavioral difficulties (EBD), attention deficit hyperactivity disorder (ADHD), autistic spectrum disorder (ASD), sensory impairments (VI—visual impairment; MSI—multisensory impairment, deaf), severe learning difficulties (SLD), speech and language impairment (SLI), Down syndrome (DS), moderate learning difficulties (MLD), and low attainers. Our collaborators worked to a common brief based on the above framework and models. Their brief was to define their focal group; to examine the category used for the group and relationships to other groups; to discuss the unique differences *versus* general differences position in relation to pedagogy, curriculum design, and teachers' knowledge in relation to relevant international research and theory; to criticize empirical evidence; and to place the analysis in an international context. This meant that contributors used their readings and critical reviews of research and theory in their selected field to respond to the common brief. Lewis and Norwich, as the project coordinators, then summarized each contribution for its key points and conclusions using a common template. This process also acted as a quality review of the individual contributions. We then summarized and synthesized in detail the range of positions taken in the preceding contributions. We presented the conclusions drawn from this group of experts in a book (Lewis & Norwich, 2004) as illustrative and not as definitive accounts about these areas of SEN.

Summary of Collaborative Study Conclusions

One of our conclusions was that although the contributors might have made claims for the usefulness of "other" category frameworks, none did so. This could be seen to reflect how well established are conventional categories, despite many misgivings about them. Most contributors commented on the nature of their SEN group as not being straightforward. For some, the group definitions came from the use of medical definitions and associated forms of causality (DS, PMLD, deaf, deaf-blind, VI). Some distinguished between medical categories and how they contrasted with functional definitions (VI). For others, the group definitions reflected presenting "symptoms" or behaviors (autism, dyspraxia, PMLD, SLI). As we expected, the environment, including social networks and systems, was represented as a significant *defining* aspect for the low attainers and MLD groups. Environmental factors were in other cases seen as *interacting* with biological and psychological factors in defining one group (ADHD), while only as *mediating* difficulties for others (autism, deaf, dyslexia, DS, and EBD).

All contributors referred to the potential, or likely, co-occurrence of difficulties, though to varying degrees (e.g., DS with mental health problems). This was emphasized particularly in the areas of ADHD, autism (ASD), deaf, dyspraxia, PMLD, MLD, MSI, and SLD. Therefore, it is unlikely that "pure" group-specific pedagogical practices based on the nature of the group could be sustained. All contributors also linked the nature of the individual group with a range of effects or impacts on learning, implying that even if hypothesized, group-related pedagogic strategies would need to be applied differentially. Thus, even with a general differences position, individual needs are at the center of pedagogic decision making.

Curriculum

The relationship between curriculum and pedagogy was assumed at the start to be one in which curriculum questions can set the determining context for questions about the commonality-specialization of pedagogy. This view was supported in several of the contributions. We were aware of alternative versions of curriculum design. This included traditional issues about curriculum design, such as academic *versus* vocational/functional orientations and process *versus* product design approaches. However, collected *versus* integrated approaches to curriculum design[2] were not identified at the start, but did emerge in the contribution about children with speech and language impairment (SLI). Curriculum design involves different levels of generality and specificity at which commonality-specialization questions can be addressed. If commonality is set at the general level of aims and goals, there is scope for flexibility at lower levels (for example, specific objectives). So, specialized programs for some children (supplementary or remedial/therapeutic programs) can be mixed with common ones. If commonality is set at the level of specific programs in particular curriculum areas, then questions of appropriateness for children with exceptional needs come to be significant.

The contributors adopted curriculum positions in their particular areas of SEN that addressed all these aspects of the starting framework. Some highlighted curriculum differences in their SEN area, whereas others took up a particular curriculum position. Both approaches were useful, though the implication is that the conclusions did not provide a definitive overview of all teaching approaches, but were illustrative of issues and positions.

For some contributors, internal differences about curriculum questions were attributed to the diversity of the needs within their SEN area. For example, differences in curriculum approach as regards deafness were presented in terms of the heterogeneity of the broad group and related to the deaf culture's use of signing. There were similarities between the deafness/hearing impairment (HI) and visual impairment (VI) areas. In the visual impairment area, additional curriculum programs concerned with mobility were relevant, though this depended on the severity of impairment. By contrast, in the PMLD area, curriculum differences were seen in terms of the adoption of a more process, or a more product, design orientation. The significance of the wider cultural context for the curriculum approach was evident not only in the deaf area (in relation to the role of signing), but also for low attainers, for whom the school curriculum can be linked to wider interventions outside the school with families and the neighborhood.

Several contributors indicated that curriculum commonality could only be at the broadest general level of common principles, as otherwise the diversity of educational needs would call for specialization. This was most explicitly argued in the contribution on ASD, which questioned the concept of a "universal curriculum design." Curriculum relevance was judged to be more important for this group than curriculum breadth. Programs for this group, it was argued, also require a therapeutic or remedial model. The contribution on PMLD implied that the curriculum had a focus on communication and covered fewer curriculum areas. This was another example of the priority being to relevance rather than breadth.

Several contributions indicated that their areas required a curriculum approach that departed from the current dominant curriculum practices in England (ADHD, ASD, low attainer, SLCN), though these variations depended on the particular area of SEN. It was argued for ASD that access and remedial orientations needed to be combined, as the current emphasis on access in special education was not enough. A similar approach was evident, though not explicitly stated, for ADHD, where it was argued that it was important to circumvent difficulties by working to strengths, while also focusing on programs to reduce inattentiveness and impulsiveness. It was also assumed in the ADHD contribution that programs needed to be more flexible and geared to pupil learning styles. The curriculum variation for children with SLI involved a move away from a collected to a more integrated approach to curriculum areas, in particular between subject learning and language learning. For the PMLD group the development of intensive interaction programs was presented as a departure from a more product- or target-based curriculum approach (Kellett & Nind, 2003). The contribution on low attainment questioned the appropriateness of traditional academic curriculum provision for those aged thirteen to sixteen years (Key Stage 4 in UK terms).

It is interesting that there were no clear links between these four areas, where contributors called for variations from dominant curriculum practices. This contrasted with the two sensory areas, hearing and visual impairment, where the need for additional curriculum programs was recognized. In the visual impairment area, there are programs focusing on mobility, use of residual vision, maximum use of senses, and special literacy routes. In the hearing impairment area, there are distinctive communication routes, though only where communication is in terms of signed bilingual or signed English approaches. In the contribution on deaf-blind, the reference to tangible symbol systems also indicated the need for additional programs.

For the other SEN areas, there was no indication of the need for specialized curriculum programs, nor departures from dominant curriculum practices. These contributions, however, identified the need for greater emphasis on certain common curriculum areas than other areas. This variation in emphasis can be termed "continua of common curriculum approaches," the curriculum version of continua of pedagogic strategies. For MLD, it was suggested that some people advocate a particular emphasis on programs focusing on problem solving and social interaction. For PMLD, curriculum emphasis was not only on communication, but also choice making, while for EBD the emphasis was more toward personal and social/emotional development. The curriculum emphasis for deaf-blind and Down syndrome was toward sensory strengths, for deaf-blind on tactile senses, and for Down syndrome on visual rather than auditory senses. By contrast, for MLD and SLD, the emphasis was not on curriculum areas, but on the degree of structure in the progression and sequence of the programs. The focus was on the sequencing of small steps in both MLD and SLD. Finally, curriculum was not treated as a significant focus compared to pedagogy and knowledge, in the contributions on dyslexia and dyspraxia, two related forms of specific learning difficulties.

Knowledge

The significance of relevant knowledge emerged strongly from contributions in the project. The nature of the required knowledge in relation to the identified SEN groups was analyzed across the different SEN areas as identified by the project contributors as spanning four foci:

Knowledge 1: The nature of the SEN group. Regardless of pedagogic relevance, such knowledge is valuable in its own right as underpinning the learner's development. This was apparent in the contributions on ADHD, ASD, deaf, Down syndrome, dyslexia, dyspraxia, PMLD, and VI. The importance of knowledge was emphasized even when the nature of the group was contested, as occurred in the case of dyslexia. For some areas, however, group-related knowledge was not relevant, as the group label was not seen as having a valid, unique identity with relevance for pedagogic decisions (low attainers, MLD). In these cases, the value of the group labels was to draw attention to the wider context of learning and the need to address, for example, the range of economic, family, and community factors which may, despite schools' best efforts, hamper school-based learning. This signaling function of the label was echoed for ADHD and dyslexia, where the group label was seen to carry orienting and specific pedagogic functions.

Knowledge 2: That relates to oneself as teacher. Three contributions (ASD, EBD, and low attainers) indicated that a further relevant aspect of knowledge relates to oneself as a teacher. Self-knowledge and professional identity may be linked with particular value positions (for example, valuing a broad and learner-centered curriculum) that operate across all learners. In this context, what seemed to be masquerading as a SEN-specific approach may conceal a position that (ideally) would be applied to all learners but, perhaps because of perceived system features, was articulated in relation to the less constrained SEN context.

Knowledge 3: That relates to the psychology of learning. This reflects a unique differences position in that knowledge about the psychology of learning would be seen as required for effective teaching of all learners. For example, one might extrapolate that a sound understanding of self-regulation and attendant processes are of value to the teacher whether working with children with ADHD, sensory needs, or a range of children with learning difficulties.

Knowledge 4: Knowledge of curriculum areas and general pedagogic strategies. This also reflects a unique differences position in that knowledge about curriculum areas and general pedagogic strategies are assumed to be important in relation to all learners.

These four aspects of knowledge can be integrated and linked to pedagogy by conceptualizing "knowledge 1" (nature of the SEN group) as a filter through which the other forms of knowledge are seen and which lead to curriculum and pedagogic decisions. Where "knowledge 1" is strongly defined (i.e., acting as a powerful filter), the resultant teaching strategy will be perceived as appearing to be very different from practice elsewhere; where "knowledge 1" is less clearly defined (weak filter), this will not be the case. For example, the area of low attainers reflects a weak "SEN" filter position (broader social and economic factors are seen as paramount), and so the label has little usefulness in terms of the knowledge base from which to plan teaching. In contrast, there is a strong "SEN" filter for VI and ADHD, given the distinctiveness of their associated knowledge base; in interaction with "knowledges 3 and 4," this can be related to points about access and specialization in the planning of teaching.

Pedagogy

The most widely made point across the contributions was the scarcity of an empirical evidence base that directly related pedagogic strategies specifically to the various SEN areas. This conclusion recognized an extensive international literature about pedagogy, but identified that this literature was often about pedagogic prescriptions based on practical experience or on applied theory and research that had little direct bearing on specific pedagogic strategies in relation to specific areas of SEN. This was partly attributed to the difficulties and complexities of undertaking systematic evaluation and research studies. It is also notable that few contributors (except the areas ADHD and EBD) approached the question of pedagogy in terms of research into classroom pedagogy as involving the teachers' thinking that lies behind teacher actions. This perspective draws on research into teaching as involving professional craft knowledge. In this tradition, pedagogy was seen to be strongly influenced by teachers' perceptions of pupil characteristics and to involve the use of ready-made categories, a "typing" process. Though typing can have negative or positive potential, it is assumed that knowledge of specific areas, like ADHD, can sharpen up less sophisticated forms of typing children, and in so doing have a positive impact on pedagogy. This perspective illustrates how knowledge about an area of SEN comes to be relevant to pedagogic matters.

Only two contributions argued for the significance of distinctive group pedagogy, ASD and ADHD. In the case of ASD, the argument was that because common pedagogic needs are relevant to children with ADHD, their individual needs are best identified through a framework of group needs. This was the most coherent case that was made in the project for a general differences pedagogic position. It is notable that the two SEN areas that took this perspective are two areas based on medically defined conditions that have come more recently to parent, public, and professional attention. The other contributions adopted a perspective that assumed generic strategies that are geared to difference by degrees of deliberateness and intensity of teaching. Many supported this position by arguing that variations on the pedagogic strategies for their SEN area can also be useful for other children. The chapters on dyslexia, dyspraxia, MLD, and SLD, for example, represent the pedagogic variations as reflecting deliberateness and intensity, in line with our initial review and the concept of a continuum of pedagogic strategies (Norwich & Lewis, 2001). In contributions about broad areas (e.g., EBD and low attainment), it was pointed out that the wide diversity within these groups reduces any pedagogic significance of the category.

Though the starting model of teaching put pedagogy in the context of curriculum, it did not spell out how these aspects interacted. This is where specific contributions showed the interrelationship between curriculum and pedagogic aspects. For example, in the visual impairment contribution there was a distinction between macro- and micro-pedagogic strategies. Whereas the macro-strategies are presented as common or generic, the micro-strategies might be distinctive to those with visual impairment, where the modality of access might be different, for example, through touch rather than sight. The interrelation between curriculum and pedagogy was also evident in other areas: deaf, EBD, PMLD, and SLCN. For EBD, for instance, there is a pedagogic tradition that is integral to a learner-centered and process curriculum model.

Individual Versus Group Differences Positions

Though the theoretical difference between these two positions depends on the presence or absence of group-specific pedagogic needs, it is important to clarify what is and is not involved in these positions. The general differences position does not imply that pedagogic decisions flow just from group membership. This position also assumes that common needs inform decisions and practices and these are attuned to individual needs. Nor is the individual differences position merely about individual needs. It assumes that a framework of common needs informs decisions and practices that are attuned to individual needs. Also, a distinctive pedagogic strategy for a child identified within a group, say PMLD, may not be relevant to another child within that diverse group. Distinctiveness may be identified at an individual level, but this does not turn the individual differences position into a general differences position. The general differences position requires a general relationship between a distinct group, however defined, and a generalized and distinctive kind of pedagogy. The project has illustrated how far we are from making these kinds of generalizations. In these circumstances, the individual differences position can be seen as a default position; if we do not take account of distinct group needs, then a reasonable alternative is to take account of common and individual needs and therefore adopt the individual differences position.

The areas where contributions endorsed the general differences position tended to be the more clearly specified ones (ADHD, ASD). General differences positions are also supported where pedagogic strategies interact with aspects of teaching access (visual impairment) and communication mode (hearing impairment). The general differences position is one that avoids simple stereotyping in terms of group-based pedagogic needs, as discussed above, because it takes account of common and individual needs. The limits of the individual differences position, however, with its continua of common pedagogic strategies, were illustrated in other areas. As strategies become more intense along continua of general pedagogic strategies, they may reach a level of intensity where they are construed as no longer a matter of difference of degree, but of kind. It is crucial to be clear that when we discuss the distinction between individual and general difference positions, we are dealing with the level of pedagogic principles, not with practical programs consisting of objectives and teaching procedures and materials. Teaching that embodies the same pedagogic principles adapted at different points along a continuum of intensity can be expected to involve different kinds of programs at the levels of practical procedures and goals. For example, to the teacher, the literacy part of the English National Primary Strategy may appear different from a program like "Alpha to Omega," designed specifically for children with dyslexic-type literacy difficulties. These programs, however, may share common pedagogic principles. This is an analysis of the principles of teaching and their specialization.

The above summary illustrates the significance of these analyses about the specialization of pedagogy for children with SEN for classifications in the field. These analyses clear theoretical ground by making conceptual distinctions (individual *versus* general differences position) based on recognition of different kinds of needs (common, group, and unique/individual). They also illustrate the interaction between different aspects of teaching (curriculum, knowledge, and pedagogy). Third, the analyses include the taking of a position on the question about commonality-specialization of teaching through highlighting the value of the *continuum* concept, which shows how differentiation or specialization can be seen as a process of *intensification*. All this leads to the tentative conclusion that traditional SEN categories used in England and internationally have *limited usefulness* in the context of planning teaching and learning in most areas. Where they are useful, the categories operate as orienting concepts and inform decision making about teaching as one of several other important elements. The project did not focus on other ways in which SEN categories may be useful, for instance, the administrative convenience in terms of additional resourcing, staffing, materials, and equipment. The analysis summarized here does, however, show that the question of specialized teaching is a significant one for the field. This contrasts with the conclusions of a recent government-funded review (Davis & Florian, 2004), which concluded that

> The questions of a separate special education pedagogy are unhelpful given the current policy context and that the more important agenda is about how to develop a pedagogy that is inclusive of all learners. (p. 34)

It is interesting that despite this conclusion the above review recognized the need for some "specialist teaching."

IMPLICATIONS FOR CLASSIFICATION OF SPECIAL EDUCATIONAL NEEDS

The tentative conclusions, discussed above, are based on traditional types of SEN classifications. They might not apply to more sophisticated classification systems. In any case, the framework presented here is based on a three-dimensional model of educational need:

- common or general needs (for all)
- distinct or specialized needs (for some)
- unique needs (for individual only)

Adopting this model means a rejection of a theoretical position that teaching is directly and mainly influenced by group specific or distinct needs. In other words, it means avoiding the view, held by many professionals and parents, that there is a specialist pedagogy. This is because there are also common/general needs relevant to all learners as well as unique ones, different from all learners. This means that the *general differences position* does not imply that general categories have direct implications for curriculum and pedagogy. In this position, general differences would be mediated through analyses of unique individual and common/general needs. It is therefore more sophisticated and goes well beyond the commonly held assumption that knowing a learner category of SEN has clear-cut implications for pedagogy and curriculum.

This leads to the question of whether this analysis of the specialization of teaching for SEN can have implications for the design of an alternative SEN classification. This question connects with the discussion in the first section of this chapter. If the traditional classifications, like the current official English SEN classification (DfES, 2003), have limited usefulness, then perhaps a more complex and multidimensional classification might be more useful. This is where several conclusions emerging from the above discussion are relevant to a classification required for pedagogic and curriculum programming purposes. Where group-based differences were seen as relevant to pedagogic decisions (ADHD and ASD), these were seen to be in terms of taking account of more specific functional difficulties, for example, attentional difficulties. Second, one of the main reasons why general categories were not seen as relevant to pedagogy/curriculum was the diversity of difficulties within the general category. Another was the high incidence of the occurrence of other difficulties. Other personal and circumstantial factors were also relevant to distancing categories from pedagogic/curriculum questions.

These point to the need for a classification that focuses on individual functional difficulties across a range of areas, while recognizing social, psychological, and possible medical/biological factors relevant to functioning. This is where the World Health Organization's *International Classification of Functioning, Disability and Health* (ICF; WHO, 2002), and the principles underpinning it, might be used to construct a classification of educational disability that has stronger relevance to curriculum and teaching decisions and practices. The ICF introduces a common language for talking about functioning, disability, and health. Disability is treated as a generic term that includes impairments, participation restrictions, and activity limitations. It shifts to a concept of functioning, where disability is not seen just as an impairment/cause. There are explicit bio-psycho-social causal assumptions that reject a polarization between medical and social models.

The ICF model represents disability in terms of the interaction of (1) bodily functions/structures, (2) activities (tasks and activities that can be executed), and (3) participation (what the person can do in current environment). These interrelated dimensions are seen as being influenced by health conditions (disorders/diseases), on the one hand, and contextual factors (environmental and personal factors) on the other. The ICF therefore identifies a person within four dimensions:

1. body function (covering physical and psychological function),

2. body structure,

3. activity and participation, and

4. contextual factors (environmental and personal factors).

The ICF has been adapted in a child and youth version, the ICF-CY (Simeonsson et al., 2003; also Simeonsson, Simeonsson, and Hollenweger, Chapter 13), using the same model and assumptions as above, but for four age groups (zero through one, three through six, seven through twelve, and thirteen through eighteen years). What is particularly interesting about the ICF system is that it is designed to monitor change over the life span. It does this through its multidimensional structure and by focusing at a level of detail about activities and participation that can gauge change. Though the system includes the effects of health conditions, activity limitations are not necessarily specific to any disorder whether physical or mental. Though the current form of the ICF-CY may not have specific relevance to educational provision, defined in curriculum and pedagogic terms, the principles of an interactive multidimensional classification might be useful. This is especially so with the greater emphasis on interservice and interprofessional planning, policy, and practice in the United Kingdom, with the establishment of Local Authority Children's Services, to replace and integrate the previously separate local education authorities and social services departments (child care and welfare services). Presenting this system at least shows that there are other classification approaches that might be more relevant to curriculum and pedagogic issues.

What might such a classification look like? It would be based on a bio-psycho-social model drawing on elements of what are commonly called medical and social models. It would distinguish between health conditions and functional difficulties that are educationally relevant. Using the ICF model, it would distinguish between *educational functional difficulties* (e.g., phonological difficulties) and *learning activity limitations* (e.g., early word reading difficulties) and *participation restrictions* (e.g., lack of additional phonologically oriented learning support in mainstream class). Also included will be environmental factors (home, school, wider community) that act as barriers and facilitators for learning, and personal factors that impact on learning activity and learning participation.

A recent example of how the ICF can inform the development of a system for assessing children with profound and multiple learning difficulties (PMLD) has been reported from the Netherlands (Tadema, Vlaskamp, & Ruijssenaars, 2005). The purpose of this assessment instrument was to enable suitable educational programming. The development level was designed to cover zero to twenty-four months for children with a mean age of ten (standard deviation 3.9). The questionnaire collected information about

1. health conditions and treatments,

2. developmental age,

3. functions (orientation, psycho-social, temperament, personality, attention, sensory, movement related, ingestion, and mental functions of language),

4. activities (learning and applying knowledge, general tasks and demands, communication, movement, and self-care), and

5. participation (general interpersonal interactions, particular interpersonal interactions).

The instrument was developed by using statements that were rated by teachers and caregivers on a three-point scale (zero through two) under the three areas of *functions* (e.g., the pupil recognizes an activity that is presented within a fixed context, the pupil has difficulty chewing food), *activities* (e.g., the pupil initiates simple actions, such as scribbling with a pencil, the pupil eats with a spoon), and *participation* (e.g., the pupil plays together with another pupil, the pupil takes part in group discussion when the caregiver addresses the pupil). The study examined the reliability of assessment across teachers and caregivers and the factor structure of the items. The authors concluded that the results showed a reliable instrument with factors that could be interpreted accurately in terms of functions, activities, and participation. They also pointed to its difference from other measures of developmental progress, as it focuses not only on child abilities, but also support required and the way children take part in group activities.

CONCLUDING COMMENTS

The Tadema et al. (2005) study illustrates how the ICF classification system can be adapted to one area of SEN in a way that supports assessment for planning teaching. There is clearly scope for further work along these lines in this and other broad areas of SEN. It may be that such developments may have to be tailored to the particular curriculum and pedagogic orientations found in different countries. Nevertheless, this approach promises some potential benefits. It would underpin an educationally specific approach to classification that recognizes the relevance of health conditions without letting such health systems dominate educational aims and methods. To do so would require focusing on learners in terms of their functional difficulties relevant to educational aims. This would enable us to distinguish between children with the same functional difficulties, but who have different activity limitations depending on participation, personal strengths and weaknesses, and environmental factors. It is worth mentioning that were such a system to be developed, the use of its general categories (e.g., orientation functioning) would be an example of a general differences position. But, as it is fine-grained and multiple categories considered in interaction within the ICF causal model, it would be distinct from the traditional broad SEN categories. Elements of unique individual factors could be incorporated into such a system. Reference to common needs, however, would also have to be taken into account in using such a system in order to draw out pedagogic and curriculum implications. All this points to the scope for some promising future developments along these lines.

NOTES

1. Details About UK Categories as Defined by the DfES (2003)

Children With Profound and Multiple Learning Difficulty (PMLD)

Pupils with profound and multiple learning difficulties have complex learning needs. In addition to very severe learning difficulties, pupils have other significant difficulties, such as physical disabilities, sensory impairment, or a severe medical condition. Pupils require a high level of adult support, both for their learning needs and also for their personal care. They are likely to need sensory stimulation and a curriculum broken down into very small steps. Some pupils communicate by gesture, eye pointing, or symbols, others by very simple language. Their attainments are likely to remain in the early P scale range (P1–P4) throughout their school careers (that is below level 1 of the National Curriculum).

Children With Severe Learning Difficulty (SLD)

Pupils with severe learning difficulties have significant intellectual or cognitive impairments. This has a major effect on their ability to participate in the school curriculum without support. They may also have difficulties in mobility and coordination, communication and perception, and the acquisition of self-help skills. Pupils with severe learning difficulties will need support in all areas of the curriculum. They may also require teaching of self-help, independence, and social skills. Some pupils may use signs and symbols but most will be able to hold simple conversations. Their attainments may be within the upper P scale range (P4–P8) for much of their school careers (that is below level 1 of the National Curriculum).

Children With Moderate Learning Difficulty (MLD)

Pupils with moderate learning difficulties will have attainments significantly below expected levels in most areas of the curriculum, despite appropriate interventions. Their needs will not be able to be met by normal differentiation and the flexibilities of the National Curriculum.

They should only be recorded as MLD if additional educational provision is being made to help them to access the curriculum.

Pupils with moderate learning difficulties have much greater difficulty than their peers in acquiring basic literacy and numerical skills and in understanding concepts. They may also have associated speech and language delay, low self-esteem, low levels of concentration, and underdeveloped social skills.

Children With Specific Learning Difficulty (SpLD)

Pupils with specific learning difficulties have a particular difficulty in learning to read, write, spell, or manipulate numbers so that their performance in these areas is below their performance in other areas. Pupils may also have problems with short-term memory, with organizational skills, and with coordination. Pupils with specific learning difficulties cover the whole ability range and the severity of their impairment varies widely.

Pupils should only be recorded as SpLD if their difficulties are significant and persistent, despite appropriate learning opportunities and if additional educational provision is being made to help them to access the curriculum.

Specific learning difficulties include dyslexia, dyspraxia, and dyscalculia.

Pupils with "low attainment": Low attainment is a general and sometimes contested term often used to refer to those pupils whose overall attainments across the curriculum are in the lowest quartile. This may arise from the interaction of many factors, but this term is not considered to be an area of special educational needs.

2. Collected Versus Integrated Curriculum Approach

A collected approach has clear boundaries between the different curriculum subject areas. By contrast, in an integrated approach the curriculum areas are interconnected, for example, through the use of projects that involve different subjects areas or the integration of language learning into other subject areas, such as science or history.

REFERENCES

Davis, P., & Florian, L. (2004). *Teaching strategies and approaches for pupils with special educational needs: A scooping study* (Research Report 516). London: Department for Education and Skills.

Department for Education. (1994). *Code of practice on the identification and assessment of special educational needs.* London: Author.

Department for Education and Skills. (2003). *Data collection by type of special educational needs.* London: Author.

Department of Education and Science. (1978). *Special educational needs: Report of the Committee of Enquiry Into the Education of Handicapped Children and Young People* (Warnock Report). London: Her Majesty's Stationery Office.

Kellett, M., & Nind, M. (2003). *Implementing intensive interaction in school: Guidance for practitioners, managers and co-ordinators.* London: David Fulton.

Lewis, A., & Norwich, B. (Eds.). (2004). *Special teaching for special children? Pedagogies for inclusion.* Maidenhead, UK: Open University Press.

Norwich, B. (1996). *Special needs education: Inclusive education or just education for all?* (Inaugural Lecture). London: University of London, Institute of Education.

Norwich, B., & Lewis, A. (2001). A critical review of evidence concerning pedagogic strategies for pupils with special educational needs. *British Educational Research Journal, 27*(3), 313–329.

Organisation for Economic Co-operation and Development. (2000). *Special needs education: Statistics and indicators.* Paris: Author.

Simeonsson, R. J., Leonardi, M., Bjorck-Akesson, E., Hollenweger, J., Lollar, D. J., & Matinuzzi, A. (2003). Measurement of disability in children and youth: Implications of the ICF. *Disability & Rehabilitation, 25*(11–12), 602–610.

Tadema, A., Vlaskamp, C., & Ruijssenaars, W. (2005). The development of a checklist of child characteristics for assessment purposes. *European Journal of Special Needs Education, 20*(4), 403–417.

World Health Organization. (2002). *International classification of functioning, disability and health: Towards a common language for functioning, disability and health.* Geneva, Switzerland: Author.

10 Disability Classification and Teacher Education

Michael L. Hardman and
John McDonnell

The preparation of teachers of students with disabilities in the United States has been aligned with disability classification and educational service delivery in the schools throughout most of the field's history. Separate schools and special classes for students classified by disability category (e.g., intellectual disabilities or emotional disturbance) required the services of a "specially trained" teacher who understood the needs and worked exclusively with a defined disability group. Within the last two decades, however, several factors have led to a reconceptualization of the role of teachers of students with disabilities and consequently the nature of their preparation. These factors include US federal education reform intent on increasing the performance of all students and manifested through standards and systemwide accountability; the No Child Left Behind Act (NCLB) and the Individuals with Disabilities Improvement Act (IDEA) of 2004; US requirements for the preparation of highly qualified teachers of students with disabilities within a standards-based system; an increasing number of students from different disability categories receiving education services together within an inclusive setting; and critical shortages in the supply of teachers of students with disabilities fueled by inadequate salaries and high attrition rates in the first three years of employment (Hardman & Mulder, 2004; Hardman & West, 2003; McLeskey, Waldron, So, Swanson, & Loveland, 2001; Rock, Thead, Gable, Hardman, & Van Acker, 2006).

In this chapter, the rationale for preparing teachers by disability category is addressed and analyzed in the context of the changing dynamic in America's schools. We propose an alternative approach to preparing teachers of students with disabilities that is more closely linked to roles and responsibilities in a standards-driven education system. The chapter concludes with a discussion of the need for general education teachers and teachers of students with disabilities to work together and move beyond the disability deficit paradigm.

PREPARING TEACHERS BY DISABILITY CATEGORY

Historically, new general education teachers and teachers of students with disabilities have been prepared for their professional roles under two different paradigms. The general education paradigm concentrated on training primary teachers to work with groups of students across basic content domains (e.g., reading, writing, math, etc.), whereas secondary teacher preparation focused within subject areas (e.g., history, science, etc.). Little attention was paid to individual type or rate of learning at either the primary or secondary level. In contrast, the preparation of teachers of students with disabilities at both the primary and secondary level evolved around the *disability-deficit paradigm: learning differences and their concomitant problems reside solely within each child.* The role of the special education teacher was to remediate learning problems by understanding student characteristics based on classification by disability category. Today, the assumptions underlying the two approaches to teacher preparation are being questioned in light of the increasing diversity in general education schools and classrooms; an emphasis on access to the general curriculum; the movement to standards-based education; and the call for both special and general educators to be accountable for improved student performance.

The Medical and Social System Models of Deviance

The preparation of teachers of students with disabilities has historically mirrored service delivery in the public schools using a mix of the medical and social system models of deviance (Hardman, 2006; McDonnell, McLaughlin, & Morison, 1997; Rock et al., 2006). In the medical model, treatment is intended to eliminate the underlying cause of disability or compensate for its effects. In the social system model, disabilities are described as discrepancies from what is normally expected. Since both models are directed at the etiology of a disability and problems that reside within the individual, the outcome has been an education system that defined and taught students on the basis of their specific deficits, be they learning, behavioral, sensory, or physical.

Reliance on the medical and social system models has resulted in the wide use of disability categories. Federal regulations for the Individuals with Disabilities Education Act (IDEA, 1997, 34 C.F.R. 300.7) prescribe separate disabling conditions. States may vary in their categorization policies, but most reflect the federal approach with some modifications in terminology. For example, where one state uses the term *mental retardation*, others may use *mental handicap*, *intellectual disabilities*, or *significantly limited intellectual capacity*. States may, however, choose to classify and serve students as noncategorical but must report to the federal government within the thirteen categories specified in law. The total reliance on separate disabling conditions was somewhat modified in the 1997 amendments to IDEA, when states and local school districts were provided the option of eliminating disability categories for children ages three through nine. Students in this age group can be defined as having a disability if they experience developmental delays in one or more areas of physical, cognitive, communication, social, or adaptive development. The United States Department of Education (2006) reported that 50% of the states have school districts that classify students on the basis of developmental delay through age nine. The remaining 50% reported student data by the number and percentage of disability-based categories. As a disability classification under IDEA, developmental delay constitutes less than 1% of the total number of students with disabilities ages six to twenty-one. These data suggest that many states continue to rely on traditional categories to determine eligibility for special education services.

Determining eligibility and classifying instructional need on the basis of disability category has often resulted in students being placed in separate (special education) schools or classrooms consistent with their identified label (Hardman, Drew, & Egan, 2006). This has been especially true for students with more significant educational needs. Students with autism are placed into "autism classes," where they learn with other students who supposedly have the same educational needs. In theory, each of the thirteen disability categories under IDEA (including "developmental delay") could result in thirteen different teacher preparation programs and thirteen different licenses. If teachers of students with disabilities are also required to establish an emphasis in either primary or secondary education, the number of licenses doubles.

Multicategorical Approaches

Although teacher preparation by disability category was the predominant model in education for most of the twentieth century, many states began moving to a multicategorical or cross-categorical approach in the 1980s. Multi-categorical state licenses for teachers of students with disabilities may be referred to as generic, comprehensive, or collaborative; exceptional children or varying exceptionalities; and mild/moderate/severe disabilities (National Association of State Directors of Teacher Education and Certification [NASDTEC], 2003). The most widely used multicategorical licenses are based on the severity of the disability (e.g., mild or severe). In most states, licensure programs in mild disabilities prepare teacher candidates to work with students who have school-related academic and/or behavioral challenges. Using disability categories, these students would be classified as having learning disabilities, mild mental retardation, or behavior disorders. Teachers working in mild disabilities provide specialized instruction that is intended to reduce or eliminate student deficits interfering with success in the general education classroom. Severe disabilities, on the other hand, is often a combination of one or more disability categories (e.g., severe mental retardation, autism, serious emotional disturbance, hearing or visual impairment) wherein students have deficits in life skills, such as communication, self-care, functional academics, or social learning.

In a 2001 study, Mainzer and Horvath found that states were almost equally divided in their use of disability category and multicategory licenses. Twenty-four states used only the multicategorical framework and twenty-three states used a combination of disability category and multicategorical approaches. Only three states offered licenses that were exclusively based on each of thirteen individual disability categories.

Although the multicategorical/severity approach in the preparation of teachers of students with disabilities has resulted in a reduction in the number of licenses, the framework does not alter the fundamental disability-deficit paradigm that has been at the foundation of teacher preparation. The essential elements of the paradigm (identifiable, internal, and discrete deficits from the norm) remain intact. Interestingly, of the twenty-four states using the multicategorical framework, fourteen were also offering a "generic" license as well. Generic licenses, such as those in Maryland and Texas, prepare teacher candidates to work with students across disability categories with a focus on understanding federal law (IDEA), assessing student needs, planning instruction, using assistive technology, organizing learning environments, and promoting participation in the general education curriculum.

Applying Disability Classification to Teacher Roles in Twenty-First-Century American Schools

The disability-deficit paradigm in education is based on two assumptions. First, the paradigm assumes that students within a specific disability category have common educational needs that require teachers to have instructional and program management skills consistent with the student's label. Second, newly prepared teachers of students with disabilities are expected to work exclusively with students classified as having a specific disability or grouping of disabilities (multicategorical).

The validity of the above assumptions has not, however, been supported by research and practice over the past thirty years. Even a superficial examination of leading categorically based textbooks used in teacher preparation programs indicates a significant overlap in the curriculum, instruction, and program management strategies presented to teacher candidates (see Hardman et al., 2006; Vaughn, Bos, & Schumm, 2005). Increasingly, researchers have acknowledged that the approaches, methods, and techniques that teachers must use to meet the educational needs of students with differing disability labels vary more in terms of intensity than type (e.g., McDonnell et al., 1997; Mercer & Mercer, 2001; Rosenberg, Sindelar, & Hardman, 2004). Intensive instruction is defined by features that include high rates of active student responding; carefully matching instruction to student skill levels; providing instructional cues, prompts, and fading to support approximations to correct responding; and detailed, task-focused feedback to the student (McDonnell et al., 1997).

The assumption that special education teachers in the United States will work exclusively with students identified as being in specific disability categories also lacks validity in today's schools. The Interstate New Teacher Assessment and Support Consortium (INTASC, 2001) suggests that disability categories have traditionally provided an organizational framework within schools. High-incidence students (e.g., students with learning disabilities or emotional disturbance) are more often educated in general education classrooms with consultative support from special education teachers. Low-incidence students (e.g., students who are deaf, students who are blind, students with severe intellectual disabilities [mental retardation]) are more likely to be placed in separate classes or separate schools with limited access to peers without disabilities. INTASC calls into question the applicability of this organizational framework for several reasons:

- A specific disability can manifest itself in individual children in a tremendous range of ways and across a continuum of mild to severe.
- Students with differing disabilities often have characteristics that overlap, making identification more complex.
- Students may have multiple disabilities and specialized needs that cross disability categories.
- The operational definitions of specific disabilities vary from state to state and district to district.

- Educational practices may be similar for individual students with different disabilities.
- Certain minority groups are disproportionately represented in specific disability categories, including the problem of over-identification for some minority groups in some disability categories.
- An increasing number of students have disabling conditions that do not fit well within the traditional disability categories (INTASC, p. 8).

Although separate categorical programs are still present in some states, national data suggest that the number is shrinking (Geiger, Crutchfield, & Mainzer, 2003; NASDTEC, 2003; United States Department of Education, 2006). Many school districts are no longer choosing to transport students to a centralized program designed to serve students with a specific disability. Increasingly, districts are serving students in their "home" school—the one they would attend if they were not disabled. In doing so, they are also developing strategies to ensure each student's access to the general education curriculum and supporting participation in classes with "typical peers." The net effect is that teachers of students with disabilities are collaborating and/or co-teaching with general education colleagues to educate students with significantly differing instructional needs regardless of the disability label.

BEYOND DISABILITY CATEGORIES: PREPARING ALL TEACHERS FOR A STANDARDS-DRIVEN SYSTEM

In the United States, the promise of the standards era and the No Child Left Behind Act (NCLB) is straightforward—all students can and will learn more than they are currently learning, and all students will succeed if schools expect the highest academic standards. If students do not succeed, then public schools must be held accountable for their failure. The definition of success is student proficiency on content specified by states and as measured by state performance standards. The promise of "all means all" includes students with disabilities. Therefore, (at least in policy) students with disabilities are assured access to the curriculum upon which the standards are based; access to assessments that measure performance on the standards; and inclusion in the reported results that determine how well a school is meeting the established performance criteria. The promise that every student will learn and succeed has been translated into public policy in the reauthorizations of the Elementary and Secondary Education Act (re-named NCLB in 2001) through a number of important provisions as described in other chapters in this volume. The 2004 reauthorization of IDEA aligns this law with the provisions of NCLB. Although public policy provides the impetus for every student to learn and succeed, the critical issue is whether the promise will become reality. One of the important provisions of NCLB and now within the IDEA is the definition of what constitutes a "highly qualified teacher."

The Highly Qualified Teacher Requirement and Its Impact on the Preparation of Teachers of Students With Disabilities

Under the NCLB, all new general education teachers working with disadvantaged children (children living in poverty) must meet specific requirements. As defined in law, a highly qualified elementary (primary), middle, or secondary education teacher is defined as an individual who has obtained full state certification (licensure), or successfully passed a state's teacher licensing examination. A highly qualified teacher must not have had state requirements waived on an emergency, temporary, or provisional basis. New elementary (primary) teachers must hold a bachelor's degree and demonstrate *subject knowledge* and *teaching skills* in basic elementary (primary) school curriculum, including, but not limited to, reading, writing, and mathematics. Subject matter competency and teaching skills must be measured by "a rigorous state test." New middle and secondary teachers must also hold a bachelor's degree and demonstrate a *high level of competency in the academic subjects they teach.* Subject matter competence must be measured by "a rigorous state subject matter test," or by completing an undergraduate major in the subject area, a graduate degree, or by completing coursework equivalent to an undergraduate academic major.

In IDEA 2004, the term "highly qualified" has the same meaning as applied to elementary (primary), middle, and secondary teachers as in NCLB. This means that new and veteran special education teachers at the elementary level must have subject knowledge and teaching skills in reading, writing, mathematics, and other areas of the basic elementary curriculum. New and veteran special education teachers at the middle and secondary level must have subject knowledge and teaching skills in academic subjects in which the teacher has responsibility for instruction.

Specifically, IDEA 2004 requires that special education teachers must hold a bachelor's degree and obtain full state certification as a special education teacher (including certification obtained through alternative routes to certification) *or* passed the state special education teacher licensing examination. In addition, special education teachers who are teaching core academic subjects "exclusively to children who are assessed against alternate achievement standards" must meet the same requirements as highly qualified elementary (primary) teachers unless the instruction is "above the elementary level." In that case, the special education teacher must have subject matter knowledge appropriate to middle or secondary level instruction. New and veteran special education teachers who teach two or more subjects at the middle or secondary level must also meet the applicable requirements in NCLB.

There was no statutory language in IDEA 2004 regarding special education teachers who only provide *consultative services* to a highly qualified general education teacher. Congressional report language for IDEA 2004, however, clarifies the intent of Congress that special education teachers in consultative roles be considered highly qualified if such individuals meet all other applicable requirements under the law.

There is considerable disagreement among educators as to whether NCLB's highly qualified standard is synonymous with the concept of "high quality." As stated by Brownell, Sindelar, Bishop, Langley, and Seo (2002), the NCLB emphasis for general educators is on a thorough knowledge of the content being taught and the verbal ability to deliver that content. It is not on pedagogy. Nonetheless, the impact of the highly qualified standard raises questions about the rationale for the continued use of the disability-deficit paradigm. Clearly, subject matter competence for teachers of students with disabilities will be particularly burdensome in schools where the special education teacher may be responsible for most, if not all, core academic subjects for students, which could be the case if only learning disability–certified teachers are permitted to instruct students with this disability classification. A potential way around this disincentive is to move to a more inclusive service delivery system in which general educators and teachers of students with disabilities collaborate in meeting the needs of all students and not focus on specific disability categorizations. School districts could choose to use teachers of students with disabilities in a more consultative role in which they work directly with or support highly qualified general education teachers who have subject matter competence. This option is consistent with the view that pedagogical expertise (assessing student performance, adapting curriculum, modifying instruction, etc.) is the hallmark of an effective teacher of students with disabilities. It also emphasizes the need for all teachers to change their practices in order to accommodate the full range of students in a school, including students with disabilities and other special needs (Cohen, McLaughlin, & Talbert, 1993; Darling-Hammond, 1997; Pugach, 2005).

The Rationale for a Collaborative Teacher Preparation Model

In this standards era, general education teachers as well as teachers of students with disabilities are expected to provide instruction and be held accountable for increasing the performance of *all* students (Rock et al.,

2006). Although teachers of students with disabilities must have the specialized knowledge and skills relevant to the needs of students with disabilities, they will also be called upon to apply this expertise to a much broader group of "high-risk students" in a collaborative educational environment. Growing student diversity will also require general educators to teach students whose needs exceed the traditionally defined "typical student." The combination of a broader definition of "typical" along with the call for students with disabilities to be taught "core academic content" makes a very strong case for the collaborative preparation of all teachers (Lipsky & Gartner, 2002). The reality is no teacher alone has the capacity to respond to the growing diversity in the schools. Collaboration is a key to raising expectations and increasing the performance of every student.

As suggested by Lipsky and Gartner (2002, p. 202),

> Special education teachers often report their lack of knowledge about the general education curriculum, whereas general education teachers often report their lack of knowledge about individualizing instruction. However, after a year of collaboration, both report greater knowledge and comfort in these areas. They use many of the same instructional strategies in the inclusive classroom that are effective for students in general classrooms. These include cooperative learning, hands-on learning, peer and cross-age tutoring and support models. . . . Special education should be understood as a service, not a place. Thus, a student (labeled either special or general education) may receive services in a variety of settings or groups. Although not a legal term, inclusion is best expressed in the student who is on the regular register, attends homeroom with her or his peers, participates equally in school activities, receives instruction suited to her or his needs, is held to the school's common standards and receives the same report card as other students.

Ensuring Access to the General Education Curriculum

The critical need to redesign preparation programs for teachers of students with disabilities has been emphasized in the last two reauthorizations of IDEA (1997 and 2004) as well as NCLB. IDEA mandates that the Individualized Education Program (IEP) must address how students will be involved and progress in the general education curriculum (Section 300.347). The statutory language implies that there should be a single curriculum, with the same high standards for all students, and that education programs should be structured to *support* the participation of students with disabilities within the curriculum. Furthermore, IDEA strengthens the relationship among all teachers in meeting the needs of students with disabilities. General educators and teachers of students with disabilities must participate on IEP teams when a student spends at least a portion of his or her day in a general education classroom.

Including students with disabilities in the general education curriculum and supporting participation in typical classes are deeply entrenched in current federal policy and school reform initiatives. Obviously, the intent of these initiatives cannot be achieved unless teachers are prepared to work collaboratively in an inclusive environment that is not grounded in the disability deficit paradigm.

Achieving Meaningful Outcomes

In order to measure student progress within the general curriculum, NCLB requires that all students, including those with disabilities, must participate in state or district performance assessments or in an alternate assessment system. This requirement recognizes that schools must be held accountable for achieving meaningful educational outcomes. The law also acknowledges that accommodations must be available to some students to allow them to participate in such assessments. From a practical standpoint, ensuring that students with disabilities participate in large-scale assessment programs will require that general and special educators collaborate in delivering instruction and identifying needed accommodations.

Effectively Using Limited Resources

Standard-based reforms have not only changed expectations for students and teachers, they have also created the need to closely examine how limited resources are used to support instruction. Schools have a variety of staff and fiscal resources available to meet the educational needs of students with disabilities or those who are at-risk of school failure (e.g., ESEA [Elementary and Secondary Education Act] Title I, IDEA). Historically, federal and state laws, school district policies, and professional conventions have driven decisions regarding how such resources are allocated within a school, not the individual needs of students. Thus, it is often the case that only students who are deemed "eligible" for government-funded special programs (such as Title I or IDEA) receive the additional instructional support and creates a system of the "haves" who can get help and the "have-nots," who need help but are not eligible for additional services. This is not only inequitable, but it also fails to take full advantage of the instructional resources readily available within a given school.

There is a need to redesign schools so that the services and supports provided through teachers of students with disabilities and other related services personnel (e.g., speech/language pathologists, physical therapists, etc.) are infused into the general education program rather than functioning as separate entities. Successfully restructuring schools in this way can only be accomplished if all educators pool their knowledge, skills, and experience to deliver programs.

Core Pedagogical and Content Skills for All Teachers

With the growing diversity in today's schools, all educators must become more student-centered in their instruction. In practice, general education teachers often assume sole responsibility for content whereas teachers of students with disabilities are expected to have the pedagogical skills to adapt instruction to the needs of students with disabilities. As such, students with disabilities may have access to teachers who have "content" expertise but are unable to accommodate unique learning needs; or they have access to teachers who have pedagogical expertise to individualize instruction, but lack content knowledge. Core expertise is needed for both general and special education teachers in order to foster an understanding of (1) the goals and purposes of schooling, (2) professional values that promote student acceptance and belonging, (3) collaboration, and (4) research-validated practice. These skills would apply across categories.

Pedagogical and Content Expertise for Teachers of Students With Disabilities

Preparing teachers with more generic skills needs to be considered within the context of what we know about teaching students with disabilities. The expertise for these teachers is predominantly pedagogical and grounded in the characteristics of effective practice: individualization, intensive instruction, and the explicit teaching of skills (Hardman et al., 2006; McDonnell et al., 1997). Special education teachers must continuously assess student performance, adjust the learning environment, modify instructional methods, adapt curricula, use positive behavior supports, and select and implement appropriate accommodations to meet the individual needs of their students (Council for Exceptional Children [CEC], 2006; Higher Education Consortium for Special Education [HECSE], 2004). Pedagogical skills, not distinct disability categories, are the foundation for teaching these students and form the basis for collaboration with general education teachers in a standards-driven system. *To develop the needed pedagogical expertise, initial preparation programs must focus less on disability categories and more on the role of teachers as support specialists.* In the role of support specialists, teachers of students with disabilities are trained to use research-validated strategies in the design and adaptation of individualized instruction within the general curriculum. Specialization areas may include academic learning, positive behavior interventions, and the teaching of functional skills.

Academic Support

General education teachers face the challenges of ensuring academic excellence, as well as responding to students with many different needs coming together in an inclusive setting. In a survey of general education teachers, Hobbs (1997) found that attempts to promote academic achievement for students with disabilities were significantly hampered by the lack of specialized assistance from a teacher of students with disabilities.

During the primary years, specialized assistance is most often needed in reading and math literacy, where students with disabilities lack strategies for problem solving, have memory problems, and are unable to work independently (Friend & Bursuck, 2002; Hallahan & Kauffman, 2006; McLaughlin, 2000). In addition to teaching the above strategies, an academic specialist at the secondary level must also have a working knowledge of the academic content taught in a class (such as history or biology) and how to accommodate or modify instruction to enhance student access to the curriculum (Dailey, Zantal-Wiener, & Roach, 2000). Assistance may also be necessary to develop student academic survival skills regardless of age level. Friend and Bursuck (2002) suggest that students who are having difficulty in academic learning often have concomitant problems related to organizational skills, completing tasks in a timely fashion, and developing positive social skills with peers and adults.

Students with learning difficulties will need additional and intense instruction in order to acquire or maintain skills in academic content. Using research-validated instructional procedures, materials, and alternative learning sequences, the academic specialist would work in conjunction with the general education teacher to enhance student performance by adapting the way instruction is delivered and by modifying the environment where the learning takes place. Possible content domains that may be included in the preparation of academic support specialists include research-validated practices in academic learning and their application to students with disabilities; designing, selecting, and using validated instructional approaches in academic content areas; and collaborative support to general education teachers.

Positive Behavior Support

Challenging behavior in schools has become a critical national issue (Children's Defense Fund, 2004; Lewis & Sugai, 1999; National Center for

Education Statistics, 2002). Although a number of approaches have been suggested to address these problems, several researchers recommend that schools move away from traditional reactive procedures of punishment, suspension, and expulsion (Hartwig & Ruesch, 2000; Lewis & Sugai, 1999; Mayer, 1999). Schools must instead place emphasis on developing and implementing systemic and proactive procedures that address problem behavior at the building and individual student levels (Taylor-Green et al., 1997). These complex interventions require highly trained professionals who can serve as resources within the schools to reduce or eliminate student problem behavior (O'Neill, Johnson, Kiefer-O'Donnell, & McDonnell, 2001).

Teaching Functional Life Skills

A functional life skills curriculum centers on the adaptive skills that enable a student to more fully participate in school, family, and community environments. Learning these skills facilitates the student's ability to cope with the demands of a given environment. In other words, an adaptive fit is created between the student and the setting in which he or she must learn to function. A life skills curriculum may include person-social development (including self-determination), communication, recreation and leisure, orientation and mobility, employment preparation, and so on. Possible content domains that may be included in the preparation of functional life skills specialists are validated practices in functional skills learning and their applications to students with disabilities; designing, selecting, and using validated instructional approaches in functional skills content areas; and collaborative support to general education teachers.

IDEA 2004 requires that students with disabilities must participate in the same statewide or district assessments of achievement as students who are not disabled. For students with disabilities requiring a modified "life skills" curriculum, these assessments are often inappropriate, and such students are excluded from taking them. Schools are still accountable, however, for the progress of these students. IDEA mandated that states must conduct alternate assessments that are aligned with alternate performance standards to ensure that all students are included in the state's accountability system.

SUMMARY AND RECOMMENDATIONS

Throughout the field's history, the education of students with disabilities in the United States has been grounded in classification by disability category. As such, the preparation of teachers of students with disabilities has also been deeply entrenched in the disability deficit paradigm. Arguments for continued categorization have focused primarily on the correlation between categorization and access to a free and appropriate public education. Proponents of categorization fear that any attempt to eliminate classification by disability category would result in a loss of services and support for students. Schools would choose to educate those students who are the easiest and least costly to serve. It can be argued, however, that although categorization has been the foundation for developing and providing services to students with disabilities, it promotes stereotyping, discrimination, and exclusion. In fact, classification by disability category is a detriment to individualization because it fails to clearly define or adequately differentiate the needs of students with disabilities (Cook, 2001; Hardman & Nagle, 2004; National Council on Disability, 2000).

In today's schools, there is a clearly defined need to prepare all teachers to work together in order to meet the educational needs of students, including those with disabilities, in a standards system that is driven by results. According to the Study of Personnel Needs in Special Education (2000), nine of ten general education teachers currently have an average of 3.5 students with disabilities in their classroom. As suggested by Pugach (2005), "The need to prepare all teachers to create classrooms that embrace students with disabilities and teach them is no longer contested" (p. 550).

This chapter has briefly examined the context in which teacher preparation takes place within the current educational environment and why we must move beyond classification by disability category. Specifically, federal policy under NCLB and IDEA dictates that schools must use evidence-based programs taught by professionals who meet the "highly qualified" teacher requirements for subject matter knowledge while at the same time ensuring that every student will achieve meaningful educational outcomes.

Although teacher preparation programs in colleges and universities have traditionally reinforced differentiated roles by separating teacher candidates, such a structure makes little sense in today's schools where there is a need for a collaborative approach to teaching and every educator must have a core skill set of knowledge and skills to improve the performance of a diverse student population. Beyond this core set of knowledge and skills, teachers of students with disabilities must be able to continuously assess student performance, adjust the learning environment, modify instructional methods, adapt curricula, use positive behavior supports, and select and implement appropriate accommodations to meet the individual needs of their students.

REFERENCES

Brownell, M. T., Sindelar, P. T., Bishop, A. G., Langley, L. K., & Seo, S. (2002). Special education teacher supply and teacher quality: The problems, the solutions. *Focus on Exceptional Children, 35*(2), 1–16.

Children's Defense Fund. (2004). *The state of America's children yearbook.* Washington, DC: Author.

Cohen, D. K., McLaughlin, M. W., & Talbert, J. E. (Eds.). (1993). *Teaching for understanding: Challenges for policy and practice.* San Francisco: Jossey-Bass.

Cook, B. G. (2001). A comparison of teachers' attitudes toward their included students with mild and severe disabilities. *Journal of Special Education, 34*(4), 203–213.

Council for Exceptional Children. (2006). *No Child Left Behind Act of 2001: Implications for special education policy and practice.* Retrieved September 17, 2006, from http://www.cec.sped.org/Content/NavigationMenu/PolicyAdvocacy/CEC PolicyResources/NCLBside-by-side.pdf

Dailey, D., Zantal-Wiener, K., & Roach, V. (2000). *Reforming high school learning: The effect of the standards movement on secondary students with disabilities.* Alexandria, VA: Center for Policy Research on the Impact of General and Special Education Reform.

Darling-Hammond, L. (1997). *The right to learn: A blueprint for creating schools that work.* San Francisco: Jossey-Bass.

Friend, M. P., & Bursuck, W. D. (2002). *Including students with special needs: A practical guide for classroom teachers* (3rd ed.). Boston: Allyn & Bacon.

Geiger, W. L., Crutchfield, M. D., & Mainzer, R. (2003). *The status of licensure of special education teachers in the 21st century* (COPSSE Document No. RS-7E). Gainesville, FL: University of Florida, Center on Personnel Studies in Special Education.

Hallahan, D. P., & Kauffman, J. M. (2006). *Exceptional learners* (10th ed.). Boston: Allyn & Bacon.

Hardman, M. L. (2006). The changing scene in education: Political, legislative, and socioeconomic factors. In L. Bullock, R. A. Gable, & K. J. Melloy (Eds.), *Effective disciplinary practices: Strategies and positive learning environments for students with challenging behaviors* (pp. 1–9). Arlington, VA: Council for Children With Behavioral Disorders.

Hardman, M. L., Drew, C. J., & Egan, M. W. (2006). *Human exceptionality: School, family, and community* (8th ed.). Boston: Allyn & Bacon.

Hardman, M. L., & Mulder, M. (2004). Critical issues in public education: Federal reform and the impact on students with disabilities. In L. M. Bullock & R. A. Gable (Eds.), *Quality personnel preparation in emotional/behavior disorders* (pp. 12–36). Dallas, TX: Institute for Behavioral and Learning Differences.

Hardman, M. L., & Nagle, K. (2004). Policy issues. In A. McCray, H. Rieth, & P. Sindelar (Eds.), *Contemporary issues in special education: Access, diversity, and accountability* (pp. 277–292). Boston: Allyn & Bacon.

Hardman, M. L., & West, J. (2003). Increasing the number of special education faculty: Policy implications and future directions. *Teacher Education and Special Education, 26*(3), 206–214.

Hartwig, E. P., & Ruesch, G. M. (2000). Disciplining students in special education. *The Journal of Special Education, 33*(4), 240–247.

Higher Education Consortium for Special Education. (2004). *Recommendations for the reauthorization of the IDEA related to the application of "highly qualified" to special education teachers.* Austin: University of Texas.

Hobbs, T. (1997). *Planning for inclusion: A comparison of individual and cooperative procedures.* Unpublished doctoral dissertation, Florida State University, Tallahassee.

Interstate New Teacher Assessment and Support Consortium. (2001). *Model standards for licensing general and special education teachers of students with disabilities: A resource for state dialogue.* Washington, DC: Council of Chief State School Officers.

Lewis, T. J., & Sugai, G. (1999). Effective behavioral support: A systems approach to proactive school wide management. *Focus on Exceptional Children, 31,* 1–24.

Lipsky, D. K., & Gartner, A. (2002). Taking inclusion into the future. In M. Byrnes (Ed.), *Taking sides: Clashing views on controversial issues in special education* (pp. 198–203). Guilford, CT: McGraw-Hill Dushkin.

Mainzer, R., & Horvath, M. (2001). *Issues in preparing and licensing special educators.* Arlington, VA: Council for Exceptional Children.

Mayer, G. R. (1999). Constructive discipline for school personnel. *Education and Treatment of Children, 22,* 36–54.

McDonnell, L. M., McLaughlin, M. J., & Morison, P. (Eds.). (1997). *Educating one and all: Students with disabilities and standards-based reform.* Washington, DC: National Research Council, National Academy Press.

McLaughlin, M. (2000). *Reform for every learner: Teachers' views on standards and students with disabilities.* Alexandria, VA: Center for Policy Research on the Impact of General and Special Education Reform.

McLeskey, J., Waldron, N. L., So, T. H., Swanson, K., & Loveland, T. (2001). Perspectives of teachers toward inclusive school programs. *Teacher Education and Special Education, 24,* 108–115.

Mercer, C. D., & Mercer, A. R. (2001). *Teaching students with learning problems.* Upper Saddle River, NJ: Merrill Publishing Company.

National Association of State Directors of Teacher Education and Certification. (2003). *The NASDTEC manual 2003.* Dubuque, IA: Kendall/Hunta Publishing Co.

National Center for Education Statistics. (2002). *Drop-out rates in the United States.* Washington, DC: Author.

National Council on Disability. (2000, January). *From privileges to rights: People labeled with psychiatric disabilities speak for themselves.* Washington, DC: Author.

O'Neill, R. E., Johnson, J. W., Kiefer-O'Donnell, R., & McDonnell, J. (2001). Preparing teachers and consultants for the challenge of severe problem behavior. *Journal of Positive Behavioral Interventions, 3,* 101–108.

Pugach, M. C. (2005). Research on preparing general education teachers to work with students with disabilities. In M. Cochran-Smith & K. M. Zeichner, *Studying teacher education: The report of the AERA panel on research and teacher education* (pp. 549–590). Mahwah, NJ: Lawrence Erlbaum.

Rock, T., Thead, B. K., Gable, R. A., Hardman, M. L., & Van Acker, R. (2006). In pursuit of excellence: The past as prologue to a bright future for special education. *Focus on Exceptional Children, 38*(8), 1–18.

Rosenberg, M., Sindelar, P., & Hardman, M. (2004). Preparing highly qualified teachers for students with emotional and behavioral disorders: The impact of NCLB and IDEA. *Behavioral Disorders, 29*(3), 266–278.

Study of Personnel Needs in Special Education. (2000). *General education teachers' role in special education* (Fact Sheet). Retrieved May 30, 2006, from http://ferdig.coe.ufl.edu/spense/

Taylor-Green, S., Brown, D., Nelson, L., Longton, J., Grassman, T., Cohen, J., Swartz, J., Horner, R. H., Sugai, G., & Hall, S. (1997). School-wide behavioral support: Starting the year off right. *Journal of Behavioral Education, 7,* 99–112.

United States Department of Education. (2006). *Twenty-sixth annual report to Congress on the implementation of the Individuals with Disabilities Education Improvement Act.* Washington, DC: Government Printing Office.

Vaughn, S., Bos, C. S., & Schumm, J. S. (2005). *Teaching exceptional, diverse, and at-risk students in the general education classroom* (3rd ed.). Boston: Allyn & Bacon.

11 Disproportionality in Special Education

A Transatlantic Phenomenon

Alan Dyson and Elizabeth B. Kozleski

INTRODUCTION

This chapter is concerned with the special education systems of two economically rich but socially unequal countries. Both England and the United States have well-resourced school systems (in comparative international terms) that are capable of making high levels of provision for children who are deemed to be in some way needy. Both countries have developed over many years elaborate special education systems that target additional resources at students who qualify for this purpose, by means of more-or-less careful processes of individual assessment and monitoring. In both countries, these processes are capable of yielding high-quality information about those students' characteristics, and of generating detailed and individualized plans for interventions that might help overcome their difficulties.

On the face of it, special education systems of this kind are both benign and rational. The targeting of need is one mark of a just society, and the use of scrupulous and scientifically based assessments is, arguably, a mark of a technologically advanced and equity-minded one. Yet in both countries, there is a puzzling phenomenon. Although students from any social group can be and are identified as in need of special education, members of some groups are more likely than others to be identified. Groups whose members tend to do badly in the general education system supply more students to the special education system. These are, moreover, precisely the groups that do least well in terms of a whole range of social indicators: health, employment, income, encounters with the penal system, and so on.

This situation is so familiar that it tends to be taken for granted by the majority of education practitioners and researchers. Yet it embodies a huge contradiction. The special education systems of England and the United States are premised on the assumption that students' difficulties are identifiable and can successfully be addressed at the *individual* level—through individual identification, assessment, and intervention. Yet those difficulties appear to be related in some way to students' membership in social *groups*. The implication is that special education typically asks the wrong question. Instead of asking, "What is wrong with this child and what can we do about it?" we should be asking, "Why does this group fare so badly and what can be done about it?" Indeed, it is arguable that special education not only asks the wrong question, but makes it less likely that the right one will get asked. By locating problems and solutions at the level of the individual and by creating a froth of activity around individual assessment and intervention, it serves to draw attention from underlying systemic and social factors. In terms of the theme of this book, the categorizations undertaken within special education are in fact category mistakes.

Such observations are hardly new. On both sides of the Atlantic (though more so in the United States), there has been a concern with the disproportional representation of certain groups in the special education system. On both sides of the Atlantic, too, there have been what Tomlinson (1995) characterizes as radical structuralist perspectives on special education that have concerned themselves precisely with the ways in which special education is produced by underlying social structures and the ways in which it acts to preserve established social orders. Interestingly, however, little of the scholarship on these issues has adopted a system-comparative perspective. Inevitably, a single country perspective focuses attention on the particularities and peculiarities of that country's system. In the United States, for instance, where critical scholars have been most active, issues of disproportionality by racial group and the role of categorization have featured prominently. The racial composition of the school population in England, however, is quite different to that in the United States (indeed, "ethnicity" rather than "race" is the usual term of analysis) and the sorts of subcategorizations that characterize the US special education system simply do not exist. Yet disproportionality—in a different form—is as real there as on the other side of the Atlantic.

Only by comparing these two systems, we suggest, is it possible to move beyond these particularities and explore underlying social processes. In the remainder of this paper, therefore, we will explore these similarities and differences, beginning with accounts of the situations in our own countries.

DISPROPORTIONALITY IN SPECIAL EDUCATION IN THE UNITED STATES

Elizabeth writes:

> My great grandfather fought in the US Civil War. He fought for the North in a war precipitated by the election of Abraham Lincoln and fueled by the great schism over slavery, the economic engine of the agrarian South. I note this because 146 years and six generations later, still in memories of living US citizens, the legacy of slavery in the United States is omnipresent. Not until the Brown decisions in 1954 and then again, in 1956 by the US Supreme Court that established the principle of "separate is not equal" did US national policy decouple race and education (Smith & Kozleski, 2005). In that same time period, as a young girl, I sat in the front of public buses traveling downtown, when the backs of the buses were still full of African American women on their way to or from work in the middle-class homes of White Americans.

Although *Brown v. the Board of Education of Topeka* pushed the boundaries of race and class, it did not tear them down. In the sixties, Governor George Wallace stood on the front steps of the University of Alabama to prevent the admission of African American students to Alabama's largest state institution of higher education. In 1967, across the Potomac River from the US capital, Thomas Jefferson High School fielded its first integrated high school football team. In 2005, the State of Virginia offered free college educations in restitution to African Americans who were shut out of completing high school in their local schools because the public schools were closed rather than comply with *Brown v. Board of Education*. In the fall of 2005, an entire city, largely African American, was devastated by Hurricane Katrina and African Americans suffered from a government unprepared and disinclined to provide safety, shelter, and subsistence. In the United States, race is the subtext. Poverty may be the agent.

Besides housing, public education is the most publicly visible arena in which race continues to have a visible impact on who is privileged and advantaged in the United States. Jonathan Kozol's 2005 book, *The Shame of the Nation: The Restoration of Apartheid Schooling in America*, provides a grim picture of the growing segregation of US schools. African American and Latino students make up more than 85% of all students served in inner city schools in the United States according to Kozol. The schools they attend are often in physical disrepair (Ferguson, Kozleski, & Smith, 2003). In 2003, a California suit brought against the state by the American Southern California Civil Liberties Union, a coalition of education activists and researchers, charged the state with violating students' right to learn based on the physical condition of many of California's inner city schools. But California's schools are not unique. From New Orleans to the District of Columbia, from Los Angeles to Chicago, children in the largest school systems in the United States do not benefit from living in the country where per capita income is among the highest in the world. Instead, they attend poorly maintained schools, overcrowded classrooms, with inadequately prepared teachers, and few instructional materials.

The War on Poverty, an initiative launched by the Johnson administration in the sixties, created the Elementary and Secondary Education Act (ESEA) that provided additional funds to support supplemental instruction in schools with high-poverty student populations. As noted by Pullin in Chapters 6 and 7, the current No Child Left Behind Act (NCLB) is the most recent reauthorization of that legislation. It focuses on decreasing the achievement gap between specific racial and ethnic and income groups in core content areas and requires public accountability for schools through the disaggregation of achievement data by racial and ethnic groups. There are many critiques of this legislation including the focus on testing as a way of measuring school quality and performance. As Kozol (2005) notes, the influence of this legislation on daily practice in schools has been immense.

As an example, Education Trust, a nongovernmental US organization, reports that 88 of every 100 White kindergartners in the United States graduate from high school. Yet only 82 of every 100 African American kindergartners graduate, 63 out of every 100 Latino kindergartners graduate, and only 58 out of every 100 Native Americans graduate from high school (Education Trust, n.d.). Although race predicts outcomes in the current US education system, it may be particularly evident in two specialized environments: juvenile justice and special education. According to data from the National Criminal Justice Reference Service Web site (n.d.), more than 80% of all individuals, eighteen years or younger serving out sentences in state and local juvenile justice systems belong to racial and ethnic minorities. African American boys constitute more than two-thirds of this group. The issue of overrepresentation is also evident in special education and has been studied twice by the National Research Council of the

National Academy of Sciences. In both 1982 (Heller, Holtzman, & Messick) and 2002 (Donovan & Cross), a panel of nationally recognized researchers reviewed the data in special education and issued a set of findings that are amazingly similar. Both reports acknowledge that students of color, particularly African Americans, are overrepresented in certain categories within special education, notably mild mental retardation and emotional disturbance. Both reports also acknowledge the interaction between ethnicity and poverty, citing the lack of opportunities to learn in classrooms in high-poverty schools where teachers are ill prepared to teach, where expectations of student learning are low, and where overcrowded classrooms lack instructional resources.

In ten of the largest school systems in the United States (Boston, Chicago, Clark County [Las Vegas], Hillsborough, Houston, Los Angeles, Memphis, Miami, New York, and Philadelphia), the percentage of children receiving special education services ranges from 10% to 25% of the total student population (Dalton, Sable, & Hoffman, 2006). Like the approximately six million students with disabilities in special education in the United States, the majority of students in these districts are identified for one of four categories: learning disabilities, emotional disturbance, mental retardation, or speech/language disabilities (United States Department of Education, n.d.). For students with these labels, often considered to be high-incidence disabilities, it is more likely to find these students in general education classes. The US Department of Education reports that a little more than half of all students with disabilities (55%) spent more than 80% of their school day in general education in the 2004–2005 school year. Of this group, 73% were in one of the four high-incidence disability categories. These data have shown little change over a ten-year period despite intervention at the federal level in the form of technical assistance, and dissemination and outreach projects. Examination of data by disability category shows that some groups of students are far more likely to be served outside the general education classroom.

Less than 20% of all students with multiple disabilities are likely to be served in general education classrooms for more than 80% of the time. As Yell and Katsiyannis (2004) have noted, students with multiple disabilities can benefit from participating in academic activities in the general education classroom. Students with intellectual disabilities, who are most likely to be identified as having mental retardation, are most frequently placed in restrictive, special education settings away from the rich, general education curriculum, and opportunities to learn among their nondisabled peers. This phenomenon continues to persist, despite the strides being made in developing literacy interventions for students with multiple disabilities as well as intellectual disabilities (Diehl, Ford, & Federico, 2005; Kliewer et al., 2004).

NCCRESt

In addition to the glacial progress on achieving the least restrictive environment standard for students with disabilities, particularly those who have severe disabilities, data from the US Department of Education, Office of Special Education Programs have also focused on reducing the inappropriate identification of children from culturally and linguistically diverse backgrounds as disabled and eligible for special education. The National Center for Culturally Responsive Education Systems (NCCRESt) was funded by the Office of Special Education Programs to provide technical assistance and dissemination to states and local school districts on one of the persistent issues in the US system of special education, namely, ethnic and racial disproportionality among students identified for special education. At a time when the nation's population is becoming culturally and linguistically diverse at an unprecedented rate (Hodgkinson, 2003), minorities (particularly African Americans, Hispanics, and Native Americans) and students living in poverty are overrepresented in three high-incidence disabilities categories (mild mental retardation, learning disabilities, and emotional/behavioral disorders; Artiles, Trent, & Palmer, 2004).

One of the features of NCCRESt's work has been to track data on the identification of students with disabilities by race and/or ethnicity, using the same six demographic categories employed by the US Census: (1) White, (2) African American, (3) American Indian and Alaska Native, (4) Asian, (5) Native Hawaiian or Other Pacific Islander, and (6) Hispanic or Latino. NCCRESt statisticians have opted to use a risk ratio to examine the relationship between a particular racial/ethnic student group identified for special education and other students in special education who fall into other racial/ethnic groups. The risk ratio is calculated by comparing two ratios. The numerator in a risk ratio is a percentage calculated using the number of students within a particular ethnic/racial group identified for special education over the number of all students in that particular ethnic racial group (e.g., the number of African American students in special education divided by the number of all students who are African American). The denominator of the risk ratio is the number of all students identified for special education divided by the total number of all other students. The risk ratio calculation was recognized in the second National Research Council report on disproportionality as the most reasonable calculation for examining disproportionality (Donovan & Cross, 2002).

NCCRESt uses two comparisons. In the first calculation, the percentage of a particular ethnicity identified for special education is compared with the percentage of all other students in special education. In a second calculation, the denominator is calculated using the White population since students who are identified as White make up the majority population in many states and local school districts. The resulting risk ratio, whether it is calculated against White students or all other students, predicts the risk that a student of a particular racial or ethnic group has for being identified for special education. A risk ratio may be calculated at the school level, the school district level, or at a state level. When calculated at the building level, attention must be given to the size of the population because small numbers make the determination of risk questionable. When the population numbers are large, at a school district or state level, however, the risk ratio calculation produces a valuable analysis, particularly computed over time.

Analysis of US Department of Education and US Census data available on the World Wide Web from the National Center for Culturally Responsive Education Systems and the National Institute for Urban School Improvement (http://nccrest.eddata.net/data) show that in the 2004–2005 academic year, while African American children represented 17% of all students attending school, they made up 22% of the children classified as having one of three categories of disability. A total of 11% of all African American children and 10% of all Native American children enrolled in public education were classified as having one or more of these disabilities. In comparison, only 8% of White and Hispanic children and 3% of Asian/ Pacific children were classified. The disproportionate overrepresentation of ethnically and linguistically diverse students in special education programs has been a concern for more than four decades beginning with Lloyd Dunn in 1968, followed by Mercer in 1973, and then by the two National Resource Council reports (Donovan & Cross, 2002; Heller, Holtzman, & Messick, 1982). In addition to overrepresentation issues, data from a variety of school systems also suggest that students who are culturally and linguistically diverse are more likely than their White, English-speaking counterparts to be placed in more restrictive settings (National Institute for Urban School Improvement, 2005–2006). As an illustration, interactive data tables downloaded from the NCCRESt Web site (www.nccrest.org) show that the identification percentages for students in three high-incidence disability categories (emotional disturbance, learning disabilities, and mental retardation) who identify as White were, in 2003–2004, about half the rate in comparison to students who identify as African American in the seven most populous states in the nation: California, Florida, Illinois, New Jersey, New York, Ohio, and Texas.

When local district data are analyzed, as NCCRESt does in collaboration with its district partners, the discrepancies between placements for students who identify as White and those that identify as African American are made even more apparent. A case in point can be made by examining data from one of the 100 largest public school systems.

This school system served about 279,000 students in the 2004–2005 academic year when the analysis was completed. About 27,000 students in the district were identified for special education. We analyzed these data at the school level to understand the risk for special education identification for students who were African American as well as those who were White. The risk for students who are African American to be identified for special education is more than three times as likely as for students from all other races and ethnicities, including students who are White. When we looked more deeply at variance across schools, we also found that variance in these rates exists at the school level with some schools more likely to over- or under-identify than other schools. Thus, within-school district variance helps to locate differences in early intervening and special education identification practices at the school level. Other researchers have found similar patterns for students who are English language learners (e.g., Artiles, Rueda, Salazar, & Higareda, 2005).

In 2004, a reauthorization of the Individuals with Disabilities Education Act (IDEA) included several provisions that were designed to address disproportionality. For one, states and territories were required to examine local school system data for indication of disproportionality, set benchmarks for determining where significant disproportionality existed, and redistribute up to 15% of federal special education funds for use in early intervening in general education to prevent excessive referrals to special education. In 2004, NCCRESt issued a conceptual framework for understanding and addressing disproportionality. This framework proposes that sustained effort to reduce disproportionality must be focused on the assumptions that undergird daily practice in schools (Klingner et al., 2005). Although curriculum and student outcomes are conceived as systemic processes, when these inert processes are brought to life in schools with particular constellations of families, children, teachers, and administrators, the activity arena known as school takes on an idiosyncratic character that is the product of all these factors in interaction with one another. Improving learning experiences for students requires policy and practice initiatives that take into consideration the social construction of schooling. The effects of the racial legacy of the United States are felt in each school and can be, at one level, examined through the lens of special education.

Special education in the United States offers a special case analysis. Although public education itself is experienced differentially by specific ethnic and racial groups, there is also evidence that gender, poverty, religion, native language, and cultural experiences complicate institutional and professional responses to individual need and promise (e.g., Utley, Obiakor, & Kozleski, 2005). The special education system in the United States allows researchers a way of examining all of these variables and their disproportionate representation. The caution in interpreting the impact of these differences on how children are educated, by whom and in what places, is in preferring some explanations over others. As schooling is a reflection of the values of the society in which it occurs, it may be more convenient and less challenging to foreground poverty over race, psychological over sociological factors, and institutional rather than individual values and beliefs (Artiles, 2003).

DISPROPORTIONALITY IN SPECIAL EDUCATION IN ENGLAND

Alan writes:

> I know less about my great grandfather than Elizabeth does about hers. Assuming he was alive in the 1860s, however, he would have been living in a country which was almost exclusively White, but which had experienced immigration from time immemorial. (Many of the early "immigrants" came equipped with swords, spears, and flaming torches, but that is another matter.) It is a fair bet that my great grandfather worked in the woollen mills of Huddersfield, where my family has lived for many generations. If so, he worked long hours, in back-breaking conditions, for little pay, and with little or no access to education, health care, or welfare benefits. This is a situation which many working-class people would recognise, with some limited amelioration, until at least the founding of the welfare state after the Second World War.

I relate this story to underline both the differences and the similarities between England and the United States. Both countries are characterized by marked inequality. England, however, though ethnically diverse for centuries, has only become "racially" diverse in recent decades. Its major forms of inequality, therefore, have related to class and gender. Its most recent civil war (in the seventeenth century) was based on class, politics, and religion, and its most recent "civil rights" movements were based on class (the Chartists and the rise of the trade unions in the nineteenth century, for instance) and gender (the women's suffrage movement in the early twentieth century). These matters seem far removed from special education, but are actually highly present within it.

Indeed, England does not, strictly speaking, have a system of special education. As Wedell (Chapter 4) notes, the 1981 Education Act, following the Warnock Report (DES, 1978), introduced a new system founded on the concept of "special educational needs" (Gulliford, 1971). The identification of children's "needs" in the new system was to be made

> Not in terms of a particular disability which a child may be judged to have, but in relation to everything about him, his abilities as well as his disabilities—indeed all the factors which have a bearing on his educational progress. (DES, 1978, par. 3.6)

Special educational needs could, therefore, arise out of any sort of educational difficulty. In consequence, assessment need not be concerned with identify disabilities and allocating children to categories of disability (which were to be abolished), and provision need not be made by placing children in special schools or other special settings. Instead, there should be an individualized assessment of the child's difficulties and appropriate individualized interventions to meet those difficulties. If those interventions could reasonably be made in regular ("mainstream") schools and classrooms, so much the better.

In principle, therefore, the English system simply responds to the difficulties students experience in schools, whether or not those difficulties arise from disability. It follows that there ought to be no question of students being misidentified as having this or that disability, and that the system should deliver intervention according to needs that can be identified through rigorous and individualized assessment processes. The reality, however, is quite different.

Ethnicity

England remains a country where the population is predominantly White British, but there are significant ethnic minority populations and these minorities are concentrated in particular places. In the 2001 census (reported by the Office of National Statistics, 2002), 7.6% of the UK population identified themselves as belonging to minority ethnic groups, with the largest groups being Indian (1.7%), Pakistani (1.3%), Black Caribbean (1.0%), Black African (0.9%), and those of Mixed backgrounds (0.8%). Minority ethnic groups, however, were more likely to live in England, where they made up 9% of the population, and to be concentrated in the industrial towns and cities of London, the West Midlands, the North West, and Yorkshire. The most recent figures show that 19.3% of primary school students and 15.3% of secondary school students have a minority ethnic background (Office of National Statistics, 2005a).

Given the ethnic diversity of the country, simple binary distinctions between majority and minority groups are necessarily crude. Nonetheless, there are some minority groups—notably the Bangladeshi, Pakistani, and Black groups[1]—that fare badly on a range of social indicators such as unemployment, income, and health (National Statistics, 2003). In terms of educational indicators, these same groups are also likely to do badly— though it is worth noting that the picture is complex. In the most recent performance figures to be published (Office of National Statistics, 2006), students within the Black, Bangladeshi, and Pakistani groups fare badly, but Chinese, Mixed White and Asian, Irish, and Indian heritage students achieve at above national average levels. The corollary, of course, is that White British students do not by any means always outperform minority ethnic groups.

These differential patterns of educational performance and social out-comes are reflected to a significant extent in the special needs education system. In the latest figures (Office of National Statistics, 2005b), 2.4% of White British children in secondary schools had statements (documents with some legal force, usually produced when students are assessed as having high levels of need with significant resourcing implications) and 14% were regarded as having special educational needs that did not require a statement. In the Black groups, these figures were 2.2% and 20.1%, respectively, 2.4% and 18% in the Pakistani group, and 2.0% and 16.2% in the Bangladeshi group. In the Indian group, however, the corresponding figures were 1.2% and 9.1%, and in the Chinese group, 1.0% and 8.0%. Put another way, children from Black backgrounds were just under one-and-a-half times more likely to be regarded as having special educational needs without a statement than White British children, and just over two-and-a-half times more likely than children from Chinese backgrounds.

Although the English system no longer allocates children to "categories of handicap" in order to make provision, in 2004 it began to collect data on the broad type of special education need that children are regarded by their teachers as having (see Norwich, Chapter 9, and DfES, 2005a, for a definition of these types). These new data have been analyzed for evidence of disproportionality by Lindsay, Pather, and Strand (2006). They calculate the odds of members of minority ethnic groups being identified as having different types of special educational needs, as compared with White British children. What they find is that the patterns of identification are different for each type of need. For instance, in the case of visual impairment, there are no significant differences between the minority groups and their White British counterparts, except in the case of children of Pakistani heritage. They suggest that genetic factors, related to a relatively high proportion of consanguineous marriages, may go some way toward explaining this overrepresentation. There are, however, no such factors to explain the differential odds ratios in respect of two other types of need—moderate learning difficulties (MLD) and emotional and behavioral difficulties (EBD). Here, for instance, the odds for Traveller children are dramatically high (5.96:1 for MLD and 2.92:1 for EBD for those of Irish Traveller heritage). The odds for other groups are also high (Black Caribbean children have odds of 1.32:1 and 2.28:1 for MLD and EBD, respectively), while those for other minority groups are much lower (for Indian children they are 0.67:1 and 0.23:1, and for Chinese children they are 0.31:1 and 0.18:1, respectively).

It may be significant that visual impairment is a "normative" disability in which professional judgment is mediated by more or less objective diagnostic criteria, whereas MLD and EBD are "nonnormative," and identification in these cases is more dependent on professional judgment. The implication is that there is something about the way professional judgment operates that makes it more or less likely that ethnic groups will be identified as having special educational needs. Whether this "something" is prejudice and discrimination on the part of education professional or emanates from the deeper interactions and constructions that characterize schools and classrooms is an interesting question. Some indications of what the answer might be are given in further analyses undertaken by Lindsay et al. (2006). In order to identify how far what appear to be the effects of ethnicity might actually be explicable in terms of other factors, they adjust their odds ratios to take account of gender, age, and socioeconomic disadvantage differences between groups. These adjusted ratios tend to be lower for minority ethnic groups than the unadjusted ratios. For instance, the odds of Black Caribbean children being identified as having EBD fall from 2.28:1 to 1.50:1. The overall pattern, however, tends to remain in that different ethnic groups have different odds, and those with higher unadjusted odds also have higher adjusted odds.

The implications this time are twofold. First, because ethnicity remains as an explanatory factor, even when other possible factors are taken into account, the English special needs education system, it seems, does indeed treat children differently on the basis of ethnicity. Second, because those other factors make a difference to the odds ratios, ethnicity is clearly not the only basis on which children are treated differently. It is to these other factors that we now turn.

Children From Poorer Backgrounds

England is a country where there are significant disparities in socioeconomic status between groups, and where these disparities are represented in educational achievement. Children and young people from poor families do worse than their peers educationally (Blanden & Gregg, 2004).

They tend to find themselves concentrated in particular schools, sometimes referred to as schools facing challenging circumstances, which are the subject of much policy activity (Chapman & Harris, 2004; Reynolds, Hopkins, Potter, & Chapman, 2001). Despite considerable recent efforts to "improve" these schools and more generally to tackle the issue of low attainment, the gap between the attainments of students from poorer backgrounds and their peers remains stubbornly wide (DfES, 2005c).

Children from poor backgrounds are much more likely than their peers to be identified as having special educational needs. The usual measure of relative poverty among school-age children is their entitlement to free school meals (FSM). In recent figures, almost 30% of pupils with special educational needs (with and without statements) were known to be eligible for free school meals in primary schools compared with around 14% of pupils with no special educational needs. In secondary schools, the comparable figures were 26% and almost 12%, respectively (Office of National Statistics, 2005b).

The evidence suggests that the disproportionate identification of children from poorer backgrounds encompasses both normative disabilities and nonnormative types of special educational need (DfES, 2005b). A large-scale survey of primary schools by Croll and Moses (Croll, 2002; Croll & Moses, 2000, 2003), however, suggests that there may be some important variations. They found an overall correlation between FSM entitlement and identification as having special educational needs of 0.43. This rose, however, to 0.45 for learning difficulties, 0.50 for emotional and behavioral difficulties, and 0.66 for what they call "discipline problems." On the other hand, it fell to 0.11 for physical sensory and health problems. The implication would seem to be that poor home background places children at somewhat greater risk of being identified as having a nonnormative type of special educational need than of having a normative disability.

Gender

England is a country where gender continues to have a significant impact on both social and educational outcomes. Women earn less than men, on average; follow different career paths; and retain responsibility for the majority of household chores and child care (Office of National Statistics, 2004). These gender differences are also apparent in education, though not perhaps in the way that might be expected from the wider social outcomes. Girls in fact outperform boys across a range of educational outcomes and across a range of social groups (Office of National Statistics, 2006).

Similar variations by gender are found in the population of children identified as having special educational needs. Boys are nearly twice as likely as girls to be identified in regular schools as having special educational needs without a statement and nearly two-and-a-half times as likely to be assessed as needing a statement (Office of National Statistics, 2005b). Again, there is evidence of some variations by type of special educational need. For instance, Croll and Moses (2003) report that boys were overrepresented both in the learning difficulties and in the emotional and behavioral difficulties types in their survey of primary schools. Similarly, Daniels, Hey, Leonard, and Smith's (1996, 1999) audit of special educational needs provision in the regular primary schools of one local authority found that more boys than girls received provision, that boys received higher levels of provision than girls, and that these differences were particularly marked in respect to MLD and, especially, EBD.

Other Factors

In addition to ethnicity, socioeconomic background, and gender, other factors bear on the likelihood of a student being identified as having special educational needs in England. For instance, age—or at least the stage a child has reached in the school system—seems to be a factor. The incidence of identified needs is highest in the middle years of schooling (with a peak at age 9), with a slow start, a decline through the secondary years, and a marked fall-off in the final year of statutory schooling (Office of National Statistics, 2005b). Our own analyses suggest that month of birth is also a factor (Dyson, Farrell, Gallannaugh, Hutcheson, & Polat, 2004). Children in England begin statutory schooling in the year in which they become five, and progress through the system with their peers who enter in the same year. This means that some children may be nearly a full year younger than others in their classes. Those who are young for their school-year group in this way are more likely to be identified as having special educational needs—an effect that holds well, surprisingly, throughout the school years.

Similarly, there is evidence that the incidence of identified special educational needs varies by time and place in a way that is difficult to explain by variations in the population. Croll and Moses (2000, 2003), for instance, find an overall 38.8% increase in the incidence of identified needs between 1981 and 1998 with, as we have seen, different patterns in groups identified as having different types of special educational need. More recently, a survey of local authority personnel by the Audit Commission reported significant perceived increases in the number of children with autistic spectrum disorders, speech and communication difficulties, and with profound and multiple learning difficulties, together with perceived decreases in moderate learning difficulties and specific learning difficulties (Audit Commission, 2002). The same survey found significant variations in the proportions of children with statements between local authorities and schools.

Finally, a series of studies have found that children whose behavior is troublesome to their teachers are particularly likely to be identified as having special educational needs (see, for instance, Galloway, Armstrong, & Tomlinson, 1994; Rees, Farrell, & Rees, 2003). Croll (2002) notes that "discipline problems" identified as special needs by schools correlate highly with poor home background, and that this correlation is in addition to any correlation with achievement. There may also be interactions with ethnicity (Gillborn & Gipps, 1996; Tennant, 2004), and certain minority ethnic groups are particularly likely to find themselves excluded from school for disciplinary reasons (DfES, 2005b).

Achievement

The patterns reported above suggest "disproportionality" in the English special needs education system cannot be understood simply through the lens of race. On the contrary, a complex set of interacting factors influence the likelihood of identification for different children. These factors include, but are not restricted to, ethnicity, class, and gender. Moreover, it would appear that, in addition to any more direct effects, these factors tend to be mediated through academic achievement. In other words, the factors associated with increased identification tend also to be associated with low achievement; and it is low achievement that leads to children being labeled as "having special educational needs." Certainly, our own study found some striking similarities between patterns of achievement in a given group and the likelihood that members of that group would be identified as having special educational needs (Dyson et al., 2004). Our finding that children who are young for their school-year group are more likely to be identified as having special educational needs can be seen as part of this pattern. Such children, we found, are also more likely to be lower achievers than their older peers, perhaps because they enter school less developmentally mature than their peers and are never enabled entirely to make up the difference.

Achievement appears as a powerful mediating factor in other studies. Both Sacker, Schoon, and Bartley (2001) and Croll (2002) find that there is a strong relationship between socioeconomic background and the likelihood of being identified as having special educational needs, but that this is mediated by achievement. When ethnicity is factored in, similar conclusions emerge. Those minority groups that are more likely to be identified as having special educational needs are also, by and large, more likely to be poor and more likely to be low-achievers (Bhattacharyya, Ison, & Blair, 2003; DfES, 2005b). We might add that, because boys tend to be lower achievers than girls, the overrepresentation of boys in the special educational needs population is not entirely surprising.

The implication of this would seem to be that, as Croll (2002) suggests, the English special needs education system, despite its apparatus of detailed assessment of individual needs, is to an important extent simply identifying low achievement. Although, therefore, the disproportional representation of social groups arises from many sources, a good deal of it arises from the differential achievements of those groups in the school system as a whole.

DISPROPORTIONALITY IN TWO COUNTRIES

We suggested at the start of this chapter that the categorization processes of special education were in fact a set of category mistakes. Looking at these two accounts, we can see that this is true in two senses.

First, there is a sense in which children are miscategorised through special education processes. This is clearest in the US system, where access to special education depends on allocation to one or other category of disability. If children from some social groups are more likely than others to be identified as disabled in this way, then we either have to believe that disabilities are distributed differentially across such groups (which seems improbable except in certain very specific cases, analogous to the incidence of visual impairment amongst Pakistani heritage children, cited above), or that children are being systematically misclassified. If the classification itself were not problem enough, it also forms the basis for differential treatment (including placement in more restrictive environments) which is inherently discriminatory.

There is no reason to believe that similar processes are not also at work in England. However, the different characteristics of the special needs education population and the different procedures in the special needs education system there suggest that a second explanation for disproportionality may also be needed. The English system requires no presumption of disability before identifying a child as having special educational needs. All that is required is that the child experiences difficulties in schooling such that her or his teachers feel the need to do something to help. Although there is the possibility that children who are doing perfectly well may be misidentified as being in difficulty, it seems unlikely that widespread disproportionality can be explained completely in this way. On the contrary, the groups that are overrepresented in special needs education do indeed do badly in the general education system. In this sense, their identification is accurate.

Similarly, it seems reasonable to suppose that some aspects of misidentification might be explicable in terms of discrimination, prejudice, and failures of cultural understanding where overrepresented groups are clearly identifiable by those professionals responsible for the identification and assessment process. The English situation, however, shows us that some clearly identifiable minority groups are actually underrepresented in special education, while "invisible" groups (most obviously, children who are young for their year groups) are overrepresented. The likeliest explanation seems to be that the overrepresentation of certain groups arises not only because of the workings of prejudice, discrimination, and misunderstanding, but also because the incidence of educational difficulties (as opposed to disabilities) is indeed higher in these groups.

These two explanations point to different kinds of category mistakes. In the former case, it is children's *difficulties* that are misclassified as disabilities; in the latter, it is the *reasons* for those difficulties. To eradicate the first kind of mistake, we need a special education system whose assessment and categorization processes are more trustworthy, and less liable to clouding by prejudice, discrimination, and misunderstanding. To eradicate the second kind of mistake, we need better analyses of why children do badly in school. Such analyses, we suggest, have to take due account of the relationship between children's educational difficulties, the characteristics of the education system where they are expected to learn, and the social and economic conditions within which they live. Above all, they must avoid treating "public issues" as though they were "personal troubles" (Mills, 1959).

The first explanation holds out a prospect for improvement within the framework of special education. We have no difficulty with the proposition that appropriate "special" interventions, appropriately targeted, can be of use to some children, even though we may have considerable doubts about many of the interventions currently offered under the aegis of special education. The second explanation, however, calls for a move from individual interventions to systemic and social action. It calls for a regular education system and, ultimately, a society in which issues of equity are taken seriously. As the US contribution to this chapter suggests, special education may be an arena in which these issues can be explored. It is not, however, an arena in which they can be resolved.

NOTE

1. The UK ethnic groupings used in this chapter are those used in national statistics. See Office of National Statistics (2001) for a discussion of some of the issues raised by this usage.

REFERENCES

Artiles, A. J. (2003). Special education's changing identity: Paradoxes and dilemmas in views of culture and space. *Harvard Educational Review, 73,* 164–175.

Artiles, A. J., Rueda, R., Salazar, J. J., & Higareda, I. (2005). Within group diversity in minority disproportionate representation: English language learners in urban school districts. *Exceptional Children, 73,* 283–300.

Artiles, A. J., Trent, S. C., & Palmer, J. (2004). Culturally diverse students in special education: Legacies and prospects. In J. A. Banks & C. M. Banks (Eds.), *Handbook of research on multicultural education* (2nd ed., pp. 716–735). San Francisco: Jossey-Bass.

Audit Commission. (2002). *Special educational needs: A mainstream issue.* London: Author.

Bhattacharyya, G., Ison, L., & Blair, M. (2003). *Minority ethnic attainment and participation in education and training: The evidence* (Research Topic Paper RTP01–03). London: Department for Education and Skills. Retrieved January 8, 2007, from http://www.dfes.gov.uk/research/data/uploadfiles/RTP01–03.pdf

Blanden, J., & Gregg, P. (2004). *Family income and educational attainment: A review of approaches and evidence for Britain.* London: London School of Economics, Centre for the Economics of Education. Retrieved April 29, 2005, from http://cee.lse.ac.uk/cee%20dps/ceedp41.pdf

Chapman, C., & Harris, A. (2004). Improving schools in difficult and challenging contexts: Strategies for improvement. *Educational Research, 46*(3), 219–228.

Croll, P. (2002). Social deprivation, school-level achievement and special educational needs. *Educational Research, 44*(1), 43–53.

Croll, P., & Moses, D. (2000). *Special needs in the primary school: One in five?* London: Cassell.

Croll, P., & Moses, D. (2003). Special educational needs across two decades: Survey evidence from English primary schools. *British Educational Research Journal, 29*(5), 731–747.

Dalton, B., Sable, J., & Hoffman, L. (2006). *Characteristics of the 100 largest public elementary and secondary school districts in the United States: 2003–04* (NCES 2006–329). Washington, DC: US Department of Education, National Center for Education Statistics.

Daniels, H., Hey, V., Leonard, D., & Smith, M. (1996). *Gender and special needs provision in mainstream schooling* (ESRC End of Award Report R000235059). (Place of publication and publisher unspecified).

Daniels, H., Hey, V., Leonard, D., & Smith, M. (1999). Issues of equity in special needs education from a gender perspective. *British Journal of Special Education, 26*(4), 184–194.

Department for Education and Skills. (2005a). *Data collection by type of special educational need.* London: Author. Retrieved August 16, 2006, from http://www.teachernet.gov.uk/docbank/index.cfm?id=5352

Department for Education and Skills. (2005b). *Ethnicity and education: The evidence on minority ethnic pupils* (Research Topic Paper RTP01–05). London: Author. Retrieved January 8, 2007, from http://www.dfes.gov.uk/research/data/uploadfiles/RTP01–05.pdf

Department for Education and Skills. (2005c). *Has the social class gap narrowed in primary schools? A background note to accompany the talk by the Rt. Hon. Ruth Kelly MP, Secretary of State for Education and Skills, 26 July 2005.* London: Author. Retrieved January 8, 2007, from http://www.dfes.gov.uk/rsgateway/DB/STA/t000597/IPPR_Speech.pdf

Department of Education and Science. (1978). *Special educational needs: Report of the Committee of Enquiry Into the Education of Handicapped Children and Young People* (Warnock Report). London: Her Majesty's Stationery Office.

Diehl, S. F., Ford, C. S., & Federico, J. (2005). The communication journey of a fully included child with an autism spectrum disorder. *Topics in Language Disorders, 25*(4), 375–387.

Donovan, S., & Cross, C. (2002). *Minority students in special and gifted education.* Washington, DC: National Academy Press.

Dunn, L. (1968). Special education for the mildly retarded: Is much of it justifiable? *Exceptional Children, 35,* 5–22.

Dyson, A., Farrell, P., Gallannaugh, F., Hutcheson, G., & Polat, F. (2004). *Inclusion and pupil achievement.* London: Department for Education and Skills. Retrieved January 8, 2007, from http://www.dfes.gov.uk/research/data/uploadfiles/ACFC9F.pdf

Education Trust. (n.d.). Retrieved May 28, 2006, from www2.edtrust.org/edtrust/

Ferguson, D. L., Kozleski, E. B., & Smith, A. (2003). Transforming general and special education in urban schools. In F. E. Obiakor, C. A. Utley, & A. F. Rotatori (Eds.), *Effective education for learners with exceptionalities* (Advances in Special Education No. 15, pp. 43–74). Oxford, UK: Elsevier Science.

Galloway, D., Armstrong, D., & Tomlinson, S. (1994). *Special educational needs: Whose problem?* London: Longman.

Gillborn, D., & Gipps, C. (1996). *Recent research on the achievements of ethnic minority pupils.* London: Her Majesty's Stationery Office. Retrieved January 8, 2007, from http://www.ofsted.gov.uk/assets/447.pdf

Gulliford, R. (1971). *Special educational needs.* London: Routledge & Kegan Paul.

Heller, R., Holtzman, W., & Messick, S. (Eds.). (1982). *Placing children in special education: A strategy for equity.* Washington, DC: Academy Press.

Hodgkinson, H. L. (2003). *Leaving too many children behind: A demographer's view on the neglect of America's youngest children.* Washington, DC: Institute for Educational Leadership.

Kliewer, C., Fitzgerald, L., Meyer-Mork, J., Hartman, P., English-Sand, P., & Raschke, D. (2004). Citizenship for all in the literate community: An ethnography of young children with significant disabilities in inclusive early childhood settings. *Harvard Educational Review, 74*(4), 373–403.

Klingner, J., Artiles, A., Kozleski, E. B., Utley, C., Zion, S., Tate, W., Harry, B., Zamora-Durán, G., & Riley, D. (2005). Conceptual framework for addressing the disproportionate representation of culturally and linguistically diverse students in special education. *Educational Policy Analysis Archives, 13*(38). Retrieved September 9, 2005, from http://epaa.asu.edu/epaa/v13n38/

Kozol, J. (2005). *The shame of the nation: The restoration of apartheid schooling in America.* New York: Crown.

Lindsay, G., Pather, S., & Strand, S. (2006). *Special educational needs and ethnicity: Issues of over- and under-representation* (Research Report RR757). London: Department for Education and Skills. Retrieved January 8, 2007, from http://www.dfes.gov.uk/research/data/uploadfiles/RR757.pdf

Mercer, J. R. (1973). *Labeling the mentally retarded.* Berkeley: University of California Press.

Mills, C. W. (1959). *The sociological imagination.* Oxford, UK: Oxford University Press.

National Center for Culturally Responsive Education Systems. (n.d.). *Interactive data tables.* Retrieved March 17, 2006, from www.nccrest.org

National Center for Culturally Responsive Education Systems, & National Institute for Urban School Improvement. (2004–2005). *Disproportionality by race and disability.* Retrieved February 8, 2008, from http://nccrest.eddata.net/data/

National Criminal Justice Reference Service. (n.d.). Retrieved January 30, 2007, from http://www.ncjrs.gov/App/QA/Detail.aspx?id=112&context=3&txtKeywordSearch=racial%20distribution <http://www.ncjrs.gov/App/QA/Detail.aspx?id=112&context=3&txtKeywordSearch=racial%20distribution>

National Institute for Urban School Improvement. (2005–2006). *What is the risk for students of a given race to be identified for special education services?* Retrieved March 21, 2006, from http://niusi.eddata.net/city5/index.php

Office of National Statistics. (2001). *The classification of ethnic groups.* London: Author. Retrieved April 18, 2006, from http://www.statistics.gov.uk/about/Classifications/ns_ethnic_classification.asp

Office of National Statistics. (2002). *Social focus in brief: Ethnicity.* London: Author. Retrieved August 28, 2006, from http://www.statistics.gov.uk/downloads/theme_social/social_focus_in_brief/ethnicity/ethnicity.pdf

Office of National Statistics. (2003). *Census 2001: Ethnicity and religion in England and Wales.* London: Author. Retrieved April 16, 2006, from http://www.statistics.gov.uk/census2001/profiles/commentaries/ethnicity.asp

Office of National Statistics. (2004). *Focus on gender.* London: Author. Retrieved April 17, 2006, from http://www.statistics.gov.uk/downloads/theme_compendia/fog2004/Gender.pdf

Office of National Statistics. (2005a). *First release: Schools and pupils in England, January 2005 (Final)* (SFR 42/2005). London: Author. Retrieved January 8, 2007, from http://www.dfes.gov.uk/rsgateway/DB/SFR/s000606/SFR42–2005.pdf

Office of National Statistics. (2005b). *Special educational needs in England, January 2005.* (SFR 24/2005 Statistical first release). London: Author. Retrieved April 20, 2006, from http://www.dfes.gov.uk/rsgateway/DB/SFR/s000584/SFR24–2005.pdf

Office of National Statistics. (2006). *First release: National curriculum assessment, GCSE and equivalent attainment and post-16 attainment by pupil characteristics in England 2005.* London: Author. Retrieved January 8, 2007, from http://www.dfes.gov.uk/rsgateway/DB/SFR/s000640/SFR09_2006.pdf

Rees, C., Farrell, P., & Rees, P. (2003). Coping with complexity: How do educational psychologists assess students with emotional and behavioural difficulties? *Educational Psychology in Practice, 19*(1), 35–47.

Reynolds, D., Hopkins, D., Potter, D., & Chapman, C. (2001). *School improvement for schools facing challenging circumstances: A review of research and practice.* London: Department for Education and Skills.

Sacker, A., Schoon, I., & Bartley, M. (2001). Sources of bias in special needs provision in mainstream primary schools: Evidence from two British cohort studies. *European Journal of Special Needs Education, 16*(3), 259–276.

Smith, A., & Kozleski, E. B. (2005). Witnessing Brown: Pursuit of an equity agenda in American education. *Remedial and Special Education, 26,* 270–280.

Tennant, G. (2004). Differential classroom interactions by ethnicity. *Emotional and Behavioural Difficulties, 9*(3), 191–204.

Tomlinson, S. (1995). The radical structuralist view of special education and disability: Unpopular perspectives on their origins and development. In T. M. Skrtic (Ed.), *Disability and democracy: Reconstructing (special) education for postmodernity* (pp. 122–134). New York: Teachers College Press.

United States Department of Education. (n.d.). Available at https://www.ideadata.org

Utley, C., Obiakor, F., & Kozleski, E. B. (2005). Overrepresentation of culturally and linguistically diverse students in special education in urban schools: A research synthesis. In J. Flood & P. Anders (Eds.), *Literacy development of students in urban schools: Research and policy* (pp. 314–344). Newark, DE: International Reading Association.

Yell, M. L., & Katsiyannis, A. (2004). Placing students with disabilities in inclusive settings: Legal guidelines and preferred practices. *Preventing School Failure, 49*(1), 28–35.

12 Classification of Children With Disabilities in the Context of Performance-Based Educational Reform

An Unintended Classification System

Katherine Nagle and Martha L. Thurlow

INTRODUCTION

The classification of children as having disabilities, and as eligible to receive special education and related services, has generated much controversy and debate over the years. Recently, these controversies have become part of the broader debate about issues of accountability in public services. Concern has been expressed about the escalating numbers of children in specific disability categories, the disproportional representation of minority groups in special education, and the need to increase system accountability for child outcomes. To address these and other longstanding concerns, President George W. Bush created the Commission on Excellence in Special Education in October 2001. The commission was charged to "recommend reforms to America's special education system and move from a culture of compliance to one of accountability for results" (President's Commission on Excellence in Special Education, 2002, p. 2). On July 1, 2002, the commission submitted its final report titled *A New Era: Revitalizing Special Education for Children and Their Families* to the White House as required by the Executive Order. Three broad recommendations formed the basis of the report, with the first major recommendation being "Focus on results—not on process." Specifically, the commission stated,

> While the law must retain the legal and procedural safeguards necessary to guarantee a "free appropriate public education" for children with disabilities, IDEA [the Individuals with Disabilities Education Act] will only fulfill its intended purpose if it raises its expectations for students and becomes results-oriented—not driven by process, litigation, regulation and confrontation. In short, the system must be judged by the opportunities it provides and the outcomes achieved by each child. (p. 12)

This recommendation accorded well with the performance-based accountability reforms already underway in general education, specifically those specified under the No Child Left Behind Act (NCLB). As the language of performance-based accountability reform has permeated special education, it has resulted in an emerging and still evolving classification of children with disabilities. This new classification system incorporates three sets of criteria for assigning children to categories based on the nature of the assessment and achievement standards to which children with disabilities are to be held.

This chapter is divided into three sections. In the first section, we present background information on current US policies relating to children with disabilities, specifically those served under IDEA, and on the assessment requirements of NCLB. In the second section, we present research findings that support the proposition of an emerging classification system for children with Individualized Education Programs (IEPs) that has its origins in current performance-based accountability reform. In the final section, we discuss the implications of this new classification system on traditional disability categories and the education of children with IEPs. In this chapter, we recognize that NCLB uses the terms "student" or "students," but for consistency with IDEA we use the term *child* or *children* for both pieces of legislation.

BACKGROUND

In the United States, achievement and school accountability have increasingly come to dominate policy reform initiatives at the state and federal levels. A longstanding concern at the federal level has been the need to ensure that disadvantaged children, including those children in high-poverty schools and members of nonmajority cultures, have the opportunity to learn challenging subject matter. It is only in the past decade, however, that children assigned to special education were specifically included in these general reforms, largely because special education was perceived as separate from the general education system. In this section, we briefly review key federal legislation that established the current performance-based accountability framework in the United States and then discuss the specific requirements for children with IEPs.

Elementary and Secondary Education Acts of 1965, 1988, 1994, and 2001

The Elementary and Secondary Education Act (ESEA) of 1965 was part of President Lyndon Johnson's War on Poverty. Title 1 of the act (see Pullin, Chapters 6 and 7) was enacted into law "to provide financial assistance . . . to local educational agencies serving areas with concentrations of children from low-income families to expand and improve their educational programs by various means, which contribute to meeting the special educational needs of educationally deprived children" (Public Law 89-10, Sec. 201, ESEA, 1965). The goal of the law remains the same, but as the reauthorizations have shown, the means for achieving this goal changed over time (Wenning, Herdman, & Smith, 2002).

In 1988, a new accountability system was established within Title I schools that required local education agencies (LEAs) to use average individual child gains on state selected standardized norm-referenced tests to identify schools with ineffective programs. The assessment requirements, however, only pertained to children in high-poverty schools receiving services under Title I (Goertz & Duffy, 2003). The 1994 reauthorization of ESEA, known as the Improving America's Schools Act (IASA), began to clearly reflect standards-based educational policy (Wenning et al., 2002). The IASA required states to establish challenging grade level academic content standards in mathematics, reading/language arts, and later, science. States were also to establish one assessment aligned with the standards and applied to all students at least once within three grade spans, third through fifth, sixth through ninth, and tenth through twelfth. The IASA required that states collect data in such a way as to enable results to be disaggregated within each state, local educational agency, and school by gender, racial, and ethnic group; English proficiency status; migrant status; and by students with disabilities as compared to nondisabled students, as well as by economically disadvantaged students as compared with students who are not economically disadvantaged. Each state, however, was to determine how it would hold schools accountable for the performance (Wenning et al., 2002).

In 2001, the ESEA was again reauthorized and included significant new assessment and accountability provisions. Among these detailed provisions, the newly named No Child Left Behind Act (NCLB) required states to annually assess the performance of all students in language arts, math, and science and to report their achievement against three levels: proficient, advanced, and basic. States have flexibility in determining what constitutes a particular achievement level and also may rename their achievement levels. States' annual academic assessments must be aligned with the content standards, measure the achievement of all children, and the results must be used to hold schools and school systems accountable for the achievement of all children within the public education system. Accountability is achieved through setting annual adequate yearly progress (AYP) performance targets for individual schools and school systems designed to ensure that all children reach grade-level proficiency in reading and mathematics by 2014.

AYP requires that three conditions are satisfied. First, not less than 95% of children in each of the following subgroups—economically disadvantaged children, children from major racial and ethnic groups, children with disabilities, and children with limited English proficiency—are to be assessed. Second, the proportion of children achieving proficient or advanced levels within each of the subgroups must meet or exceed the annual measurable objectives (AMO) set by the state for all students as well as meet the state target in at least one other indicator (e.g., attendance, graduation). School districts and schools that fail to make AYP toward statewide achievement are subject to mandatory and increasingly severe sanctions aimed at getting them back on course to meet state standards. Schools that meet or exceed AYP objectives or close achievement gaps will be eligible for academic achievement awards.

The Individuals with Disabilities Education Act

The 1997 reauthorization of IDEA was the first time that special education policy specifically addressed how children with disabilities would participate in the general state level assessment and accountability programs by specifying that these children are to be provided with appropriate testing accommodations as specified in their IEPs. Policymakers also recognized that some children with disabilities need alternate ways to participate in assessment programs. Thus, the 1997 IDEA amendments required the state or local educational agency to develop guidelines that allowed "for the participation of children with disabilities in alternate assessments for those children who cannot participate in state and district-wide assessment programs" (§ 612(a)(17)(A)(i)).

The 2004 IDEA Amendments

To further align the major legislative and regulatory requirements affecting states, the 2004 reauthorization of IDEA addressed how children with disabilities would be included in state accountability systems established by NCLB. Specifically, IDEA 2004 reaffirmed the IDEA 1997 requirement that all children with disabilities are to be included in state- and districtwide general assessment programs, including academic assessments for accountability purposes. To this end, children with disabilities must be provided with appropriate accommodations and alternate assessments where necessary and as indicated in their IEPs. Furthermore, states must develop guidelines for the provision of appropriate accommodations and develop assessment guidelines for the participation of those children who cannot participate in general assessments.

NCLB and IDEA 2004 Regulations and Guidance

The NCLB and IDEA 2004 recognize the right of children with IEPs to a free and appropriate public education (FAPE). Both specify additional options and flexibility for this population. In this section, we address in detail academic achievement standards options and alternate assessment options that are emerging from the US Department of Education's (ED) attempts to better align education policy for this group of children. These provisions have particular importance to the emerging classification schemes we discuss later in the chapter.

Alternate Academic Achievement Standards

In December 2003, the ED recognized that it was not appropriate to measure all children with IEPs against grade-level achievement standards and that not all children with IEPs could participate in the regular statewide assessment. The department issued final regulations for the inclusion of children with "the most significant cognitive disabilities" in

ESEA Title I assessments (ED, 2003, p. 68,702). Under this regulation and additional nonregulatory guidance released in August 2005 (ED, 2005a), states were granted the flexibility to measure the achievement of children with the most significant cognitive disabilities against alternate achievement standards (34 C.F.R. § 200.1(d)) and to develop alternate assessments based on alternate achievement standards. Because the concept of alternate achievement standards was new to educational practice, the US Department of Education defined an alternate achievement standard as "an expectation of performance that differs in complexity from a grade-level achievement standard" (ED, 2005a, p. 20). States are permitted to define who they consider to be children with the most significant cognitive disabilities.

The US Department of Education made it clear that alternate achievement standards were appropriate for only a small percentage of children with disabilities. In an attempt to deter states and districts from assigning too many children with disabilities to alternate achievement standards as a means of improving the system's AYP scores, the department placed a cap on the percentage of proficient and advanced scores achieved through alternate assessment procedures that could be included in district- and state-level AYP calculations. The number of proficient and advanced scores that are allowed to be counted as such must not exceed 1% of all children in the grades tested, which totals about 9% of all children with disabilities across the United States. In any specific state, this percentage might differ, however. In states with larger percentages of children with disabilities, the percentages will be smaller (e.g., in Maine, where the percentage of six- to seventeen-year-old children with disabilities is 14.97%, the 1% figure translates to about 7% of children with disabilities). In states with smaller percentages of children with disabilities, the opposite is true (e.g., in Colorado, where the percentage of six- to seventeen-year-old children with disabilities is 8.90%, the 1% figure translates to about 11% of children with disabilities).

Modified Academic Achievement Standards

In May 2005, the US Department of Education responded to concerns from the field concerning NCLB's requirement that all children but those with the most significant cognitive disabilities would be held to the same grade-level academic achievement standards by creating a new policy (ED, 2005b, 2005d). Although this new policy was not yet final at the time of writing, it is directed toward a second group of children with IEPs. According to the proposed regulations on modified achievement standards, there is a group of children with IEPs whose progress in response to high-quality instruction is such that these children are not likely to achieve grade-level proficiency within the school year covered by their IEPs. For this limited group of children, states can develop and implement modified achievement standards (ED, 2005c). The proposed regulations do not define who may take a test based on modified achievement standards. Instead, they require that states have in their guidelines for IEP teams certain key criteria (defined by the US Department of Education) in order to ensure that children with IEPs are not inappropriately held to modified achievement standards. In the proposed regulation, modified achievement standards must be aligned with the state's academic content standards for the grade in which the child is enrolled; provide access to a grade-level curriculum; and not preclude the child from earning a regular high school diploma. In addition, under the proposed regulation states and LEAs would be permitted to include in their AYP determinations the proficient and advanced scores from assessments based on modified achievement standards, not to exceed 2% of children assessed, or approximately 20% of children with disabilities (§ 200.13(c)(2)(ii)).

Alternate Assessments

To take advantage of the flexibility offered by the US Department of Education, states must develop alternate assessments or modify their existing assessments. Alternate assessments based on alternate achievement standards are required to (1) be aligned with the state's content standards, (2) yield results separately in both reading/language arts and mathematics, (3) be designed and implemented in a manner that supports use of the results as an indicator of AYP, and (4) meet the requirements for high technical quality including validity and reliability. Assessments based on modified achievement standards are required to (1) be aligned to grade-level content standards, (2) yield separate results in reading/language arts and mathematics, (3) meet the requirements for high technical quality including validity and reliability, and (4) fit coherently in the state assessment system by adopting the performance levels of basic, proficient, and advanced.

In addition to the two groups of children who take an alternate assessment based on either alternate achievement standards or modified achievement standards, there are two other common categories of assessment participation recognized by NCLB and IDEA 2004. These common categories of assessment participation are (1) children who take the regular assessment without accommodations and (2) children who take the regular assessment with accommodations. The term "accommodations" here is used to mean "test or test administration changes that are not considered to alter the construct measured" (Sireci, Scarpati, & Li, 2005, p. 460). In its proposed regulations on modified achievement standards, the US Department of Education pointed out that under Title 1 a child must receive a valid score on an assessment in order to be considered a participant for AYP purposes. If the proposed rule is implemented, states will be required to develop guidelines for IEP teams requiring that each child be validly assessed. IEP teams will also be required to identify any accommodations that would result in an invalid score.

The IDEA introduced another category of alternate assessment—alternate assessments based on grade-level achievement standards. Currently, only a few states have alternate assessments based on grade-level achievement standards (Thompson, Johnstone, Thurlow, & Altman, 2005) and participation rates in these vary from less than 1% of children with disabilities tested (Massachusetts) to as high as 20% (Vermont) or 21% (Kansas; Government Accountability Office, 2005). Table 11.1 shows the national average percentages of children with disabilities in the general and the alternate assessments based on alternate achievement standards.

Table 11.1 Participation of US Children With Disabilities in 2003–2004 Regular Assessment and Alternate Assessments Based on Alternate Achievement Standards

	Regular Assessment			Alternate Assessment Based on Alternate Achievement Standards		
	Elementary	*Middle*	*High*	*Elementary*	*Middle*	*High*
Reading	86%	85%	82%	11%	11%	10%
Math	88%	86%	81%	9%	11%	10%

SOURCE: Thurlow, Moen, & Altman, 2006.

School systems are under increasing pressure to meet steadily increasing AYP goals for children and significant subgroups as the year 2014 draws closer. In the remainder of this chapter, we posit that in the current climate of performance-based accountability the disability categories familiar to special education are becoming less useful to school systems. Schools and school systems are now paying close attention to whether they will make AYP. It is now possible for children with IEPs to be categorized by the type of assessment they take, by the achievement standards against which they will be measured, and by the proximity of their score to the proficient level on state assessments.

PERFORMANCE-BASED ACCOUNTABILITY: A NEW CLASSIFICATION SYSTEM

In this section, we present research findings from a five-year study involving four states, conducted by the Education Policy Reform Research Institute (EPRRI). This institute was funded by the US Department of Education's Office of Special Education Programs (OSEP) in 2000 to investigate and describe the impact of including children with disabilities in state educational accountability systems as required by the 1997 IDEA. Two school districts in each of four states (California, Maryland, New York, and Texas) were selected to participate in the study. EPRRI researchers used two complementary strategies to collect qualitative data, namely, analysis of extant data and in-depth interviewing. In addition, a variety of documents were collected and analyzed as well as information from state Web sites. Between October 2001 and January 2002, EPRRI researchers conducted 35 interviews at the state level and 44 at the district level. The following typologies emerged from analyses of these interviews.

Categorization Based on Assessment Type

The current regulations defining how students with disabilities will participate in state-mandated assessments may have unintentionally created a new categorization system: those children with IEPs who are held to grade-level achievement standards take the regular assessment, with or without accommodations, and those children who are held to alternate or modified achievement standards and take an alternate form of assessment.

Interviews revealed that it was increasingly common for teachers and administrators to refer to children with disabilities based on the state assessment they take. For example, informants in one of EPRRI's study states referred to children who took the state's alternate assessment as "IMAP kids." Similarly, in another state several teachers, both regular and special education teachers, referred to children who participated in the state's alternate assessment as "Alt assessment kids." In yet another state, children with IEPs who participated in the regular assessment were referred to as "TAAS kids." Although modified assessments were not available in the states in which EPRRI conducted its research, the students who are seen as eligible for these assessments have previously been labeled "gap kids" or "gray area kids" (Almond, Quenemoen, Olsen, & Thurlow, 2000; Nagle, Yunker, & Malmgren, 2006). The educational implications of categorizing children by the assessment they take may be a form of expectancy setting resulting in students being denied access to the general curriculum at a challenging and rigorous level. As with other types of labels, expectancy effects loom large. Evidence of low expectations for children with IEPs emerged from *Education Week*'s 2004 survey ("Quality Counts," 2004) of 800 special and general education teachers. Results from that survey indicated that more than eight in ten teachers believed that *most* special education children should be expected to meet a separate set of academic standards, rather than the same standards as others their age. Nearly as many said that special education children should be given an alternate assessment, rather than the same tests as general education children. Findings from the EPRRI study also supported the belief among educators that children with disabilities should not be held to the same achievement standards as other children (Nagle & Crawford, 2005; Nagle, Yunker, & Malmgren, 2006). Most policymakers at the state and district levels, however, expressed the belief that this attitude was slowly changing as the performance of children with IEPs improved and as these students took the regular assessment. For example, a state-level informant from one of EPRRI's study states reflected,

> Historically, we underestimate the ability of children with disabilities generally. We usually set up our instructional programs around those estimates and expectations, which mean that they are almost always lower than they should be. We want to force people to reconsider their expectations and then get on with allowing children to have opportunities they haven't had before. (Nagle, 2004, p. 16)

Categorization Based on Performance Level

Further evidence from the research conducted by EPRRI suggests that schools are also categorizing children with IEPs based on their performance on state assessments. The findings from interviews suggest three categories. First are the children with IEPs who meet or exceed the state's proficient level of performance on the state general or alternate assessments. Second are children with disabilities who scored just below proficient and who narrowly missed making the cut score on the state's assessments. Finally, there are the children whose scores are solidly within the category of basic.

The practice of labeling children by their performance level encourages schools to engage in what Booher-Jennings (2005) referred to as "educational triage." For children who fall in the proficient and advanced categories of achievement, there is a risk that their educational needs will be neglected because they are above the accountability "radar." In other words, a state's proficiency bar becomes a ceiling for children. For children with and without IEPs in this group, there is also a risk that other academic needs may go unaddressed. Indeed, EPRRI researchers found considerable evidence that schools were not directing instructional time or resources toward improving the achievement of the children in the proficient or advanced group. This is not really surprising because once children are proficient there is little incentive to improve their performance.

On the other hand, there is considerable evidence that schools are focusing their resources on interventions on any child who is right below the proficient cutoff. The emphasis is placed on the "almost-passing child," or "bubble" kids, identified by Booher-Jennings (2005). According to Booher-Jennings, schools concentrate on this category of children because they have a chance at moving them over the proficiency bar and improving their ability to make AYP. EPRRI's research supported this contention as practitioners in the majority of schools involved in EPRRI's research indicated that they concentrated their resources on this category of children, *regardless* of whether the child had or did not have an IEP. Teachers and administrators indicated that the school or district had a range of instructional initiatives in place to focus on improving the achievement of these children.

For the children whose performance is well within the basic range, there is a real risk that they may be perceived as "lost causes" and possibly marginalized in school improvement efforts. The school-level practitioners involved in EPRRI's study were particularly perplexed by this group of children with disabilities because they did not believe that there was a way to raise their performance. Many of the individuals interviewed believed that a large proportion of these children fell "in the gap" between the general and alternate state assessments. They felt that a third assessment might be better able to capture progress of these students.

DISCUSSION

In this chapter, we identified and discussed two ways of categorizing children within a performance-based classification system: (1) categorization based on assessment participation and achievement standard, and (2) categorization based on performance level. These categories are not mutually exclusive, although it may be that they build on one another. For example, children may first be categorized according to the type of state assessments they take. Only after a child is categorized by assessment type is he or she categorized by academic achievement standard. Similarly, categorizing based on performance level may occur only after a certain period of time, or for a certain subgroup of children.

Whether these categorizations are evident in the practices of teachers and administrators across all states is not known. Also unknown are the consequences of these new categorizations of children. The extent to which these labels are beneficial, detrimental, or a mixture of both remains to be seen. If performance-based classification results in increased opportunity for children with disabilities to learn academic subject matter then the categorization may be neutral. As the process of referring to performance level is part of the general education lexicon, it may encourage, for some children at least, further inclusion into the larger education system and greater access to general education services and supports. Categorization by assessment or achievement level, however, may create challenges that will be difficult for some children with disabilities to overcome.

REFERENCES

Almond, P., Quenemoen, R., Olsen, K., & Thurlow, M. (2000). *Gray areas of assessment systems* (Synthesis Report No. 32). Minneapolis: University of Minnesota, National Center on Educational Outcomes. Retrieved May 12, 2005, from www.nceo.info/OnlinePubs/Synthesis32.html

Booher-Jennings, J. (2005). Below the bubble: Educational triage and the Texas Accountability System. *American Educational Research Journal, 42*(2), 231–268.

Goertz, M. E., & Duffy, M. C. (2003). Mapping the landscape of high-stakes testing and accountability programs. *Theory Into Practice, 42*(1), 4–11.

Government Accountability Office. (2005). *Most children with disabilities participated in statewide testing, but inclusion options could be improved* (GAO-05–618). Washington, DC: Author.

Nagle, K. M. (2004). *Emerging state-level themes: Strengths and stressors in educational accountability reform* (Topical Review No. 4). University of Maryland: Education Policy Reform Research Institute.

Nagle, K. M., & Crawford, J. (2005). Opportunities and challenges: Perspectives on NCLBA from special education directors in urban school districts. *Journal of Special Education Leadership, 18*(2), 8–13.

Nagle, K. M., Yunker, C. A., & Malmgren, K. W. (2006). Students with disabilities and accountability reform: Can a rising tide raise all boats? *Journal of Disability Policy Studies, 17*(1), 28–39.

President's Commission on Excellence in Special Education. (2002). *New era: Revitalizing special education for children and their families.* Washington, DC: US Department of Education.

"Quality counts: Count me in." (2004, January 8). *Education Week* (Special issue).

Sireci, S. G., Scarpati, S. E., & Li, S. (2005). Test accommodations for children with disabilities: An analysis of the interaction hypothesis. *Review of Educational Research, 75*(4), 457–490.

Thompson, S., Johnstone, C., Thurlow, M. L., & Altman, J. (2005). *2005 state special education outcomes: Steps forward in a decade of change.* Minneapolis: University of Minnesota, National Center on Educational Outcomes. Retrieved May 12, 2005, from http://cehd.umn.edu/nceo/OnlinePubs/2005StateReport.htm

Thurlow, M., Moen, R., & Altman, J. (2006, June). *Annual performance reports: 2003–2004 state assessment data.* Minneapolis: University of Minnesota, National Center on Educational Outcomes. Retrieved May 18, 2005, from www.nceo.info/OnlinePubs/APR2003–04.pdf

United States Department of Education. (2003). *Title I. Improving the Academic Achievement of the Disadvantaged: Final Regulations.* Retrieved September 1, 2005, from http://www.ed.gov/legislation/FedRegister/finrule/2003–4/120903a.html

United States Department of Education. (2005a). *Alternate achievement standards for children with the most significant cognitive disabilities: Non-regulatory guidance.* Retrieved September 1, 2005, from http://www.ed.gov/admins/lead/account/saa.html#guidance

United States Department of Education. (2005b, May). *Flexibility for states raising achievement for children with disabilities* (Fact Sheet). Retrieved August 6, 2005, from http://www.ed.gov/policy/elsec/guid/raising/disab-factsheet.html

United States Department of Education. (2005c, December). *Notice of proposed rulemaking: Children with disabilities and modified achievement standards.* Retrieved February 13, 2006, from http://www.ed.gov/policy/speced/guid/modachieve-nprm-summary.doc

United States Department of Education. (2005d, May). Spellings announces new special education guidelines, details workable, "common-sense" policy to help states implement *No Child Left Behind (Press Release).* Retrieved August 6, 2005, from: http://www.ed.gov/news/pressreleases/2005/05/05102005.html

Wenning, R. J., Herdman, P. A., & Smith, N. (2002). *No Child Left Behind: Who is included in new federal accountability requirements?* Alexandria, VA: New American Schools. (ERIC Document Reproduction Service No. ED469962)

Part III

New Approaches to the
Classification Dilemma

13

International Classification of Functioning, Disability and Health for Children and Youth

A Common Language for Special Education

Rune J. Simeonsson, Nancy E. Simeonsson, and Judith Hollenweger

Special education has preceded the development of a useful taxonomy for children with special needs. The time for addressing the issues both scientifically and in practice is surely upon us now. (Reynolds, 1994, p. 241)

I t is only within the last three decades that children with disabilities have gained the right to education in Western countries; the right to early childhood intervention is even more recent. In many parts of the world, these rights are yet to be realized. Implementation of the right to education of children with disabilities has taken the form of legislative and societal initiatives in the United Kingdom, the United States, and many other countries (United Nations Children's Fund [UNICEF], 1999, 2001; United Nations Educational, Scientific and Cultural Organization [UNESCO], 1994). A prerequisite for implementing the rights of children to education and interventions has been to establish criteria for eligibility. This has typically implied a process of assessing children to determine if the nature and severity of their disability meets established criteria for eligibility. In this context, their conditions are identified and named within some categorical or classification system.

From a historical (Shalick, 2000) as well as contemporary perspective (Munn, 1997; Neville, 2000), it is clear that approaches to classification of children with disabilities not only convey information but also assign value to their conditions. The significance of naming and classification activities related to childhood disability is that they influence perceptions of children's needs and the way in which those needs should be met (Florian et al., 2006). The purpose of this chapter is to examine issues related to the definition and classification of children with disabilities and advance the *International Classification of Functioning, Disability and Health for Children and Youth* (ICF-CY; World Health Organization [WHO], 2007) as a common language for special education. Specifically, this chapter will (a) review issues in defining and classifying childhood disability, (b) identify current problems related to the classification of students with disabilities in educational settings, (c) describe the dimensional paradigm of disability, and (d) advance the ICF-CY as a framework and classification for serving students with disabilities in special education.

DEFINING AND CLASSIFYING CHILDHOOD DISABILITY

In a series of lectures given more than a century ago, Down (1887) described the state of knowledge about the nature of disabilities among children, under the heading "Some of the Mental Affections of Childhood and Youth" (p. 49). Focusing on the terms assigned to define conditions of disability, he concluded that terms such as "idiot" and "imbecile" were used casually and without precision. His position was that such terms needed to be replaced and that more appropriate terms should reflect the concept of limited intellectual ability. The term "moron" should be assigned to describe children whose condition had a congenital etiology whereas the term "feebleminded" would be applicable for children whose condition had a postnatal onset and was characterized by a gradual deterioration of function. In addition to changes in naming, Down also proposed a two-level system to classify problems of mental development among children. The first level of the classification was based on the dimension of ethnicity, in which features of a person corresponding to those of an ethnic group formed the basis for assignment. In this context, Down concluded, "Being able to refer to the child to an ethnic type other than Caucasian settles beyond question that the cause of the malady . . . was antecedent to birth" (p. 49). Included among the ethnic types were Malay, North American Indian, Negroid, Mongolian, and Aztec. A second classification was based on etiology encompassing three subgroups: congenital, accidental, and developmental. Conditions of a congenital nature were those with a hereditary base. Children assigned to the accidental subgroup were those identified on the basis of postnatal insults or injury being identified as "born or ready to be born with all the potentiality of intelligence, but whose brains became damaged by traumatic lesions, by medications or by inflammatory disease" (p. 49). The third subgroup of conditions identified under the heading developmental, encompassed conditions of childhood due to "cases which break down by over-excitement in babyhood and by over-pressure in schools at second dentition and puberty" (p. 49).

Although Down's classification of childhood problems on the basis of ethnicity is inconsistent with contemporary conceptions of disability, the other three components proposed by Down in 1887 can be seen to have anticipated current classification approaches based on a medical model of disability. Some of the medical conditions in his classification can be identified under diagnostic entries in the *International Statistical Classification of Diseases and Related Health Problems* (ICD–10; WHO, 1992), and others of a more psychiatric nature in the *Diagnostic and Statistical Manual of Mental Disorders* (*DSM–IV–TR*; American Psychiatric Association, 2000). Historically, however, the absence of a single taxonomy of disability has resulted in substantial variability of naming of childhood disability across disciplines and service settings. The ICD-10, for example, has been used to document etiology. Documentation of mental disorders is primarily done with the *DSM–IV–TR* in psychiatric and mental health settings. In educational settings, on the other hand, a list of selected categories, usually medically based, is used in the absence of an established taxonomy.

A key problem of medically based disability categories in education is inconsistency in the use of terms. Terms such as "visual impairment," "visual disability," and "visual handicap" are often used interchangeably. Similarly, "learning impairment," "learning disabilities," and "learning disorders" are terms used without clear distinction. Do these terms refer to the same condition and do they describe the same populations, respectively? If they have an equivalent meaning, why are different terms used to define the deficit? Terminological variability and lack of consistency in referring to children with disabilities reflect a significant semantic problem in special education. Inconsistencies in terminology are particularly problematic in more prevalent groups in special education, such as children with learning difficulties, emotional or behavior problems, or limited cognitive ability. A review of literature provides illustrations of such inconsistencies in that children with emotional or behavioral problems have been referred to by the following terms: "emotionally behaviorally disturbed," "emotional and behavioral disorder," "seriously emotionally disturbed," "behavioral disabilities," and "severe behavior handicapped." With reference to mental retardation, students have been referred to as "mildly mentally retarded," "mildly handicapped," "mild MR," and "handicapped students." In regard to children with learning difficulties, the following terms are represented in the literature: "learning disorder," "learning disability," "moderate learning difficulties," and "mild LD."

In addition to variability of terms in special education and other services for children with disabilities, are problems associated with the casual use of adjectives, presumptive application of qualifiers, inconsistent use of terminology, and labeling with nouns. Casual use of adjectives in the literature, for example, include the "swallowing impaired child," "communication disabled child," "multihandicapped child," and "crawling, crippled child." The word "disorder" has seen increased use with a common practice being one in which it is preceded by a specific condition. Examples include "neurodevelopmentally disordered child," "conduct disordered child," "phonologically disordered child," "behavior disordered child," and "language disordered child." Inconsistent terminology is also evident in the variety of terms used to describe the condition of limited cognitive ability. In this case, the word "mentally" is combined with terms such as "deficient," "retarded," "handicapped," "challenged," and "impaired." The question that can be asked is, do these different names define different conditions or reflect a common underlying condition? Among the most problematic form of naming is using words defining the condition to assign labels to individuals such as "multiply impaired," "spastics," "deaf-mutes," "autistics," and "mental retardates." Each of these terms reflects a status of denigration with adjectives converted to nouns. A final naming misuse is when terms used to define disability in persons are extended to objects, such as "handicapped parking," "handicapped room," "handicapped permit," "disabled room," and "disabled parking." These problems of inconsistency and misuse in naming illustrate the lack of a standard conception and language of disability.

CLASSIFICATION PROBLEMS IN EDUCATION

The right to education of children with disabilities, as that of all children, is embodied in international declarations and national legislation. The

United Nations Convention on the Rights of the Child (UN, 1989), paragraph 23, has defined the rights of children with disabilities in broad terms based on principles of equality of opportunity, participation, and independence for full citizenship. "Education for All" is a representative declaration endorsing such rights, but its implementation brings challenges of identification of children with disabilities and provision of services (Hollenweger, 2003). The Special Educational Needs and Disability Act (SENDA) in the United Kingdom (Sanderson-Mann & McCandless, 2005) and the Individuals with Disabilities Education Act (IDEA) in the United States (http://idea.ed.gov) are legislative acts affirming that all students with disabilities have the right to education. These acts have advanced ideals for policies and services to enhance the development and quality of life of individuals with disabilities from infancy through adolescence. Their implementation and translation into appropriate interventions have raised significant questions about defining disability, determination of eligibility, provision of clinical services, and formulation of policy. Key challenges associated with these questions have been the lack of a comprehensive conceptual model of disability, a corresponding classification system, and functional assessment. Policies and practices in special education may vary across countries with approaches to defining disability based on some conception of diagnoses, categories, and special needs without a consistent conceptual frame. Usually, disability has been defined within a medical model and drawn on etiological or diagnostic criteria. The variable base for the categorical system has contributed to problems in defining eligibility, designing individualized interventions, and in the transition of students from one educational level to another as well as from one service system to another.

Variability in classification of childhood disability has been problematic in health and education in terms of conceptual, methodological, as well as measurement issues (Simeonsson, 2006). Fundamental to these issues is how disability in childhood is viewed. In the United Kingdom and some other European countries, the approach in education is to view the child as having "special needs," whereas in the United States the child is viewed as having a disability defined in terms of one of thirteen diagnostic categories. As noted in previous chapters, children in the United Kingdom identified as having special education needs (SEN) are those who (1) manifest significantly greater learning difficulties than their age peers or (2) have a disability that prevents or restricts them from using the educational facilities generally provided for their age peers. A similar concept of children with special education needs is also the basis for special education policy in Spain (Gonzalez & Valle, 1999). Holt (2003) has expressed concern about the conception of special needs in SENDA in its vagueness with reference to a norm of deviance and location of disability in the child. A challenge within a "special needs" perspective is to operationalize the nature and severity of the child's learning difficulties and to account for restrictions accessing environmental resources. With reference to diagnostic categories in the United States, representative questions have been raised about attention deficit hyperactivity disorder (Bussing, Zima, Pervwien, Belin, & Widawski, 1998; Silver, 1990), traumatic brain injury (Clark, 1996; Savage, DePompei, Tyler, & Lash, 2005), and conceptual and applied issues regarding learning disability as a diagnostic group (Finlan, 1994). Semantic and conceptual issues in turn contribute to scientific problems such as instability of categorical assignment (Halgren & Clarizio, 1993), the sociocultural dimensions of learning disabilities (Keogh, Gallimore, Weisner, & Weisner, 1997), and more broadly to the need for greater recognition of individual differences in order for special education to be effective (Detterman & Thompson, 1997).

Compounding the above problem associated with the categorization of children in special education is loss of information when data are aggregated at local or national levels. The current practice in the United States is to utilize the thirteen categories to derive head counts of the population served in special education at the state and federal level. Although the nature and number of these categories in the United States have remained relatively constant across the legislative dates from 1976 to the present, changes have occurred in this list with deletions of some categories and the addition of others. A change occurred in the 1991 reauthorization of IDEA with replacement of the word "handicap" with the word "disability." This was, however, simply a change in terminology and not a change in an underlying distinction between the concepts of handicap and disability. Assignment to the thirteen current IDEA categories differs on the basis of eligibility in terms of etiology (e.g., traumatic brain injury), diagnoses (e.g., autism, mental retardation), and health conditions (e.g., other health impairment). As such, they do not represent dimensions of an underlying conceptual framework. Given reliance on diagnostic categories that are often operationalized differently from one system or locale to another, it is difficult to compare data aggregated at the national level. Another problem pertains to the fact that overlap is likely in the assignment of children to a category of disability. Thus, it is not clear to what extent a child may have co-occurring disabilities or impairments. These and other representative concerns are in keeping with Reynolds' (1994) position that special education practice has been carried out in the absence of a consistent definitional approach or systematic taxonomy.

Inconsistencies in the conceptualization, classification, and functional assessment of childhood disability thus constitute persistent problems influencing eligibility determination, provision of educational and related clinical services, and research efforts in special education. Classification approaches with infants and young children at risk or with disabilities may vary as a function of age and policies of the early intervention service system with resulting variability likely for determination of eligibility (Simeonsson, 1991). Variability is likely in the way disability is defined in special education programs as well as other social service agencies. In a review of federal statutory definitions of disability in the United States, for example, Domzal (1995) identified eleven different federal acts with accompanying definitions pertaining to children. In these acts, not only did terminology vary for the population including such terms as "handicapped children," but the definitional criteria varied substantially as well. Variability of definitional criteria at the federal level is often exacerbated at the state level. This variability is in no small part attributable to the lack of a common conceptual framework of disability. The result of this variability and lack of definitional consistency is not only that eligibility for services varies as a function of age and agency, but also that it precludes statistical summation of early intervention populations and comparative research (Aron, Loprest, & Steuberle, 1996).

A wide range of terms is used to describe the population served in special education and allied health fields. Definitions of disabilities vary as a function of age groups with disability defined differently in adults from disability in school-age children who differ in turn from infants and toddlers. Problems in defining and classifying childhood disability have from time to time led to the search for approaches to conceptualize disability in alternative and more coherent ways. A prime example of the search for an alternate classification approach was the work of Hobbs (1975a, 1975b) and his colleagues in the 1970s. As noted by Burke and Ruedel in Chapter 5, Hobbs and his colleagues (Hobbs, 1975b), in response to a directive from the US secretary of health, education, and welfare, reviewed the issue of disability classification of children. In a follow-up volume, Hobbs (1975a) concluded that whereas there were real problems with the categorical approach, it served bureaucratic functions of the service systems in terms of determining eligibility for the provision of services. Hobbs did propose an alternative system based on a functional perspective of children's needs that

> should emphasize services required, not types of children; it should link etiology, current status, intervention and outcome; it should identify assets as well as liabilities; it should be sensitive to the developmental status of the child, to his strengths as well as weaknesses; it should include the matrix of other persons significant in the life of the child, as well as settings; and it should be dated and its validity bound to a limited period of time. (Hobbs, 1975a, p. 234)

Although this comprehensive system was not implemented, its major premises are consistent with calls for a functional approach to assessment and classification of disability in childhood over the last decade.

There has been growing interest in a functional basis for assessment and classification in health, rehabilitation, and educational contexts. Models of disabilities (Munn, 1997) and approaches, however, have not been based on a comprehensive conceptual framework that could integrate disability across developmental stages, across different conditions, and across different service systems. More recently, there has been growing interest in documentation at the population level of limitations of functioning (Halfon & Newacheck, 1999; Hughes, Halfon, Brindis, & Newacheck, 1996; LaPlante & Carlson, 1995; Mudrick, 2002) and emotion (Costello et al., 1996; Costello, Mustillo, Erkanli, Keeler, & Angold, 2005). Further, these approaches have not readily related to special education categories for an integrated approach to disability data.

The above review has identified a number of issues related to the special needs and categorical approaches to define disabilities of children in special education. Central to both of these major approaches has been the lack of a conceptually based, comprehensive framework for defining characteristics associated with disabilities. To have a useful classification system, a conceptually based framework is needed that is sufficiently comprehensive to encompass the dimensions of functioning in children and compatible with issues related to transition to adulthood (Hallum, 1995). Given the mandate of special education, such a classification should be particularly inclusive of dimensions relevant to the learning and social demands of schooling. This is in keeping with Reynolds' (1994) suggestion that "classification of children in the schools should probably be based mainly on progress in curriculum and oriented mainly to problems of instruction" (p. 240). The availability of a comprehensive conceptual model and a taxonomical system to classify disability in a consistent manner across different points of development would clearly serve an important role in practice, policy, and research.

THE DIMENSIONAL PARADIGM OF DISABILITY

Basic to a comprehensive approach for defining and classifying disability in childhood is to build on current bio-psycho-social (Engel, 1992) and social (Colver, 2005; Shakespeare, 2005) models of disability. A major premise of these models is recognition of the functioning and disability as the interaction between the person and the environment. There is an associated premise that etiology and underlying health conditions are different from manifestations of function and performance of activities (Bickenbach, Chatterji, Badley, & Ustun, 1999).

Within this perspective, the primary focus of classification of disability in special education should be identification of the characteristics that define the nature and extent of children's performance limitations in meeting the physical, social, and psychological tasks encountered in the school environment. With reference to the educational context, a more direct focus on functions associated with learning should be part of a comprehensive classification of disability in special education. Research in educational and experimental psychology has provided ample documentation of functional limitations of children with disabilities such as looking, listening, attending, short- and long-term memory, and comprehension skills. Classification of these functional skills would provide comprehensive documentation of problems of learning, information processing, and social adaptation among students in special education. Of related importance is documentation of behaviors essential to relationships and social participation. Classification of such behaviors is also of value given their role in mediating student performance on individual and social tasks.

The importance of distinguishing between underlying health conditions and their consequences has served as the basis for the development of several conceptual models of disability (Table 12.1). These models have drawn on the concept of disablement as a process in which an underlying health condition is manifested at different levels of human functioning, typically defined as the body, person, and societal level (Institute of Medicine, 1991; Nagi, 1965; National Center for Medical Rehabilitation Research [NCMRR], 1993). For three of the conceptual models, there are associated taxonomies—the first one being the experimental version of the *International Classification of Impairments, Disabilities and Handicaps* (ICIDH; WHO, 1980). The ICIDH represented a visionary contribution to the field of disability when it was published in that it distinguished underlying health conditions from their consequences of impairments, disabilities, and handicaps. It also provided a taxonomy for documenting those consequences in terms of impairments as abnormalities of structure; disabilities as reduced abilities to perform basic skills; and handicaps as disadvantage in fulfilling roles expected for age, gender, and culture. The ICIDH was characterized by conceptual and content limitations, including lack of coverage of disability of childhood (Simeonsson, Lollar, Hollowell, & Adams, 2000), but saw some experimental use as a taxonomy to document the nature and distribution of disability (Diderichsen et al., 1990). The second model of disablement with an associated classification, the Life Habits Assessment (LIFE-H) was developed by the Quebec Committee on the ICIDH (Fougeyrollas, 1995; Fougeyrollas et al., 1998). Application of this classification has been primarily with adults although it has been used to assess the experience of disability of children with cerebral palsy (LePage, Noreau, Bernard, & Fougeyrollas, 1998).

Table 12.1   Dimensional Paradigms of Disability

Classification Model	Underlying Cause/Etiology	Limitations at Body Level	Limitations at Person Level	Limitations at Societal Level	Environment
Nagi/Institute of Medicine	Pathology	Impairment	Functional limitations	Disability	
NCMRR	Pathology	Impairment	Functional limitations	Disability	Societal limitations
1980 ICIDH	Disease, injury	Impairment	Disability	Handicap	
Quebec Committee Classification (LIFE-H)	Risk factors	Organ systems	Capacities	Life habits	Environment
2001 ICF	Health conditions	Body functions and structures	Activities	Participation	Environment

The experimental nature of the ICIDH and a number of associated limitations led to the initiation of a revision of the ICIDH beginning in the early 1990s. Main considerations underlying the revision effort were to address linear assumptions of the ICIDH and to build on the concept of disablement that recognized disability as dynamic and a product of interactions with the environment (Halbertsma et al., 2000; Verbrugge & Jette, 1994). The result of that revision was the publication of the *International Classification of Functioning, Disability and Health* (ICF) by the World Health Organization in 2001. Disability is presented as an umbrella term in the ICF, incorporating problems of body function and structure, performance of activities, and participation. This is evident in the structure of the taxonomy as illustrated in the interaction of components in Figure 12.1 (WHO, 2001). In the ICF, health and functioning are classified across the three dimensions of body function, body structures, and activities, and participation with the environment constituting a fourth classification domain allowing documentation of the extent to which environmental factors serve as barriers or facilitators.

Although publication of the ICF offered a comprehensive taxonomy of functioning and disability, it was recognized that it was not inclusive of the developing characteristics of children and youth (Simeonsson, Leonardi, Lollar, Björck-Åkesson, Hollenweger, & Martinuzzi, 2003). To that end, a derived version of the ICF for children and youth (ICF-CY) was prepared by an international work group and published in 2007. Reflecting the dimensional models shown in Table 12.1, the ICF-CY offers an integrated

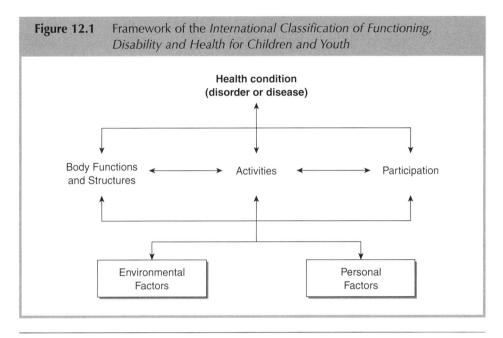

Figure 12.1 Framework of the *International Classification of Functioning, Disability and Health for Children and Youth*

SOURCE: Adapted from the World Health Organization (WHO) (2007).

conceptualization of disability in childhood. First, the dimensional approach of the ICF-CY provides a perspective of disability as a multifaceted phenomenon. Second, documenting manifestations across dimensions serves to classify functional characteristics, not classification of diagnoses or persons. Documentation of characteristics across dimensions has direct implications for identifying resources and supports for individuals or populations. Building on these contributions, a third benefit is that the ICF-CY provides a framework for greater specificity in selecting measures to assess the dimension of relevance for providing interventions. It should be noted that the Quebec, ICF, and ICF-CY taxonomies offer frameworks for the documentation of individual functioning in environmental contexts. The value of a dimensional model for special education is that the unit of classification would be shifted from the child's diagnosis to functional characteristics of the child. This is an important distinction and in keeping with a holistic and non-stigmatizing approach to disability.

TOWARD A COMMON LANGUAGE OF DISABILITY IN SPECIAL EDUCATION

The publication of the ICF-CY in the WHO family of classifications offers a comprehensive framework with broad implications for children in terms of policy, epidemiological studies, service provision, and research. Important applications include (1) classification of functioning and health for children served in a variety of service sectors, (2) identifying national goals for reducing inequalities in access to child health care, and (3) documenting profiles of functional limitations of children in clinical and related service settings. In regard to services, the ICF-CY can provide a framework for specifying the intended domain of impact in terms of body function or structure, performance of activities, or participation in social and societal roles.

Within the ICF-CY framework, the focus of classification is on the child's response to the demands of schooling in terms of activity limitations and participation restrictions experienced by a child rather than the diagnosed condition. The value of differentiating functional manifestations from underlying conditions can be illustrated in the categorical basis for special education eligibility of two children. Eligibility on the basis of traumatic brain injury or learning disabilities would be premised on distinct differences associated with diagnosed conditions. Both children, however, may share common functional limitations of attending, recalling, performing academic tasks, and participating in class and social activities. Thus, for both children, documented problems of recall would be classified as impairments of body function, reading difficulties as limitations of performance in school activities, and problems taking turns in class discussions as restrictions of participation.

With publication of the ICF in 2001 and publication of the ICF-CY in 2007, there is growing interest in their application in various fields including physical medicine, rehabilitation, psychology, and nursing (Heinen, van Acthenberg, Roodbol, & Frederiks, 2005; Institute of Medicine, 2006; Kearney & Pryor, 2004; Müller-Staub, Lavin, Needham, & van Achtenberg, 2006; Simeonsson et al., 2003). The applicability of the ICF for early childhood assessment and intervention (Almqvist, Hellnas, Stefansson, & Granlund, 2006), for special education (Florian et al., 2006; Hamlin & Simeonsson, 2006), and for the field of mental retardation (Simeonsson, Granlund & Björck-Åkesson, 2006) has also been recognized. In Japan, the National Institute on Special Education has published a manual for the use of the ICF as a guide to practice (Tokunaga, 2006). In the United States, a limited set of ICF codes has been included in a handbook for data managers (Early Intervention Data Handbook, n.d.).

Two specific contributions of the ICF-CY can be identified for child health and education settings. First, it provides a conceptual model consistent with a holistic and interdisciplinary approach to childhood disability (Simeonsson, 2006). The major goal of early intervention, special education, and rehabilitation is to prevent or reduce the disablement process and to minimize the consequences on the child's quality of life. A second contribution is that it provides a comprehensive taxonomy to document separate dimensions of human functioning and the impact of environmental factors. Documentation of the extent to which child functioning is associated with adaptation to social roles with participation codes of ICF-CY often corresponds to dimensions currently of interest in measurement of quality of life.

There are at least seven contributions of the ICF-CY that can be considered for special education. At a universal level, the ICF-CY may serve as a standard reference for defining the rights of children. The UN Convention on the Rights of the Child (UN, 1989) has defined the rights of children with disabilities in terms of principles of equality of opportunity, participation, and independence. Embedded in these rights are access to care, education, and support, and protection from neglect and exploitation. Although such rights are often implicit in legislation of Western countries, the ICF-CY may provide the basis for explicit documentation of rights (Corker & Davis, 2000; Lansdown, 2000). This may be of particular significance in developing countries where the right to education of children is often abridged and where children with disabilities are unlikely to have access to schooling (Simeonsson, 2003; Simeonsson, Björck-Åkesson, & Bairrao, 2006). To this end, restricted access to education may be documented with ICF-CY codes serving as evidence of the deprivation of rights of the individual child or a population.

A second contribution of the ICF-CY is a framework for integrating multidisciplinary efforts (Allan, Campbell, Guptill, Stephenson, & Campbell, 2006). The model of the ICF-CY components (Figure 12.1) can frame the multidisciplinary activities of assessment, intervention, and monitoring of progress and outcomes. In this regard, assessment typically involves the domains of body functions, body structures, and activities whereas intervention focuses on improving performance of activities and achieving participation outcomes. Identification of barriers and supports with environmental factors is an important element of each component of interdisciplinary work. Of particular relevance to the school setting is that the disciplines of special education, allied health, nursing, and psychology can share the common language of the ICF-CY in documenting characteristics of the child and identifying needed interventions and environmental supports. This contribution can reduce the problem of discipline-specific languages that may restrict a holistic and integrated view of the child.

A third way in which the ICF-CY can contribute to special education practice is in the derivation of profiles of child functioning. Instead of classifying students, the ICF-CY can yield a profile of the students' problems of body function or structure, activities, and participation. This is a key distinction and in keeping with a holistic and nonstigmatizing approach to disability. Further, identification documentation can be made of environmental factors that represent barriers to performance of activities and participation.

As the characteristics of children with disabilities reflect performance limitations, eligibility for special education should in turn be based on profiles reflecting the nature and extent of their functional limitations in meeting the demands of the school environment. Accompanying such profiles should be documentation of significant environmental barriers. Within the ICF-CY framework, the IDEA definition of children eligible for special education in the United States could be rewritten for example as:

> Children with disabilities means (1) children with functional limitations in activities of . . . listening, communicating, attending, learning, undertaking tasks, managing behavior, relating to others, and (2) who by reason thereof need special education and related services.

A fourth contribution of the ICF-CY is that profiles of functional characteristics can also be used to plan individualized interventions by matching characteristics with needed supports or resources. The profiles are descriptive of those factors that define a child's difficulties in meeting the demands of schooling with documentation of environmental factors that mediate learning and adaptation. The profiles should have direct implications for the derivation of individualized plans for instruction.

A fifth contribution is that the ICF-CY can guide the selection of measures for assessment or outcome monitoring (Granlund, Eriksson, & Ylven, 2004). In this regard the ICF-CY framework can promote the development of new instruments with more direct correspondence to the important domains of activities (Wells & Hogan, 2003), participation (Forsyth & Jarvis, 2002), and environmental factors. In a related manner, the ICF-CY can also provide the basis for defining relevant domains for outcome documentation in special education. The ICF-CY components of body functions, body structures, and activities offer content for assessment measures and participation codes are consistent with the identification of intervention outcomes. The component of environmental factors can address the lack of available instruments to assess children's environments. The current focus on evidence-based practice suggests that outcomes can be defined by changes in participation. Thus, the child's mastery of skills, personal independence, social integration, and developmental or academic transitions would constitute outcomes of special education consistent with ICF-CY participation codes.

In a related area, a sixth contribution of the ICF-CY is the use of severity qualifiers and codes to document change of child functioning. A reduction in the value of the severity qualifier for a code of functioning from severe (3) to mild (1) can reflect a positive gradient of change from an earlier to a later assessment. A shift from a lower code to a higher code within a hierarchy, for example, completing a simple task (ICF-CY-d2104.2) to completing a complex task (ICF- CY-d2105.2), could serve to document a qualitative nature of outcome.

It is also clear that there will be increased utilization of technology in the definition and assessment of biological and functional manifestations of disability. From the biological side, contributions from research on the human genome will allow increasingly more precise identification of etiology and markers of specific syndromes. Thus it is likely that students will be identified on the basis of specific syndromes rather than by categories such as mental retardation, learning disabilities, or speech and language disabilities. For example, it is becoming common to find children referred to as a child with "Williams syndrome," "Asperger syndrome," or "Rett syndrome" (Leonard, Fyfes, Leonard, & Msall, 2001). Children with each of these syndromes present with unique physical, behavioral, and/or psychological characteristics that differentiate them from other children with disabilities. However, description of their characteristics as well as that of any child with disabilities should capture impairment and disability as variations of human functioning. This is consistent with recommendations to view children with chronic conditions in a noncategorical framework (Stein & Silver, 1999, 2002). It is also recognized that there will be a continued need to aggregate data to document the nature and distribution of functional manifestations of congenital or acquired conditions of children (McDougall & Miller, 2003) extended to special education. The use of the ICF-CY could increase the precision of statistical databases with significant implications for documenting the type of resources used and for projecting future resource needs as a function of changing prevalence patterns. Further, from a perspective of functions, technological advances will improve our understanding of structure-function relationships through imaging techniques and neuropsychological tests. Research advances in these and other areas can benefit from the common language of the ICF-CY in documenting independent and dependent variables related to disability in childhood.

Recognition of the central role of the environment (Bronfenbrenner, 1999) and its documentation is one of the significant contributions of the ICF-CY with important implications for children and adults with disabilities. Ongoing advances in the engineering of the physical and social environment and availability of assistive technology will result in expanded opportunities for achievement and school participation. Tasks required of students in the school environment are of direct relevance for assessment and documentation under relevant chapters and codes of the ICF-CY.

Current research on disability verifies that limitations and restrictions of activities and participation experienced by children and adults with disabilities are as dependent on access to physical and social contexts as on etiological factors. A priority for research is identification of environmental factors that are effective in promoting student functioning and performance in school settings. To that end, a common language for matching characteristics of the child with the environment can enhance the educational experience of students with disabilities and contribute to a fuller realization of their potential.

REFERENCES

Allan, C. M., Campbell, W. N., Guptill, C. A., Stephenson, F. F., & Campbell, K. E. (2006). A conceptual model for interprofessional education: The *International classification of functioning, disability and health* (ICF). *Journal of Interprofessional Care, 20*(3), 235–245.

Almqvist, L., Hellnas, P., Stefansson, M., & Granlund, M. (2006). "I can play!" Young children's perceptions of health. *Pediatric Rehabilitation, 9*(3), 275–284.

American Psychiatric Association. (2000). *Diagnostic and statistical manual of mental disorders* (4th ed., text revision). Washington, DC: Author.

Aron, L. Y., Loprest, P. J., & Steuberle, C. E. (1996). *Serving children with disabilities: A systematic look at the programs.* Washington, DC: Urban Press.

Bickenbach, J. E., Chatterji, S., Badley, E. M., & Ustun, T. B. (1999). Models of disablement, universalism and the *International classification of impairments, disabilities and handicaps. Social Science & Medicine, 48,* 1173–1187.

Bronfenbrenner, U. (1999). Environments in developmental perspective: Theoretical and operational models. In S. L. Friedman & T. D. Wachs (Eds.), *Measuring environment across the life span: Emerging methods and concepts* (pp. 3–28). Washington, DC: American Psychological Association.

Bussing, R., Zima, B. T., Pervwien, A. R., Belin, T. R., & Widawski, M. (1998). Children in special education programs: Attention deficit hyperactivity disorder, use of services, and unmet needs. *American Journal of Public Health, 88*(6), 880–886.

Clark, E. (1996). Children and adolescents with traumatic brain injury: Reintegration challenges in educational settings. *Journal of Learning Disabilities, 29*(5), 549–560.

Colver, A. (2005). A shared framework and language for childhood disability. *Developmental Medicine and Child Neurology, 47,* 780–784.

Corker, M., & Davis, J. M. (2000). Disabled children: (Still) invisible under the law. In J. Cooper (Ed.), *Law, rights, and disability* (pp. 217–238). London: Jessica Kingsley.

Costello, E. J., Angold, A., Burns, B. J., Erkanli, A., Stangl, D. K., & Tweed, D. L. (1996). The Great Smoky Mountains Study of Youth: Functional impairment and serious emotional disturbance. *Archives of General Psychiatry, 53*(12), 1137–1143.

Costello, E. J., Mustillo, S., Erkanli, A., Keeler, G., & Angold, A. (2003). Prevalence and development of psychiatric disorders in childhood and adolescence. *Archives of General Psychiatry, 60,* 837–844.

Detterman, D. K., & Thompson, L. A. (1997). What is so special about special education? *American Psychologist, 52*(10), 1082–1090.

Diderichsen, J., Ferngren, H., Hansen, F. J., Lindman, C., Kallio, T., Lagergren, J., et al. (1990). The handicap code of the ICIDH, adapted for children aged 6–7 years: Classification group of the Nordic Neuropediatric Association. *International Disability Studies, 12,* 54–60.

Domzal, C. (1995). *Federal statutory definitions of disability.* Falls Church, VA: Conwal Incorporated. Unpublished manuscript.

Down, J. L. (1887). Abstracts of the Lettsomian lectures on some of the mental affections of childhood and youth. *British Medical Journal, 8,* 49–50.

Early Intervention Data Handbook. (n.d.). Available at http://www.ideadata .org/EarlyInterventionDataHandbook.asp

Engel, G. L. (1992). How much longer must medicine's science be bound by a seventeenth century world view? *Psychotherapy and Psychosomatics, 57,* 3–16.

Finlan, T. G. (1994). *Learning disability: The imaginary disease.* Westport, CT: Bergin & Harvey.

Florian, L., Hollenweger, J., Simeonsson, R. J., Wedell, K., Riddell, S., Terzi, L., & Holland, A. (2006). Cross-cultural perspectives on the classification of children with disabilities: Part 1. Issues in the classification of children with disabilities. *Journal of Special Education, 40*(1), 3–45.

Forsyth, R., & Jarvis, S. (2002). Participation in childhood. *Child: Care, Health and Development, 28*(4), 277–279.

Fougeyrollas, P. (1995). Documenting environmental factors for preventing the handicap creation process: Quebec contributions relating to ICIDH and social participation of people with functional difference. *Disability & Rehabilitation, 17*(3–4), 145–153.

Fougeyrollas, P., Noreau, L., Bergeron, H., Cloutier, R., Dion, S. A., & St-Michel, G. (1998). Social consequences of long term impairments and disabilities: Conceptual approach and assessment of handicap. *International Journal of Rehabilitation Research, 21*(2), 127–141.

Gonzalez, J. E. J., & Valle, I. H. (1999). A Spanish perspective on LD. *Journal of Learning Disabilities, 32*(3), 267–275.

Granlund, M., Eriksson, L., & Ylven, R. (2004). Utility of the *International classification of functioning, disability and health* participation dimension in assigning ICF codes to items for extant rating instruments. *Journal of Rehabilitation Medicine, 36*(3), 130–137.

Halbertsma, J., Heerkens, Y. F., Hirs, W. M., Kleiijn-de Vrankrikjer, M. W., Van Ravensberg, C. D., & Napel, H. T. (2000). Towards a new ICIDH. *Disability and Rehabilitation, 22,* 144–156.

Halfon, N., & Newacheck, P. (1999). Prevalence and impact of parent reported disabling mental health conditions among U.S. children. *Journal of the American Academy of Child and Adolescent Psychiatry, 38*(5), 600–609.

Halgren, D. W., & Clarizio, H. F. (1993). Categorical and programming changes in special education services. *Exceptional Children, 59*(6), 547–555.

Hallum, A. (1995). Disability and the transition to adulthood: Issues for the disabled child, the family and the pediatrician. *Current Problems in Pediatrics, 25*(1), 12–50.

Hamlin, T., & Simeonsson, R. J. (2006). Special education. In G. L. Albrecht (General Ed.), *Encyclopedia of disability* (pp. 565–572). Thousand Oaks, CA: Sage Publications.

Heinen, M. M., van Acthenberg, T., Roodbol, G., & Frederiks, C. M. (2005). Applying the ICF in nursing practice: Classifying elements of nursing diagnoses. *International Nursing Review, 52*(4), 304–312.

Hobbs, N. (1975a). *The futures of children: Categories, labels, and their consequences.* San Francisco: Jossey-Bass.

Hobbs, N. (Ed.). (1975b). *Issues in the classification of children: A sourcebook on categories, labels, and their consequences* (2 vols.). San Francisco: Jossey-Bass.

Hollenweger, J. (2003). Internationale perspektiven einer pädagogik für alle. *Schweizerische Zeitschrift fur Heilpädagogik, 1*(04), 6–12.

Holt, L. (2003). (Dis)abling children in primary school micro-spaces: Geographies of inclusion and exclusion. *Health & Place, 9,* 119–128.

Hughes, D., Halfon, N., Brindis, C., & Newacheck, P. (1996). Improving children's access to health care: The role of decategorization. *Bulletin of the New York Academy of Medicine, 73,* 237–254.

Individuals with Disabilities Education Act. (2004). Available at http://idea.ed.gov

Institute of Medicine. (1991). *Disability in America: Toward a national agenda for prevention.* Washington, DC: National Academy Press.

Institute of Medicine. (2006). *Workshop on Disability in America: a new look.* Washington, DC: National Academy Press.

Kearney, B. P. M., & Pryor, J. (2004). The *International classification of functioning, disability and health* (ICF) and nursing. *Journal of Advanced Nursing, 46*(2), 162–170.

Keogh, B. K., Gallimore, R., Weisner, T., & Weisner, T. S. (1997). A sociocultural perspective on learning and learning disabilities. *Learning Disabilities Research & Practice, 12,* 107–113.

Lansdown, G. (2000). Implementing children's rights and health. *Archives of Disease in Childhood, 83,* 286–288.

LaPlante, M., & Carlson, D. (1995). *Disability in the United States: Prevalence and causes, 1992* (Report of the Disability Statistics Rehabilitation Research and Training Center). Washington, DC: National Institute on Disability and Rehabilitation Research.

Leonard, H., Fyfes, S., Leonard, S., & Msall, M. (2001). Functional status, medical impairments, and rehabilitation resources in 84 females with Rett syndrome: A snapshot across the world from the parental perspective. *Disability and Rehabilitation, 23,* 107–117.

LePage, C., Noreau, L., Bernard, P-M., & Fougeyrollas, P. (1998). Profile of handicap situations in children with cerebral palsy. *Scandinavian Journal of Rehabilitation Medicine, 30,* 263–272.

McDougall, J., & Miller, L. T. (2003). Measuring chronic health condition and disability as distinct concepts in national surveys of school-aged children in Canada: A comprehensive review with recommendations based on the ICD-10 and ICF. *Disability and Rehabilitation, 25*(16), 922–939.

Mudrick, N. R. (2002). The prevalence of disability among children: Paradigms and estimates. *Physical Medicine and Rehabilitation Clinics of North America, 13,* 775–792.

Müller-Staub, M., Lavin, M. A., Needham, I., & van Achtenberg, T. (2006). Meeting the criteria of nursing diagnosis classification: Evaluation of ICNP®, ICF, NANDA and ZEFP. *International Journal of Nursing Studies, 44*(5), 702–713.

Munn, P. (1997). Models of disability for children. *Disability and Rehabilitation, 19*(11), 484–486.

Nagi, S. Z. (1965). Some conceptual issues in disability and rehabilitation. In M. B. Sussman (Ed.), *Sociology and rehabilitation* (pp. 100–113). Washington, DC: American Sociological Association.

National Center for Medical Rehabilitation Research. (1993). *Research plan for the National Center for Medical Rehabilitation Research.* Washington, DC: National Institutes of Health.

Neville, B. (2000). Tertiary pediatrics needs a disability model. *Archives of Disease in Childhood, 83,* 35–37.

Reynolds, M. C. (1994). Child disabilities: Who's in, who's out. *Journal of School Health, 64,* 239–241.

Sanderson-Mann, J., & McCandless, F. (2005). Guidelines to the United Kingdom Disability Discrimination Act (DDA) 1995 and the Special Educational Needs and Disability Act (SENDA) 2001 with regard to nurse education and dyslexia. *Nurse Education Today, 25,* 542–549.

Savage, R. C., DePompei, R., Tyler, J., & Lash, M. (2005). Paediatric traumatic injury: A review of pertinent issues. *Pediatric Rehabilitation, 8*(2), 92–103.

Shakespeare, T. (2005). Review article: Disability studies today and tomorrow. *Sociology of Health and Illness, 27*(1), 138–148.

Shalick, W. O. (2000). Children, disability and rehabilitation in history. *Pediatric Rehabilitation, 4*(2), 91–95.

Silver, L. (1990). Attention deficit-hyperactivity disorder: Is it a learning disability or a related disorder? *Journal of Learning Disabilities, 23*(7), 394–397.

Simeonsson, R. J. (1991). Primary, secondary and tertiary prevention in early intervention. *Journal of Early Intervention, 15*(2), 124–134.

Simeonsson, R. J. (2003). *Early childhood development and children with disabilities in developing countries* (Commissioned report for the World Bank). Washington, DC: World Bank.

Simeonsson, R. J. (2006). Defining and classifying childhood disability. In *Workshop on Disability in America* (pp. 67–87). Washington, DC: Institute of Medicine, National Academy Press.

Simeonsson, R. J., Björck-Åkesson, E., & Bairrao, J. (2006). Children's rights. In G. L. Albrecht (General Ed.), *Encyclopedia of disability* (pp. 257–259). Thousand Oaks, CA: Sage Publications.

Simeonsson, R. J., Granlund, M., & Björck-Åkesson, E. (2006). The concept and classification of mental retardation. In H. Switzky & S. Greenspan (Eds.), *What is mental retardation? Ideas for an evolving disability in the 21st century* (pp. 247–266). Washington, DC: American Association on Mental Retardation.

Simeonsson, R. J., Leonardi, M., Lollar, D., Björck-Åkesson, E., Hollenweger, J., & Martinuzzi, A. (2003). Applying the *International classification of functioning, disability and health* to measure childhood disability. *Disability & Rehabilitation, 25*(11–12), 602–610.

Simeonsson, R. J., Lollar, D., Hollowell, J., & Adams, M. (2000). Revision of the *International classification of impairments, disabilities and handicaps:* Developmental issues. *Journal of Clinical Epidemiology, 53,* 113–124.

Stein, R. E. K., & Silver, E. J. (1999). Operationalizing a conceptually based noncategorical definition. *Archives of Pediatric and Adolescent Medicine. 153,* 68–74.

Stein, R. E. K., & Silver, E. J. (2002). Comparing different definitions of chronic conditions in a national data set. *Ambulatory Pediatrics, 2*(1), 63–70.

Tokunaga, A. (2006). Trends and perspectives of the use of the *International classification of functioning, disability and health* (ICF) on special needs education in Japan. *Journal of Special Education in the Asia Pacific, 2*, 17–30.

United Nations. (1989). *Convention on the Rights of the Child.* New York: Author.

United Nations Children's Fund. (1999). *The state of the world's children 1999.* New York: Author.

United Nations Children's Fund. (2001). *The state of the world's children 2001.* New York: Author.

United Nations Educational, Scientific and Cultural Organization. (1994). *The Salamanca statement and framework for action.* Geneva, Switzerland: UNESCO, Special Education, Division of Basic Education.

Verbrugge, L., & Jette, A. (1994). The disablement process. *Social Science and Medicine, 38*(1), 1–14.

Wells, T., & Hogan, D. (2003). Developing concise measures of childhood activity limitations. *Maternal and Child Health Journal, 7*(2), 115–126.

World Health Organization. (1980). *International classification of impairments, disabilities, and handicaps.* Geneva, Switzerland: Author.

World Health Organization. (1992). *International statistical classification of diseases and related health problems* (Rev. 10th ed.). Geneva, Switzerland: Author.

World Health Organization. (2001). *International classification of functioning, disability and health.* Geneva, Switzerland: Author.

World Health Organization. (2007). *International classification of functioning, disability and health for children and youth.* Geneva, Switzerland: Author.

14 Learning Disabilities in the United States

Operationalizing a Construct

Deborah L. Speece

The notion of learning disability is alive in the United States despite an inability to precisely define and diagnose the construct of unexpected underachievement that characterizes it. It is assumed that a condition called learning disability (LD) exists and, given this assumption, it would be logical to infer that LD is a cross-cultural phenomenon. It is, however, an American invention as few other countries use the term in quite the same way. Norwich (in Chapter 9) argues for dyslexia to be recognized as a classification of reading disorders, but dyslexia is not the broad construct implied by the term learning disability as used in the United States. In the United States, LD comprises all learning disorders in academic domains (i.e., math, written language) and is not limited to reading, although some estimate that as many as 80% of children identified as LD have reading disabilities. Oral expression and listening comprehension are other areas that, if deficient, can be the basis of an LD diagnosis. In this chapter, I focus on the concept of learning disabilities from the perspective of US policy, practice, and research as a specific instance of classification. The intent is to examine proposals to operationalize the construct and reflect on the meaning of a learning disability.

Doris (1986) noted that interest in learning disabilities among scientists and practitioners outstrips our actual knowledge of the condition. As presented by Hallahan and Mercer (2002), the roots of LD in the United States are found in Europe in the early work of Gall and Hinshelwood on brain injury and reading difficulty. Orton, an American, built upon their ideas by proposing specific brain functions that were impaired and advocating direct phonics instruction for children with reading impairments. Werner and Strauss, working in both Germany and the United States, are credited with focusing on more generalized learning problems that were ultimately captured by Kirk who introduced the term "learning disabilities" to the educational lexicon in the 1960s (Hallahan & Mercer). In early work, assessment and remediation of LD were closely linked as seen in Monroe's emphasis on error analysis to guide instruction. Instead of focusing on test scores, her approach was to develop a profile of child strengths and weaknesses from which to generate instructional recommendations. The connection between assessment and instruction was lost in the 1977 regulations to Public Law 94-142 (Education for All Handicapped Children Act) in which learning disability was defined as unexpected underachievement *and* a severe discrepancy between achievement and intelligence (Speece & Hines, 2007). Unexpected underachievement is now considered the representation of the LD construct, whereas severe discrepancy was proposed in 1977 as the method to operationalize the construct. The guiding assumption of discrepancy is that low achievement is unexpected in the face of an average or above intelligence test score.

Within the United States, learning disabilities is arguably the most controversial disability category and it is the only category of disability (out of thirteen) whose criteria for diagnosis are defined in law. The federal definition of a specific learning disability as stated in the Individuals with Disabilities Education Act (IDEA) is,

(A) **In General.**—The term "specific learning disability" means a disorder in one or more of the basic psychological processes involved in understanding or in using language, spoken or written, which disorder may manifest itself in imperfect ability to listen, think, speak, read, write, spell, or do mathematical calculations.

(B) **Disorders Included.**—Such term includes such conditions as perceptual disabilities, brain injury, minimal brain dysfunction, dyslexia, and developmental aphasia.

(C) **Disorders Not Included.**—Such term does not include a learning problem that is primarily the result of visual, hearing, or motor disabilities, of mental retardation, of emotional disturbance, or of environmental, cultural, or economic disadvantage. (IDEA Amendments of 2004, § 602(30), p. 118)

Until the passage of the Individuals with Disabilities Education Improvement Act of 2004 (IDEA), the federal regulations that support the above definition, although occasionally challenged, did not undergo any serious modification since the original 1977 regulations to Public Law 94-142 (Education for All Handicapped Children Act) were put in place. The statutory definition that includes psychological processing problems coupled with academic difficulties was unchanged and, apparently, unopposed. The central concept of aptitude-achievement (or IQ-achievement) discrepancy remained intact until the *proposed* regulations to IDEA 2004 were written. It was widely anticipated, based on the proposed regulations, that the discrepancy language would be seriously altered in the *final* regulations. It was further anticipated that a new method of operationalizing unexpected underachievement, referred to as Response to Intervention (RTI), would largely supplant IQ-achievement discrepancy. As it turned out, the final regulations retained both approaches to identifying LD, permitting but not requiring the use of RTI, which either pleased no one or everyone, depending on one's perspective.

It is here that the controversy begins. There are two primary issues with the current LD definition. The first is that the states *must not require* an aptitude-achievement discrepancy. The discrepancy criterion is a proxy for psychological/cognitive processing problems that remain part of the law (the terms "psychological processing" and "cognitive processes" are used interchangeably in this chapter). If a discrepancy is present, processing problems are inferred to be the cause of low achievement given normal intelligence. Cognitive processes refer to a number of constructs including intelligence, memory, and attention.

The second issue is allowing the process called Response to Intervention (RTI) to be used as one means of documenting LD. In the new regulations, states *must permit* the use of an RTI approach to identify LD. RTI reflects a system that links frequent assessment with instruction and instructional decisions. Instruction is conceptualized as increasingly intensive levels of instruction, or "tiers," that children receive if it is determined they have not responded well to the current instructional arrangement. Children who enter a third level of instruction are thought to be eligible for further assessment for an LD diagnosis, although the connection between LD and RTI is not fully specified. Entering a third level of instruction is not necessarily synonymous with LD even though a child without a significant cognitive disability who does not respond to two or three phases of instruction likely meets the spirit of "unexpected" underachievement. US law requires a multifaceted assessment prior to diagnosis, so how lack of responsiveness is to be tied to such an assessment has yet to be determined.

The seeming equality policymakers gave to these two disparate approaches to operationalizing LD sets the stage for examination of how the construct of LD (i.e., unexpected underachievement) should be operationalized. Although the regulations explicitly allow the possibility of using either a discrepancy approach or RTI (or both), comments in the proposed regulations by the US Department of Education suggest that RTI approaches are favored by the department (see www.wrightslaw .com/idea/law.htm).

As would be expected, there are critics and proponents of cognitive processing and RTI approaches to defining LD. The following provides an idea of the flavor of the arguments concerning the new proposals for LD identification.

Hale, Naglieri, Kaufman, and Kavale (2004) wrote,

> We strongly believe that practitioners must use standardized intellectual, cognitive, and neuropsychological assessment measures to identify process deficits as well as integrities. (p. 6)

In response to Hale et al. (2004), Fletcher and Reschly (2005) wrote

> There is no evidence that such [cognitive processing] assessments are related to intervention or help sort [specific learning disabilities] according to putative cause. As such, the notion expressed . . . can only be characterized as the opinion of four people with vested interests in current practices who formed what they described as an ad hoc committee that met over a weekend. (p. 10)

Heated exchanges notwithstanding, it is instructive to review what Cromwell, Blashfield, and Strauss (1975) listed, in Hobbs (1975, Vol. 1), as important criteria for a classification system: reliability, coverage, logical consistency, clinical utility, and acceptability to users. The issue is the extent to which either cognitive processing definitions (including aptitude-achievement discrepancy) or RTI conceptualizations meet these criteria. The research evidence for each position is briefly reviewed keeping in mind the Cromwell et al. criteria.

COGNITIVE PROCESSES

The term "psychological processes" has been retained as part of the definition of learning disabilities in every reauthorization of IDEA. This is so despite (1) early dissatisfaction with the term that led to the 1977 federal regulations instituting intellectual ability-achievement discrepancies as a criterion for identification rather than psychological processes (Reschly, Hosp, & Schmied, 2003; Torgesen, 2002), and (2) consistent research findings from earlier eras that the psychological processing approaches to assessment and intervention were not valid (e.g., Kavale & Mattson, 1983; Klenck & Kirby, 2000).

Current proponents of cognitive processing say these earlier efforts failed to gather support because the measure of intelligence used for the processing conceptualization of LD lacked a theoretical basis (Kavale, Holdnack, & Mostert, 2005; Naglieri, 2003). They argue that the conceptual base for IQ-achievement discrepancy is not flawed but rather its measurement is. It appears the number of professional writers who support this position is limited; however, practitioners may be in agreement. Manchik and Nelsen (2005) reported that 75% of the school psychologists they surveyed endorsed assessment of cognitive processes in diagnosing LD and more than 60% endorsed using IQ-achievement discrepancies.

A review of the validity evidence presents a mixed picture (Speece & Hines, 2007). Newer measures of intelligence like the Woodcock-Johnson Cognitive Battery (III) (Woodcock, McGrew, & Mather, 2001) and the Cognitive Assessment System (Naglieri & Das, 2005) present evidence of criterion-related validity. The criterion measures, however, are tests of achievement. If achievement is the important validity criterion for cognitive processes, what do cognitive processing scores add to the diagnosis of learning disability? Proponents of cognitive processing need to make the case that profiles of performance have an added value and are not simply redundant with achievement.

Another validity question is the extent to which performance informs instruction. Speece and Hines (2007) concluded that whereas attempts to make this connection are in the literature, interpretation is severely limited by the lack of experimental designs and a need for larger samples and testable hypotheses. Others reached similar conclusions (Meikamp, 2005), with Fletcher, Coulter, Reschly, and Vaughn (2004) stating that "anecdotal links between cognitive processing and instruction are at best appealing experimental hypotheses that have not been validated despite extensive efforts over the past 30 years" (p. 321).

It bears stating that professionals in the field of LD would likely agree that cognitive processing differences underlie the condition we call learning disabilities. Current understanding of processing operations and their relationship to learning, however, are not sufficiently developed for either diagnosis or intervention. This conclusion does not mean it will never be possible to assess cognitive processes in a meaningful way, only that the necessary evidence is not currently available. The issue of diagnostic relevance is essential when evaluating measures of cognitive processing. Two questions arise: Are measures of cognitive processing effective in diagnosing students with LD and are they helpful in designing interventions? It seems that there is not solid evidence to support their relevance in either area.

These conclusions suggest that few if any of the Cromwell et al. (1975) criteria are met through a cognitive processing approach to identifying LD. The lone criterion that may have some support is user acceptability and even that conclusion lacks consensus. It seems that this line of thinking has not progressed much beyond what was written in 1975 about the classification of learning disabilities.

RESPONSE TO INTERVENTION (RTI)

Background

About the time that research findings converged on the invalidity of aptitude-achievement discrepancies (e.g., Fletcher et al., 1994), Fuchs and Fuchs (Fuchs, 1995; Fuchs & Fuchs, 1998) suggested that treatment validity (now known as RTI) may provide a method of identifying children for LD services. They credited Messick (1984) with the idea that instruction could be the mechanism for special education placement that would reduce disproportionate placement of minority children in special education. Fuchs and Fuchs operationalized treatment validity/RTI with curriculum-based measurement, frequent progress monitoring, and several phases of instruction. This general approach has gained favor with researchers and practitioners.

In the context of the regulations for the implementation of IDEA 2004, there is a two-pronged test for LD eligibility: (1) the child does not *achieve commensurate* with his or her age or grade level standards in one of seven domains despite appropriate instruction, and (2) the child fails to make *sufficient progress* in meeting state-approved results. One of two methods is allowed to judge the latter criterion. The first is an RTI method. The second criterion requires a pattern of strengths and weaknesses either alone or in conjunction with *intellectual ability* that the multidisciplinary team believes is relevant for an LD diagnosis. The regulations maintain the exclusionary clauses that include sensory impairments, mental retardation, and economic and cultural differences. In addition, IDEA 2004 specifically states that a child may *not* be identified as LD if there was a lack of appropriate instruction in reading or math or if the child has limited English proficiency.

Absent from the regulations is the requirement for a severe discrepancy between achievement and intellectual ability that has been a hallmark of LD identification since the first regulations were put in place in 1977. Although the new regulations leave the door open for considering intellectual ability, state education agencies (SEAs) may not require discrepancy models, and must allow local education agencies to use RTI models (see www.wrightslaw.com/idea/law.htm). Also absent from the final regulations is the statement that appeared in the proposed regulations that SEAs may *prohibit* the use of discrepancy models. Thus, both ways of operationalizing LD are equal from a policy perspective.

RTI is an umbrella term encompassing a variety of different assessment and instructional approaches (e.g., Fuchs, Mock, Morgan, & Young, 2003; Marston, Muyskens, Lau, & Carter, 2003). There is some consensus, however, on conceptualizing RTI as three tiers of increasingly intense instruction with ongoing monitoring of progress. Tier 1 is general education instruction in which all children are receiving instruction deemed to be effective. Prior to the new regulations, general education was assumed to be effective without any substantiation. The thrust of the regulations is a more rigorous approach to documenting the quality of general education emphasizing instruction and curricula that have scientific support. Another proposal for assessing quality is monitoring student progress. When most students are making progress, the instruction is presumed effective (Fuchs, 1995; Fuchs & Fuchs, 1998). The extent to which this will mean monitoring all children is not clear, but several authors urge universal screening at a minimum if not regular monitoring of all children (e.g., Fuchs, 1995; Speece & Case, 2001).

Tier 2 instruction, conceptualized as more intensive than general education, may occur in the general education classroom (e.g., Fuchs & Fuchs, 1998; O'Connor, 2000; Speece & Case, 2001) or as an extra-classroom supplement (e.g., Vaughn, Linan-Thompson, & Hickman, 2003; Vellutino et al., 1996). Tier 2 may include two learning trials for a child considered at risk for learning problems, each lasting from eight to twelve weeks. If the first trial does not result in improved learning, instruction is further modified and a second trial is undertaken. Tier 3 is often associated with assessment for eligibility as LD as well as more intensive instruction and continued monitoring of progress. Tier 3 is the most poorly defined of the three tiers with no clear consensus on what further assessment may include, how LD will be defined, or how instruction will differ from Tier 2.

Research

The bulk of the research evidence suggests that some RTI methods identify a group of children who experience serious learning problems. Methods that include growth as a criterion in addition to level of performance identify a reasonable number of children (i.e., 4 to 10%) who differ significantly and often substantially from children who do not have academic growth and level deficits (Case, Speece, & Molloy, 2003; Fuchs, 2003; Fuchs et al., 2005; McMaster, Fuchs, Fuchs, & Compton, 2005; Speece & Case; 2001; Speece, Case, & Molloy, 2003). These studies provide evidence of construct validity. Whether these children should be identified as learning disabled is open to debate and further inquiry. The data base is limited to early elementary schoolchildren and reading, with few exceptions. This limited coverage of developmental levels and academic domains is of concern given federal initiatives to support RTI approaches to the identification of LD. Studies are needed that incorporate larger and more diverse samples and a wider array of measures and domains. Another issue that hinders evaluation is that RTI criteria are arbitrary. For example, to identify students for further intervention, Speece and Case (2001) defined dual discrepancy as 1.0 standard deviation below the mean level and slope of classmates who were not considered at risk for reading problems. McMaster et al. (2005), however, defined dual discrepancy as 0.5 standard deviation below the mean level and slope of all average-achieving students in the study. Thus, the case for RTI construct validity is positive but, as stated above, limited in scope to children in early elementary school and reading.

RTI fares a bit better against the Cromwell et al. (1975) criteria for classification. Although user acceptability awaits further investigation, surveys of school psychologists and researchers concluded that RTI was viewed as a desired element in LD identification (Manchik & Nelsen, 2005; Speece & Shekitka, 2002). It is likely that RTI will produce better coverage compared to aptitude-achievement discrepancies in that discrepancy approaches do not identify nondiscrepant children who have reading difficulties as severe as discrepant children (Fletcher et al., 1994; Speece & Case, 2001). Because RTI methods are based on achievement, poor readers who do not meet discrepancy criteria would still be identified. Whether the ranks of LD swell under RTI approaches remains to be seen. Classification reliability will depend on how well the many parts of RTI can be standardized (screening, fidelity of intervention, progress monitoring, adequate response). IQ-achievement discrepancy approaches are criticized in that children may or may not qualify depending on the school district. There is little about RTI to lead us to believe the same will not be true of it.

The benefit of RTI lies in the potential for logical consistency and clinical utility. Cromwell et al. (1975) stated that a useful classification would have elements of a typology (condition is present or absent) as well as dimensions. Up to this point, LD has been viewed as a typology even though there is ample evidence of dimensions. For example, Case et al. (2003) identified three groups of at-risk children based on their degree of responsiveness judged in relation to their classmates. One at-risk group was never identified as nonresponsive across three years, one at-risk group was infrequently judged as such (three or fewer times), while the third at-risk group was frequently judged as not responding (four or more times). The groups were validated on teacher ratings of academic competence, number of school services received, and reading achievement. The "infrequent" group is interesting in that these children went in and out of risk across the three years of the study as befits the meaning of "at risk" as a probability statement, not a hard and fast category. This finding is in line with the view that reading disability is most properly thought of as a continuum rather than a typology (Pennington & Lefly, 2001; Snowling, Gallagher, & Frith, 2003). RTI may be able to further a dimensional approach to reading/learning disability given that "responsive" represents a continuum.

There may be other dimensions to consider beyond responsiveness and this may be the key to elaborating the ambiguous Tier 3. Batsche et al. (2005) suggest the federally required multidimensional assessment is conducted at this point in addition to intensive intervention and continued progress monitoring. These authors cite level and rate differences, documented adverse impact, and adherence to exclusion factors as the elements of eligibility under an RTI view. This appears to suggest that RTI data provide most of what the school team needs to make a classification decision even though the authors also note the regulations require assessment in all areas related to the disability. Thus, there is a gap in suggested practice between RTI data and the need for further assessment. Does this mean that published, nationally normed achievement measures are to be administered at this point? To what purpose? Is it possible that a student would exhibit repeated failure to respond but score in the normative range on a different test? Not likely, making administration of a nationally normed achievement test moot. Or, are there other valid instruments, beyond those used to document treatment responsiveness, that provide insight for instructional modification? It is well-known that commonly used, published, norm-referenced achievement instruments provide limited instructional information. Exactly what the additional assessments should be requires elaboration. The regulations suggest assessment of health, vision, hearing, social and emotional status, general intelligence, academic performance, communicative status, and motor abilities, as appropriate (Batsche et al., 2005). These could be condensed to dimensions of physical health, mental health, and achievement/aptitude, each viewed as a continuum with dimensions assessed as needed.

Speece and Hines (2007) suggested that recognition of co-morbid conditions in federal guidelines would better reflect the reality of children's learning problems. The continued reliance on exclusion factors to define LD in the law (i.e., visual, hearing, or motor disabilities; mental retardation; emotional disturbance; environmental, cultural, or economic disadvantage cannot be the putative cause of the learning problem) works against a dimensional view in that a learning disability is viewed as a single, orthogonal category. In contrast to federal guidelines, the most recent edition of the *Diagnostic and Statistical Manual of Mental Disorders* (*DSM-IV-TR*; American Psychiatric Association, 2000) supports co-morbid LD diagnosis, including not only the co-occurrence of more than one academic difficulty but also cross-classification diagnosis with mental retardation, pervasive developmental disorder, and communication disorder. Although co-morbid diagnosis is not explicitly prohibited, federal reimbursements are based on number of students identified, not number of handicapping conditions identified, resulting in states' reluctance to acknowledge co-morbidity (Handwerk & Marshall, 1998). This may be particularly true of co-morbid conditions requiring additional treatment, such as emotional disturbance, rather than of those requiring accommodations or pharmacological interventions, such as attention deficit hyperactivity disorder (ADHD). Furthermore, because ADHD is not listed as an exclusionary factor in the LD definition, practitioners may be more willing to consider it in assessment. A broader view of LD that incorporates multiple dimensions, including responsiveness to instruction, number of academic markers, oral language skills, and social/emotional functioning, may complicate the diagnosis in an RTI Tier 3 but would likely provide some needed guidance on the comprehensive assessment that is still required.

Simeonsson, Simeonsson, and Hollenweger (Chapter 13) suggest a more radical change to classification that may be appropriate for LD. They describe a system in which description of functions rather than classification of persons into diagnostic categories operates as the primary method for understanding and treating disabilities. This approach, embodied in the *International Classification of Functioning, Disability and Health* (ICF), eschews a medical model of disability in favor of understanding the child in context. Philosophically, the ICF makes a great deal of sense. Realistically, it is complex and, possibly too cumbersome to implement in schools. Nonetheless, approaches that take a holistic view of the child deserve systematic evaluation.

INTENDED AND UNINTENDED CONSEQUENCES

In the analysis of validity, Messick (1989) cautioned us to examine unintended as well as intended consequences of measurement procedures. This advice is particularly important given that the US Congress legislated alternative approaches to identifying learning disabilities. What will be gained and lost, or is it a zero sum game? The following are a few issues to consider.

Constructs

The construct that underlies LD is unexpected underachievement. This construct was originally operationalized as a discrepancy between achievement and intelligence that aligns with the cognitive processing deficit perspective. Is the construct lost when LD is defined as RTI? Some (Hale et al., 2004; Kavale et al., 2005; Scruggs & Mastropieri, 2002) believe that RTI essentially dismantles the construct of LD with the real possibility of eliminating the category. They argue, essentially, that measurement of intelligence is central to the construct and that more careful attention to implementation of current criteria would improve identification. On the other hand, RTI is at its essence a reflection of unexpected underachievement. A child not responding to instruction that is benefiting most other children makes nonresponsiveness unexpected, assuming that the child does not have a severe cognitive impairment. In fact, it has been argued that when a child does not respond to good instruction, cognitive processing deficits may be inferred (Fuchs & Fuchs, 1998). The problem with cognitive processes, from an RTI perspective, is that they cannot be measured, not that they are unimportant.

Incidence

What is the likelihood that increased (or decreased) numbers of children will be identified as LD under RTI compared to aptitude-achievement discrepancy or other cognitive-processing approaches? The regulations to IDEA 2004 stipulate that children who have not received good instruction in reading and math and those who are learning English cannot be identified as LD. If implemented, these provisions could mean a decrease in identification rates as children receiving poor instruction or who do not know English would not be misidentified as they might be if discrepancy formulas were applied indiscriminately. The obvious problems are defining good instruction and the potential bias that would preclude LD services for English language learners who nonetheless exhibit unexpected underachievement. When the original regulations for Public Law 94-142 were under consideration, many were concerned about the number of children who could be identified and a cap of 2% was introduced (Weintraub, 2005). The cap was lifted when severe discrepancy was introduced as discrepancy was intended to achieve the 2% cap. Over the past thirty years, the percentage of school-age children identified as LD grew from 1.8% to 5.9% of the school-age population (Zirkel, 2006). There are few data on this issue but there is some indication that the percentages will be stable (Case, Speece, & Molloy, 2003; Speece & Case, 2001). These estimates, however, are based on projections from research studies and not actual practice. Another consideration is that states can conceivably use both RTI and discrepancy methods to identify LD. If this situation occurs, it is possible that incidence will increase. Speece and Case reported only a 25% overlap between children identified with RTI and discrepancy methods so use of both methods would identify more children than either alone. This situation would further blur the meaning of LD as the heterogeneity of the LD group would likely be as high as that associated with all children not so identified.

Identification and Entitlement

In the United States, classification as disabled entitles children and parents to services and protections. Is it possible that RTI becomes a never-ending series of tiers in which no one is ever declared disabled and, thus, not afforded the protections specified by special education law? Proponents of RTI list early identification and intervention as major goals with the corresponding emphasis on Tier 1 (general education classrooms) and Tier 2 (more intensive instruction) and relatively little thought to what happens in Tier 3. Using RTI to identify LD was a clear goal in early conceptualizations (Fuchs & Fuchs, 1998), but there is little guidance on what will be accomplished in the third tier and how rights will be protected. Since federal funds are tied to identification, LD most likely will not go away but the murkiness of operationalizing LD based on RTI is troubling.

Standardization

LD diagnosis is more than either discrepancy or RTI. It involves multidisciplinary teams, a variety of assessments, observations, team meetings, and decisions. Regardless of the central defining feature, there is a lot of room for variability in practice. This is demonstrated in the different percentages of children identified as LD by different states, most of which use discrepancy criteria. One could easily make the case that the variability in who is identified will increase under RTI given the number of new dimensions subsumed by the concept: responsive (how to define?), scientifically based instruction (what counts as evidence?), progress monitoring (which measures, how often?), tiers of instruction (how many? who is responsible?). Proponents have not claimed that RTI will reduce variability. It will be important to consider if variability will, in the end, swamp the construct making LD meaningless. Again, proponents will refute this prospect and it likely is not the goal. But it could possibly be an unintended consequence if there are no means to standardize the identification process.

CONCLUSIONS

Our failure to operationalize the construct of learning disabilities is troubling for researchers and practitioners. This is not a new problem but is further complicated by the federal endorsement of two seemingly different approaches to operationalizing the construct. Retaining both methods speaks to the power of politics in American education. It is well established scientifically that discrepancy methods are fraught with methodological and substantive problems (e.g., Fletcher et al., 1994; Stuebing et al., 2002) but elements remain. By the same token, RTI is a concept with little evidence to support its use at the national level yet it is featured in federal legislation. It is reasonable to assume that efforts of lobbyists were at work on both issues.

It is fascinating that LD classification in the United States is legislated. Classification is a well regarded scientific activity and scientists should be the ones to solve the problems. Scientists cannot, however, provide legislators with a clear roadmap of how one gets to an LD diagnosis. The elephant in the room is etiology. Proponents of discrepancy likely believe the construct will be lost if discrepancy is dropped because they believe that discrepancy is the behavioral manifestation of difficulty at the neurobiological level, where "real" LD resides. Their arguments may have less to do with the value of discrepancy per se and more to do with etiology. Proponents of RTI may be characterized as pragmatists. They likely have no problem with assuming neurobiological underpinnings of LD; but their interpretation of the evidence leads to the conclusion that, currently, there are no behavioral markers of neurobiological influences on learning disabilities. Thus, classification of LD in schools should rest on failure to respond to solid instruction with an empirical basis delivered faithfully and monitored regularly.

As is often the case, a pertinent example can be drawn from the medicine. Trans fat is now unequivocally associated with heart disease, the leading cause of death in the United States. The strength of this connection convinced legislators in New York City to ban trans fat in restaurants. Ideally, the science precedes legislation as exemplified by this example. The field of LD needs to provide evidence of "trans fat," so to speak, and then identify the behavioral markers needed for diagnosis. Researchers are tackling the issues from both the neurobiological and behavioral perspectives (e.g., Pugh et al., 2001; Temple et al., 2003), but conclusions about cause await further experimentation.

In medicine and education, it is important to bear in mind that today's truths may become yesterday's fictions. This holds particularly for classification, which is a dynamic and fundamental science (Gould, 1989) where change is expected and embraced. To wit, thirty years ago vegetable oil with trans fat was considered a healthy replacement for saturated fats like butter (Santora, 2005).

NOTE

Portions of this chapter are based on Speece and Hines (2007).

REFERENCES

American Psychiatric Association. (2000). *Diagnostic and statistical manual of mental disorders* (4th ed., text revision). Washington, DC: Author.

Batsche, G., Elliott, J., Graden, J. L., Grimes, J., Kovaleski, J. F., Prasse, D., et al. (2005). *Response to intervention: Policy considerations and implementation.* Alexandria, VA: National Association of State Directors of Special Education.

Case, L. P., Speece, D. L., & Molloy, D. E. (2003). The validity of a response-to-instruction paradigm to identify reading disabilities: A longitudinal analysis of individual differences and contextual factors. *School Psychology Review, 32,* 557–582.

Cromwell, R. L., Blashfield, R. K., & Strauss, J. S. (1975). Criteria for classification systems. In N. Hobbs (Ed.), *Issues in the classification of children: A sourcebook on categories, labels, and their consequences* (Vol. 1, pp. 4–25). San Francisco: Jossey-Bass.

Doris, J. (1986). Learning disabilities. In S. J. Cecil (Ed.), *Handbook of cognitive, social, and neuropsychological aspects of learning disabilities* (Vol. 1, pp. 3–53). Hillsdale, NJ: Lawrence Erlbaum.

Fletcher, J. M., Coulter, W. A., Reschly, D. J., & Vaughn, S. (2004). Alternative approaches to the definition and identification of learning disabilities: Some questions and answers. *Annals of Dyslexia, 54,* 304–331.

Fletcher, J. M., & Reschly, D. J. (2005). Changing procedures for identifying learning disabilities: The danger of perpetuating old ideas. *The School Psychologist, 59,* 10–15.

Fletcher, J. M., Shaywitz, S. E., Shankweiler, D. P., Katz, L., Liberman, I. Y., Stuebing, K. K., et al. (1994). Cognitive profiles of reading disability: Comparisons of discrepancy and low achievement definitions. *Journal of Educational Psychology, 86,* 6–23.

Fuchs, D., Mock, D., Morgan, P. L., & Young, C. L. (2003). Responsiveness to intervention: Definitions, evidence, and implications for the learning disabilities construct. *Learning Disabilities Research and Practice, 18,* 157–171.

Fuchs, L. S. (1995, May). *Incorporating curriculum-based measurement into the eligibility decision-making process: A focus on treatment validity and student growth.* Paper presented at the Workshop on IQ Testing and Educational Decision Making, National Research Council, National Academy of Science, Washington, DC.

Fuchs, L. S. (2003). Assessing intervention responsiveness: Conceptual and technical issues. *Learning Disabilities Research & Practice, 81,* 172–186.

Fuchs, L. S., Compton, D. L., Fuchs, D., Paulsen, K., Bryant, J. D., & Hamlett, C. L. (2005). The prevention, identification, and cognitive determinants of math difficulty. *Journal of Educational Psychology, 97*(3), 493–513.

Fuchs, L. S., & Fuchs, D. (1998). Treatment validity: A unifying concept for reconceptualizing the identification of learning disabilities. *Learning Disabilities Research and Practice, 13,* 204–219.

Gould, S. J. (1989). *Wonderful life.* New York: W. W. Norton.

Hale, J. B., Naglieri, J. A., Kaufman, A. S., & Kavale, K. A. (2004, Winter). Specific learning disability classification in the new Individuals with Disabilities Education Act: The danger of good ideas. *The School Psychologist, 6*–14.

Hallahan, D. P., & Mercer, C. D. (2002). Learning disabilities: Historical perspectives. In R. Bradley, L. Danielson, & D. P. Hallahan (Eds.), *Identification of learning disabilities: Research to practice* (pp. 1–79). Mahwah, NJ: Lawrence Erlbaum.

Handwerk, M. L., & Marshall, R. M. (1998). Behavioral and emotional problems of students with learning disabilities, serious emotional disturbance, or both conditions. *Journal of Learning Disabilities, 31,* 327–338.

Hobbs, N. (Ed.). (1975). *Issues in the classification of children: A sourcebook on categories, labels, and their consequences* (2 vols.). San Francisco: Jossey-Bass.

Kavale, K. A., Holdnack, J. A., & Mostert, M. P. (2005, Winter). Responsiveness to intervention and the identification of specific learning disability: A critique and alternate proposal. *Learning Disability Quarterly, 28,* 3–16.

Kavale, K. A., & Mattson, P. D. (1983). One jumped off the balance beam. *Journal of Learning Disabilities, 16,* 165–173.

Klenk, L., & Kirby, M. W. (2000). Re-mediating reading difficulties: Appraising the past, reconciling the present, constructing the future. In M. E. Kamil (Ed.), *Handbook of reading research* (Vol. 3, pp. 667–690). Mahwah, NJ: Lawrence Erlbaum.

Manchik, G. R., & Nelsen, J. M. (2005). *Identifying reading disabilities: A survey of past and proposed practices.* Unpublished manuscript, University of Montana.

Marston, D., Muyskens, P., Lau, M., & Carter, A. (2003). Problem-solving model for decision making with high-incidence disabilities: The Minneapolis experience. *Learning Disabilities Research and Practice, 81,* 187–200.

McMaster, K. L., Fuchs, D., Fuchs, L. S., & Compton, D. L. (2005). Responding to nonresponders: An experimental field trial of identification and intervention methods. *Exceptional Children, 71,* 445–463.

Meikamp, J. (2005). Das-Naglieri Cognitive Assessment System [Review of the test] [Electronic version]. *Mental Measurements Yearbook, 14.* Retrieved August, 2005 from ephost@epnet.com

Messick, S. (1984). Assessment in context: Appraising student performance in relation to instructional quality. *Educational Researcher, 13,* 3–8.

Messick, S. (1989). Validity. In R. L. Linn (Ed.), *Educational measurement* (3rd ed., pp. 13–103). New York: Macmillan.

Naglieri, J. A. (2003). Current advances in assessment and intervention for children with learning disabilities. *Advances in Learning and Behavioral Disabilities, 16,* 163–190.

Naglieri, J. A., & Das, J. P. (2005). Planning, attention, simultaneous, successive (PASS) theory. In D. P. Flanagan & P. L. Harrison (Eds.), *Contemporary intellectual assessment: Theories, tests, and issues* (2nd ed., pp. 120–135). New York: Guilford.

O'Connor, R. (2000). Increasing the intensity of interventions in kindergarten and first grade. *Learning Disabilities Research and Practice, 15,* 43–54.

Pennington, B. F., & Lefly, D. L. (2001). Early reading development in children at risk for dyslexia. *Child Development, 72,* 816–833.

Pugh, K. R., Mencl, W. E., Jenner, A. R., Katz, L., Frost, S. J., Lee, J. R., et al. (2001). Neurobiological studies of reading and reading disability. *Journal of Communication Disorders, 34,* 479–492.

Reschly, D. J., Hosp, J. L., & Schmied, C. M. (2003). *And miles to go . . . : State SLD requirements and authoritative recommendations.* Washington, DC: US Department of Education, Office of Special Education Programs.

Santora, M. (2005, August 11). Hold that fat, New York asks its restaurants. *New York Times.* Retrieved December 10, 2006, from http://www.nytimes.com/2005/08/11/nyregion/11fat.html

Scruggs, T. E., & Mastropieri, M. A. (2002). On babies and bathwater: Addressing the problem of the identification of learning disabilities. *Learning Disability Quarterly, 25,* 155–168.

Snowling, M. J., Gallagher, A., & Frith, U. (2003). Family risk of dyslexia is continuous: Individual differences in the precursors of reading skill. *Child Development, 74,* 358–373.

Speece, D. L., & Case, L. P. (2001). Classification in context: An alternative approach to identifying early reading disability. *Journal of Educational Psychology, 93,* 735–749.

Speece, D. L., Case, L. P., & Molloy, D. E. (2003). Responsiveness to general education instruction as the first gate to learning disabilities identification. *Learning Disabilities Research and Practice, 18,* 147–156.

Speece, D. L., & Hines, S. J. (2007). Learning disabilities. In E. J. Mash & R. A. Barkley (Eds.), *Assessment of childhood disorders* (4th ed., pp. 598–635). New York: Guilford.

Speece, D. L., & Shekitka, L. (2002). How should reading disabilities be operationalized? A survey of experts. *Learning Disabilities Research and Practice, 17,* 118–123.

Stuebing, K. K., Fletcher, J. M., LeDoux, J. M., Lyon, G. R., Shaywitz, S. E., & Shaywitz, B. A. (2002). Validity of IQ-discrepancy classifications of reading disabilities: A meta-analysis. *American Educational Research Journal, 39,* 465–518.

Temple, E., Deutsch, G. K., Poldrack, R. A., Moiller, S. L., Tallal, P., Mersenich, M., & Gabrieli, J. D. E. (2003). Neural deficits in children with dyslexia ameliorated by behavioral remediation: Evidence from functional MRI. *PNAS, 100,* 2860–2865.

Torgesen, J. K. (2002). Empirical and theoretical support for direct diagnosis of learning disabilities by assessment of intrinsic processing weaknesses. In R. Bradley, L. Danielson, & D. P. Hallahan (Eds.), *Identification of learning disabilities: Research to practice* (pp. 565–613). Mahwah, NJ: Lawrence Erlbaum.

Vaughn, S., Linan-Thompson, S., & Hickman, P. (2003). Response to treatment as a means of identifying students with reading/learning disabilities. *Exceptional Children, 69,* 391–409.

Vellutino, F. R., Scanlon, D. M., Sipay, E. R., Small, S. G., Pratt, A., Chen, R. S., et al. (1996). Cognitive profiles of difficult to remediate and readily remediated poor reader: Early intervention as a vehicle for distinguishing between cognitive and experiential deficits as basic causes of specific reading disability. *Journal of Educational Psychology, 88*, 607–638.

Weintraub, F. (2005). The evolution of LD policy and future challenges. *Learning Disabilities Quarterly, 28*, 97–99.

Woodcock, R. W., McGrew, K. S., & Mather, N. (2001). *Woodcock-Johnson® III NU Tests of Cognitive Abilities*. Itasca, IL: Riverside.

Zirkel, P. A. (2006). *The legal meaning of specific learning disabilities for special education eligibility*. Reston, VA: Council for Exceptional Children.

15 Beyond the Dilemma of Difference

The Capability Approach in Disability and Special Educational Needs

Lorella Terzi

INTRODUCTION

Conceptualizing differences among children, and in particular differences relating to disability and special needs, is a complex educational problem. What counts as a disability or a special educational need is much debated in education. The debate is characterized, on the one hand, by positions that see disability and special educational needs as caused by individual limitations and deficits and, on the other, by positions that see them as limitations and deficits of the schooling systems in accommodating the diversity of children. A crucial aspect of this debate concerns the use of classifications of disability and related forms of "categorizations" (Florian et al., 2006, p. 37). Whereas some perspectives (see, for example, MacKay, 2002) endorse the use of these classifications as necessary to ensure appropriate educational provision, other views critically highlight their possible discriminatory effects.

At the core of this contentious educational debate lies a fundamental difficulty, known as the "dilemma of difference" (Dyson, 2001; Norwich, 1993, 1996). The dilemma lies in the choice between identifying children's differences in order to secure appropriate provision, with the risk of labeling and discriminating, and accentuating learners' "sameness" and offering common provision, with the risk of not paying due attention to their needs. The dilemma entails the interplay of two fundamental dimensions: a theoretical level that relates to issues of conceptualization, and a political one that relates to the equal entitlement of *all* children to education.

In this chapter, I argue that the capability approach, developed by Amartya Sen, provides an innovative and important perspective that takes the educational debate beyond the dilemma of difference in significant ways. The capability approach is a normative framework for assessing inequality, that is, it is an ethical and political perspective concerned with determining how social institutions *ought* to be designed. Proponents of the approach assert that the just design of social arrangements should be evaluated in the space of capability, that is, in the space of the real freedoms that people have to promote and achieve their own well-being. Considerations of human diversity in terms of the interrelation between individual, social, and circumstantial factors are central in the evaluation of people's capabilities and, therefore, of their well-being. My main contention in this chapter is that conceptualizing disability and special educational needs through the capability approach helps in resolving the theoretical dimension of the dilemma because it allows defining disability and/or the difficulties children experience in learning as specific aspects of human diversity emerging from the interaction of individual and social elements, without necessarily implying classification procedures. At the same time, this conceptualization locates the debate within a normative framework aimed at justice and equality, thus addressing the political issue of the equal educational entitlement of *all* children and thereby accentuating "sameness" in treating all children as equal.[1]

The chapter is divided into three sections. The first part critically outlines how current positions in special and inclusive education, in juxtaposing individual and social elements, lead to partial understandings that do not capture the complexity of a disability or special educational need. The second section presents elements of the capability approach. It highlights how this approach allows for an understanding of a person's disability or special educational needs as emerging from the interrelation of individual and circumstantial elements, thus overcoming the duality of current perspectives. The final part presents a conceptualization of special educational needs in terms of capabilities, and shows how this approach provides new and fruitful answers to the dilemma of difference.

CONCEPTUALIZING DIFFERENCES IN EDUCATION: DISABILITY AND SPECIAL EDUCATIONAL NEEDS

However much they stand in contrast, educational approaches to disability and special educational needs all address the relation between children's diversity and school systems. The debate is characterized, on the one hand, by perspectives that causally relate children's difficulties to their individual characteristics, often seen as individual limitations and deficits. On the other hand, some attribute learning difficulties to the inability of schooling institutions to address children's differences. My argument in this section will be that the perceived duality of individual and social elements is artificial, and leads to limited and unsatisfactory conceptualizations of disability and special needs. More specifically, I will argue that perspectives emphasizing individual limitations end up overshadowing the role played by the design of schooling institutions in determining learning difficulties. Conversely, perspectives that identify schooling factors as key causes of learning difficulties tend to overlook elements related to individual characteristics. In order to substantiate my critique, I need to distinguish between impairment and disability (a distinction that will be further elaborated in later sections of the chapter). In short, impairment is an individual feature, such as the lack of a limb or the loss of a function, for instance, a hearing loss. It need not result in a disability; whether it does or not depends both on the possibility of overcoming the impairment and on social arrangements. A disability is a functional limitation or an inability to perform some significant activity, which in an educational context can result in a barrier to learning. For example, a hearing impairment can become a learning disability if teaching is not appropriately provided. Disabilities, then, are relational both to impairments and to the design of social arrangements. With this view in mind, I will now turn my attention to the limits of current approaches to disability and special educational needs of children.

Educational perspectives that explain children's learning difficulties as causally linked to their personal features conceptualize disability as related to individual impairment and limitation. These perspectives endorse the adoption of classificatory systems and categories of disability and learning difficulties that are considered essential for identifying children's needs and for securing appropriate provision. Proponents of these views criticize perspectives based on the social model of disability—the model supported by disabled people's organizations—for failing to analyze the complexity of disability and for simplifying it under the "neat umbrella of disability" as socially constructed (MacKay, 2002, p. 160). MacKay expresses concern about the fact "that many cohorts of experienced teachers . . . have been taught that impaired hearing is not a barrier to learning, because real barriers have to be construed socially" (MacKay, 2002, p. 160).

Such perspectives display limits in their understanding of children's difficulties. As I have noted above, impaired hearing can certainly become in itself a barrier to learning, and hence a disability, when teaching is not provided to accommodate children with that impairment. If teaching were conducted in diverse ways, for instance by specific methods of facilitating language development (see, for example, Gregory, 2005), then hearing impairment would remain an impairment but would not result in a disability. Consequently, category-based positions end up emphasizing the "individual" aspect of the relation between children's difficulties and school, thus seriously overlooking the relevance of the schooling factor in determining learning difficulties and, therefore, failing to express the complexity of disability and special needs as differences in education.

Similar considerations apply to the concept of special educational needs adopted in the United Kingdom following the Warnock Report (Department of Education and Science [DES], 1978) and the 1981 Education Act, as discussed in detail by Wedell in Chapter 4. While aiming at emphasizing the relational aspect of learning difficulties, and bringing the theory and practice of special education beyond the use of categories, the concept of special educational needs not only remains inscribed in a "within-child model," but also substantially introduces a new overarching category, that of special needs. This category still presents special needs as essential to the individual child, and de facto separates children with special needs from those without (Norwich, 1993, p. 45). Furthermore, the concept of special educational needs appears theoretically unspecified and practically unworkable. This leads, on the one hand, to a conceptual proliferation of needs, for instance, in ideas of exceptional needs (Norwich, 1996, p. 34) or notions of "individual needs" (Ainscow & Muncey, 1989). On the other hand, the unspecified nature of the concept leads to the reintroduction of the categories it aimed to abolish, for example, "sensory impairment" or "emotional and behavioral difficulties." Thus, the notion of special needs remains conceptually a "within-child model" and fails to capture the complexity of disability.

Opposed to these views are perspectives that identify children's learning difficulties as caused by the limitations of the schooling systems in meeting individual differences. These positions maintain that disabilities and special needs are wholly socially constructed, thus neither inherent nor essential to the child. Dyson, for instance, states,

> Special needs are not the needs that arise in a child with disabilities with regard to a system that is fixed. Rather they are needs that arise between the child and the educational system as a whole

when the system fails to adapt itself to the characteristics of the child. (1990, p. 59)

As Norwich has rightly pointed out, there seems to be an inconsistency in arguing for an interaction between child and school and then asserting only the limitations on the part of the school (Norwich, 1993, p. 50).

Some sociologists of education influenced by the social model of disability maintain that disability and special needs in education are socially constructed, in that they are the products of disabling barriers and exclusionary and oppressive educational processes (Armstrong, Armstrong, & Barton, 2000; Barton, 2003; Corbett, 1999; Oliver, 1996; Tomlinson, 1982). They see disabilities and difficulties as caused by institutional practices that marginalize and discriminate through the use of labeling procedures and disabling categories and methods. These positions critique the use of categories of disability for their arbitrary, socially situated, and discriminatory effects. The use of categories is seen as aimed at separating and, until recently, segregating children on the basis of their presumed "abnormality," and as labeling and devaluing disabled children and children with special needs. Consequently, according to proponents of this perspective, "difference is not a euphemism for defect, for abnormality, for a problem to be worked out through technical and assimilationist education policies. Diversity is a social fact" (Armstrong et al., 2000, p. 34). Differences and diversity, therefore, instead of posing a "dilemma," have to be promoted and celebrated.

This perspective shows relevant theoretical problems. First, stating that learning difficulties and special educational needs are socially constructed presents obvious elements of over-socialization, and significantly overlooks the individual factors related to impairments (Terzi, 2004). To refer to the example used above, a hearing impairment has to be recognized and acknowledged for provision to be made in order to avoid educational barriers. Hence, simply stating that hearing impairment is a difference to be celebrated does not seem to be a sufficient means to the end of educating the child, and even less so when the aim is the enactment of equal entitlements.[2] This becomes more evident in the case of children with multiple disabilities. Second, the abandonment of any use of categories and classifications of disability and special needs in favor of a generic celebration of differences is in itself a problematic and, to a certain extent, counterproductive position. How can policies be designed to celebrate differences, and specifically differences related to impairment and disability, in the absence of any specification of the concept of difference? Consequently, educational perspectives that advocate the abandonment of categories of disability and special educational needs and assert that they are solely socially constructed seriously overlook the relevance of individual factors and the importance of the relation between individual factors and the design of schooling systems in determining learning difficulties.

As we have seen, the opposition between individual and social elements presents consistent theoretical limits, which are mainly related to the unilateral causality and to the fixed dichotomy proposed. According to Norwich,

> Individual difficulty versus the organizational inflexibility is a false causal opposition. The social and the individual are not exclusive alternatives between which causal accounts are chosen. We need accounts which can accommodate the individual personal with the social organizational. (1996, p. 20)

I maintain that the capability approach provides exactly a normative framework where individual personal and social organization can be accounted for in their interaction. The next section outlines the fundamental elements of the capability approach. It shows how this approach takes the understanding and theorization of impairment and disability to an important, relational dimension.

RECONCEPTUALIZING DISABILITY: THE CAPABILITY APPROACH[3]

The capability approach is a normative framework for the assessment of poverty, inequality, and the design of social institutions. It provides an answer to the "equality of what" question, which is central to debates in political philosophy and, specifically, in liberal egalitarianism, and concerns what elements social institutions and policies should aim to equalize. Closely linked to the "equality of what" question are two further issues: first, the choice of the space in which to assess equality and, second, the kind of measurement that should be used in comparing people's relative advantages and disadvantages.

The capability approach argues that equality and social arrangements should be evaluated in the space of capabilities, that is, in the space of the real freedoms people have to achieve valued functionings that are constitutive of their well-being. It maintains that, rather than the means to freedom, what is fundamental in assessing equality is the extent of people's freedom to choose among valuable functionings. Functionings are the beings and doings that individuals have reason to value. Walking, reading, being well nourished, being educated, having self-respect, or acting in one's political capacity are all examples of functionings. Capabilities are the real opportunities and freedoms people have to achieve these valued functionings. Capabilities are therefore potential functionings or, as Sen says,

> Various combinations of functionings (beings and doings) that the person can achieve. Capability is, thus, a set of vectors of functionings, reflecting the person's freedom to lead one type of life or another . . . to choose from possible livings. (Sen, 1992, p. 40)

Sen provides a useful example that helps us to understand the distinction between functionings and capability by comparing the situation of a starving person to that of someone fasting (Sen, 1992, p. 111). Clearly the person starving is deprived of the capability—that is, the real, effective freedom—of choosing whether to eat or to fast, whereas the person who fasts retains her freedom to choose, and hence she has the relevant capability. For the capability approach, what is fundamental in the assessment of equality is "what people are actually able to be and to do" (Nussbaum, 2000, p. 40), and hence the set of capabilities available to them, rather than the set of achieved functionings they can enjoy at any given time. The focus of the capability approach is, therefore, on the real effective freedoms people have and on their choice among possible bundles of functionings. Ultimately, this allows for the pursuit of people's individual well-being, and facilitates their life planning on the basis of individual choice (Robeyns, 2003).

Capabilities, as we have seen, constitute the space for assessing and seeking equality. The evaluation of equality, however, and the comparisons of individuals' relative advantages and disadvantages within this space entail the use of some kind of measurement. Fundamental to the capability metric is the centrality of human diversity. Sen claims, "Human diversity is no secondary complication (to be ignored, or to be introduced 'later on'); it is a fundamental aspect of our interest in equality" (Sen, 1992, p. xi). According to Sen, human beings are diverse in three fundamental ways. First, they are different with respect to personal characteristics such as gender, age, physical and mental abilities, talents, proneness to illness, and so forth. Second, individuals are different with respect to external circumstances, such as inherited wealth and assets, environmental factors including climatic differences, and social and cultural arrangements (Sen, 1992, pp. 1, 20, 27–28). Third, and fundamentally, they are different in terms of their ability to convert resources into valued functionings (Sen, 1992, p. 85). For example, a lactating woman, due to her specific condition, needs a higher intake of food for her functionings than a similar but nonlactating woman. The variations entailed by these differences are central to the capability metric and have to be accounted for when addressing the demands of equality. I maintain that this intrinsic interest in human heterogeneity thus defined is crucial for reexamining impairment, disability, and special needs within a concern for justice.

What does Sen's capability approach offer to the understanding of impairment and disability? I maintain that it provides two main insights. The first, which draws on Sen's specific understanding of personal heterogeneities, concerns how we can think of impairment and disability as aspects of human diversity. This raises considerations concerning the relational aspect of disability, with respect both to impairment and to social institutions. The second fundamental insight concerns the centrality of human diversity in the evaluation of people's relative advantages or disadvantages, which thus entails the evaluation of disability in relation to the distributive patterns of relevant freedoms, and hence, ultimately, in terms of justice. These insights constitute an important framework for reconceptualizing impairment and disability. I shall now proceed to substantiate these claims.

The first fundamental insight provided by the capability approach for the reconceptualization of disability relates to its specific and complex understanding of human heterogeneity as encompassing personal, external, and circumstantial elements, including the individual differential conversion of resources into valuable functionings. This allows for a conceptualization of disability as emerging precisely from the interlocking of these personal, social, and circumstantial factors. This conceptualization, furthermore, sees disability as relational both with respect to impairment and to the design of social arrangements. Let us see why. Impairment, on this understanding, is a personal feature that becomes a disability—an inability to perform some significant class of functionings on average performed by someone's reference group under common circumstances (Buchanan, 2000, p. 286)—when it interacts with specific social and environmental structures. Disability is, therefore, relational both with respect to impairment and to the design of social institutions. In this sense, for example, a visual impairment becomes a disability in relation to the specific functioning of reading text messages on computer screens when, and if, no use of Braille displays and speech output screen readers is provided (Perry, Macken, Scott, & McKinley, 1996, p. 4). In this case, although the visual impairment is not overcome, the functioning of reading messages on screens is, nevertheless, achieved through an alternative functioning made possible by the adjustment of the environmental design. Consider also the case of a hearing impaired person who has lost the hearing functioning in a certain range of frequencies of sounds, which is on average detected by people. If the range of sounds undetectable by the impaired person is irrelevant to the functionings in that person's social environment, then she is not a disabled person[4] (Buchanan, 2000, p. 287). Consider, finally, the possibility of designing cars where the functioning of seeing is played, say, by a computerized monitor. In this case, a visually impaired person would be able to drive, and hence her impairment would not result in a disability for that specific functioning. True, this person would still be able to choose only to drive a certain type of car, due to her impairment, but the opportunity of achieving the relevant functioning of driving would still be available. Consequently, whether impairments do or do not result in disability depends both on the possible overcoming of the impairment itself as well as on the specific design of the social and physical environment. What these examples aim to show, ultimately, is that within a capability framework, disability is seen as inherently relational, both with respect to impairment and to social arrangements. Furthermore, the capability approach provides a specific conception of disability as one aspect of human heterogeneity, without suggesting monolithic and direct notions of diversity as abnormality, and this appears to be fundamental in overcoming the discrimination and oppression denounced by disabled people's movements as inherent to current categories of normality, abnormality, and diversity.

It is perhaps worth mentioning here, albeit briefly, how the capability approach, in suggesting a truly relational understanding of impairment, disability, and the design of social environment, compares with some versions of the social model of disability,[5] recently proposed, for instance, by scholars such as Carol Thomas (1999, 2002, 2004), or by Tom Shakespeare and Nick Watson (2001), in their critique of the social model. Whereas the more accredited version of the social model strongly denies any relational causality between impairment and disability, and presents disability as caused by social oppression and discrimination (see, for instance, Oliver, 1996), some disabled scholars, and in particular Thomas, have recently called for a reintroduction of considerations of impairments and "impairment effects" within what constitutes disability. Thus, Thomas asserts the importance of the experience of impairments in restricting activity, and maintains that this has to be accounted for in a social relational conceptualization of disability. In line with the social model, however, Thomas sees disability as the restriction of activity caused by social structures and as distinct from the restriction of activities relating to impairment effects (Thomas, 2004, p. 581). Although Thomas' perspective presents an important and more theoretically coherent and justified position than other versions of the social model, I maintain that there are at least two important new theoretical dimensions offered by the capability approach with respect to the social relational model. The first concerns the conceptualization of disability as restriction of functionings, relating both to individual impairment and the design of social environments. The capability approach sets this conceptualization within a unified theoretical framework. This, in turn, helps in avoiding the theoretically questionable "proliferation" of understandings of disability in terms of restriction of activity caused by oppressive social structures as separate and distinct from the restriction of activity caused by impairment (the impairment effects in Thomas' view). Moreover, the unified view offered by the approach is fundamentally inscribed in a framework aimed at justice and fairness, thus within a normative perspective where the just claims of disabled people are comprehensively considered. This leads to my second, main point.

The second insight into the capability approach's innovative potential with respect to current understandings of disability relates to the centrality of human diversity in assessing equality in the space of capability. In repositioning human diversity as central to the evaluation of individual advantages and disadvantages, Sen's capability approach promotes an egalitarian perspective that differs from others in that it deals at its core with the complexity of disability. Sen's concept of human diversity, as we have seen, suggests a conceptualization of disability as emerging from the interlocking of personal, social, and circumstantial factors. This enables the overcoming of current understandings of impairment and disability as biologically or socially determined in a unilateral way.[6] Moreover, the capability approach promotes an egalitarian perspective in which entitlement does not depend on the causal origin of disability. Thus, the capability approach shifts attention away from the biological or social causes of disability to the full set of capabilities one person can choose from, and the role that impairment and disability play in this set of freedoms. Ultimately, the capability approach provides an egalitarian framework where disability is evaluated in the light of the distributive patterns of relevant capabilities, or, in other words, of effective opportunities for well-being (see Terzi, 2005b, p. 209). This has fundamental consequences for the design of social policies and institutions, and consequently has fundamental implications for the design of educational policies and schooling systems.

An example may help in illustrating these insights. Consider, for instance, the functioning of reading and how it enables more complex functionings, like accessing written information, or communicating via electronic mail, thus allowing the performance of a wide range of tasks, including, for instance, the possibility of working in an office environment. Now consider the situation of a visually impaired person who uses Braille resources. In determining the full set of capabilities that a Braille user has to achieve her valued ends, the capability approach looks at how this specific functioning, reading Braille, interacts with circumstantial factors, such as the physical environment where the person lives and the presence of Braille resources and output speech devices, and how it interacts with personal conversion factors, such as her general strength and attitudes. This approach also considers the interplay between Braille use and the ends that the person values, one of which could, for example, be working in an office. The capability approach allows us to say that being a visually impaired person in relation to certain functionings is a disadvantage, when the specific resources are not provided or the physical environment is not designed appropriately. The provision of Braille resources and the appropriate design of the environment are matters of justice in the capability approach, because these contribute to the equalization of the capability to pursue and achieve individual well-being (see Terzi, 2005b, p. 209).

Ultimately, the two insights outlined so far provide a fundamental framework for reexamining impairment and disability. In what follows, I shall outline some (provisional) elements of a capability perspective on disability.

Reconceptualizing impairment and disability within the capability approach implies reframing these concepts in terms of functionings and capabilities. Impairment is a personal feature that may affect certain functionings and, therefore, become a disability. Consequently, disability is a restriction of functionings. This is the result of the interlocking of personal with social and circumstantial features. Because functionings are constitutive of a person's being, and capability represents the various combinations of functionings that a person can achieve and hence her freedom to choose one type of life or another (Sen, 1992, pp. 39–40), a restriction in functionings results in a restriction of the set of functionings available to the person. Consequently, it results in a narrower range of capability. Ultimately, within this framework, disability is conceptualized as a limitation on relevant capabilities and is seen in its relational aspect, both with respect to impairment and to the design of environmental and social arrangements. In this sense, disability is evaluated as a "vertical inequality," or as a kind of difference that—in affecting the individual set of valuable capabilities, and unlike a "horizontal inequality" such as the color of one's eyes (Pogge, 2004)—has to be addressed as a matter of justice. Hence, rethinking impairment and disability in terms of capabilities implies considering what the full sets of capabilities one person can choose from are and evaluating the impact of impairment on these sets of freedoms. It implies, moreover, considering the interface between the individual and the environmental characteristics in assessing what circumstantial elements may lead impairment to become disability, and how this impacts capabilities. In this sense, impairment and disability are elements to be accounted for, both in theories of justice and in social policy, when considering what a person is actually able to be and to do.

On the basis of the above, I suggest then that this conceptualization of disability in terms of capability has important theoretical and normative implications for education. The next section applies elements of the capability approach to the "dilemma of difference." The capability approach is a normative philosophical framework. As such, it is not an educational theory, nor a system of classification or categorization. Although its operationalization in education needs further analysis, applying the theoretical framework of the approach to educational issues might help in reflecting on the values informing policy, and in clarifying concepts, thus leading to necessary reconceptualizations (Brighouse, 2002, 2006; McLaughlin, 2000; Robeyns, 2006).

BEYOND THE DILEMMA OF DIFFERENCE: THE CAPABILITY APPROACH IN EDUCATION

The capability approach advances our understanding of disability and special educational needs in relevant ways. I maintain that it resolves the dilemma of difference by significantly addressing the tensions at its core.

How is the dilemma resolved within the capability perspective? The capability approach provides a framework that allows the interplay between the theoretical dimension of conceptualizing disability and special educational needs as aspects of human diversity (the difference) and the political level of responding to the equal entitlement of *all* children to education (the sameness).

The theoretical level of the dilemma relates to definitions of disability and special educational needs as specific differences. Within the capability approach, disability and special educational needs are considered aspects of human diversity, and are seen as inherently relational, thus accounting for the relation between children's individual characteristics and the features of schooling systems. Furthermore, in capability terms, disability and difficulties in learning are conceptualized in relation to individuals' full sets of functionings and capabilities. These include alternative ways of functionings as well as more typical ones, all part of a comprehensive view that does not rely on predetermined assumptions of normality. This responds positively to some of the concerns expressed with regard to existent understandings of disability and special educational needs. Some examples in education can help in explaining this aspect. Consider, for instance, dyslexia. Dyslexia may considerably affect the achievement of basic functionings such as reading and writing, and hence it may result in a consistent limitation of immediate functioning achievements and of future capabilities. In this sense, dyslexia is an individual disadvantage in certain aspects of education, namely, all those related to literacy where the individual may experience "learning difficulties." Yet when the educational environment is appropriately designed to address the learning modalities of an individual with dyslexia, and the individual is receptive to it, this potential restriction in functionings may not become a disability, and thus not be a realized functioning restriction. The capability framework looks precisely at this relational aspect of how the individual child interacts with her schooling environment and how she converts resources into functionings, while at the same time considering how the environment is designed. In this sense, no emphasis is placed on within-child factors over educational factors, or vice versa because the focus of the framework is on the interaction between the two elements. Moreover, no unilateral causal relation is established between individual or indeed circumstantial features and disability or learning difficulties. Furthermore, this approach takes into account not only the interaction but also the complexity of both dimensions, individual and circumstantial, as these elements are part of the metric proposed by the approach.

Consider now hearing impairment. Understanding hearing impairment involves looking at how this has an impact on related functionings and capabilities sets within education. Hearing enables other basic functionings such as, for instance, listening and communicating. The latter, while being fundamental to all dimensions of learning, play a specific role—for example, in language acquisition. Hence, prima facie, a complete hearing loss, as in the case of deafness, significantly restricts basic functionings and relevant capabilities. However, there may be a second way of considering hearing impairment and of looking at its specific implications with regard to education. We need to refer here to alternative functioning or doing the same in different ways. It is widely recognized that deaf people can effectively "listen" to vocal messages by way of "lip-reading" and that they can communicate through sign language. For example, in the community of Martha's Vineyard, the wider population commonly and effectively adopted both English and sign language, learning them from infancy and thus virtually allowing the communicative functionings of the deaf group of the community to be exercised (Ree, 2000, p. 201). Yet our social arrangements are not designed like Martha's Vineyard, and are instead based almost exclusively on vocal languages. Without exploring here the reasons and the implications of such arrangements, it is worth considering the concept of alternative functioning in education. Education can play a significant role in expanding capabilities for deaf children while providing for the functionings, including the alternative functionings that they can achieve. In this sense, many hearing impaired people may become effectively competent in terms of understanding, if not in terms of production, of two languages.

Conceptualizing disability and special needs in education in terms of functionings limitations and related restrictions in capabilities, therefore, provides fruitful answers to the theoretical tension of the dilemma of difference. Before addressing the second level of the dilemma, that is, its political dimension, it is worth touching upon the possible implications of the capability perspective on disability and special needs thus outlined for classificatory systems in education. The perspective I have presented so far does not necessarily presuppose any specific system of classification of disability or indeed special educational needs, nor does it encourage the use of particular forms of categorizations. It does not imply, however, the uselessness of medical or psychological understandings of certain disabilities or learning difficulties. Rather, the approach outlines the variety of possible functionings and the restrictions that may occur in relation to specific impairments in their interaction with particular social arrangements. Thus, although differences pertaining to disability and special needs are specifically conceptualized and accounted for in the capability approach, they do not appear to be stigmatized or used in discriminatory ways.

The second level of the dilemma of difference entails considerations about the just entitlement of *all* children to education. In short, it is the problem of treating all children as *equals,* thus accentuating their "sameness." Reconsidering differences and diversity in terms of functionings and capabilities implies seeing these as central in the evaluation of individuals' capabilities, that is, of their effective opportunities for educational functionings. This, in turn, relates to issues of justice and equalization in people's opportunities to achieve well-being. In view of these considerations, let us now analyze how the capability metric evaluates, for example, dyslexia and hearing impairment in relation to education.[7] Dyslexia, as we have seen, impairs reading and writing functionings, and in this sense a child with dyslexia is disadvantaged in certain aspects of her education when compared to a non-dyslexic child. Because being literate has intrinsically and instrumentally important values, dyslexia limits not only the achievement of reading and writing functionings but also of those prospective relevant capabilities yielded by education. Consequently, dyslexia is considered a difference that, in affecting functionings, constitutes an identifiable disadvantage. This is not an absolute disadvantage, but a relative one, depending on the design of educational systems. Suppose, for example, that there is an educational system completely based on visual arts curricula. In such an education, dyslexia would certainly have a very different impact from the one it has on literacy-based systems. Ultimately, in capability terms dyslexia constitutes a vertical inequality, and, as such, addressing it in terms of additional resources in literacy-based systems is a matter of justice. Likewise, the capability metric considers functioning in alternative ways, such as that of hearing impaired children—a personal feature that stands as a vertical inequality with respect to the functional demands of dominant educational arrangements.

In conclusion, in light of the specific role of education in expanding capabilities, a child's functionings limitations result in limitation of the child's future capabilities. In this sense, the capability metric highlights disability as a vertical inequality[8] when compared to nondisability, or as a kind of difference that, in limiting functionings, has to be addressed as a matter of justice because this contributes to the equalization of the individual's capability to achieve well-being. The capability approach highlights the equalization of people's effective freedoms, their capabilities, as the main goal of social, and therefore educational institutions, and suggests that within their design, the inequality related to disability has to be addressed through the deployment of additional resources (I have outlined a principled framework for a just distribution of resources to disabled learners in Terzi, 2005c, 2005d). These, I maintain, are important and fundamental insights provided by the capability approach to disability and special educational needs.

CONCLUSION

Conceptualizing differences among children, and specifically differences entailed by disability and special needs, is a difficult educational problem.

In this chapter, I have argued that current understandings of disability and special needs present a duality between individual and social factors that does not capture the complexity of disability, but leads instead to partial and limited accounts. I have furthermore suggested that the capability approach provides a framework that responds to the tensions of the dilemma of difference in ways that take the debate to new and important theoretical and ethical dimensions.

I would like to conclude my paper with a note of caution. What I have suggested in this contribution is a possible conceptualization of impairment and disability based on the capability approach. How this conceptualization can inform school practices, or education policy, needs further investigation.[9] The capability approach helps in clarifying understandings of disability and related inequalities and to ascertain the legitimacy of just claims for educational resources, broadly understood. In light of these insights, I believe that the capability approach constitutes an important and interesting normative framework that can contribute substantially to the advancement of educational theories and practice.

ACKNOWLEDGMENTS

I am very grateful to Professor Harry Brighouse and to the late Professor Terry McLaughlin for providing me with invaluable support. I acknowledge the Philosophy of Education Society of Great Britain for generous research funding. The material in this chapter was originally presented at the Third Anglo-American Symposium on Special Education and School Reform, Cambridge, UK, June 9–12, 2004. Subsequently, it was presented at the annual conference of the British Educational Research Association in Manchester, UK, in 2004; the Colloquium in Philosophy and Education at Teachers College, Columbia University, in February 2005; and finally at the annual conference of the Philosophy of Education Society of Great Britain at New College, Oxford, UK, in 2005. I am grateful to all those present for their insightful questions and comments.

Finally, the reviewers of this chapter, Professors Lani Florian, Margaret McLaughlin, and Sheila Riddell, provided extremely valuable and challenging comments to an earlier version of the chapter.

NOTES

This chapter is a version of my article of the same title, published in the *Journal of Philosophy of Education* (Terzi, 2005a). An abridged version of the chapter is published in Cigman (2007), which includes a foreword by Mary Warnock.

1. I have thoroughly addressed this level of the debate in Terzi, 2005c.

2. I have based this reading of the literature mainly on the work of scholars in the United Kingdom who support the view of "full inclusion," which does not require the identification of differences, nor additional educational provision. The work of other researchers endorsing the social model of disability does not entirely support this reading. What these scholars debate relates primarily to how best to respond to impairment. I am grateful to the editors of this volume for alerting me to this difference.

3. This section draws on Terzi, 2005b.

4. This, however, raises the question of considering the person's capabilities, and hence the functionings she may wish to have. What if this limitation, although not relevant in her dominant social framework, still hinders the person's set of valuable beings and doings? Here the discussion leads to the aspect of preference formation and the influence of processes of ambition-affecting socialization that are problematic aspects of the capability approach. Some of these problems have been effectively addressed, albeit within a different framework and for different purposes, in Arneson (1989). I am grateful to an anonymous referee of the *Journal of Philosophy of Education* for pointing out this connection.

5. I have extensively addressed some of the theoretical and political limitations of the social model of disability in Terzi, 2004.

6. I owe this insight to discussions with Harry Brighouse.

7. These and following considerations draw on Brighouse and Unterhalter, 2003.

8. Considering disability as restrictions of functionings equates disability to a vertical inequality, thus to a kind of difference that has to be addressed as a matter of justice (see preceding section for a precise understanding of this point in relation to the presence of an impairment not resulting in a restriction of functionings, thus not becoming a disability). In the example provided here, dyslexia is understood as emerging from neurological conditions (as suggested by current literature) and thus relating both to the specific individual feature as well as to the design of literate societies. As such, dyslexia results in difficulties in literacy that require appropriate adjustments not needed, for example, by the majority of non-dyslexic children, including those generically defined as "slow or poor readers" (however imprecise and questionable these understandings may be). The debate on how dyslexia differs from other forms of learning difficulties, and whether a "slow reader" has learning difficulties or not, is beyond the point made in this paper. It follows, however, from previous points that where a slow reader has no identifiable impairments relating to restrictions in functionings, the reader is not disabled. He or she may experience restrictions in reading functionings, for example, but the latter are not the result of a disability, and as such are beyond the scope of this particular analysis. I am grateful to an anonymous reviewer for raising these important points.

9. These insights are carefully and thoroughly examined in Robeyns, 2006.

REFERENCES

Ainscow, M., & Muncey, J. (1989). *Meeting individual needs.* London: David Fulton.

Armstrong, F., Armstrong, D., & Barton, L. (2000). *Inclusive education: Policy, contexts and comparative perspectives.* London: David Fulton.

Arneson, R. (1989). Against Rawlsian equality of opportunity. *Philosophical Studies, 93*(1), 77–112.

Barton, L. (2003). *Inclusive education and teacher education: A basis for hope or a discourse of delusion.* London: Institute of Education.

Brighouse, H. (2002). *Egalitarian liberalism and justice in education.* London: Institute of Education.

Brighouse, H. (2006). *Values and evaluation in school reform.* Unpublished manuscript.

Brighouse, H., & Unterhalter, E. (2003, September). *Distribution of what? How will we know if we have achieved education for all by 2015?* Paper presented at the Third Conference of the Capability Approach, Pavia, Italy.

Buchanan, A. (2000). Genetics and the morality of inclusion. In A. Buchanan, D. W. Brock, N. Daniels, & D. Wikler (Eds.), *From choice to chance: Genetics and justice* (pp. 258–303). Cambridge, UK: Cambridge University Press.

Cigman, R. (Ed.). (2006). *Included or excluded? The challenge of mainstream schools for some SEN children.* London: Routledge.

Corbett, J. (1999). *Bad-mouthing: The language of special needs.* London: Falmer Press.

Department of Education and Science. (1978). *Special educational needs: Report of the Committee of Enquiry Into the Education of Handicapped Children and Young People* (Warnock Report). London: Her Majesty's Stationery Office.

Dyson, A. (1990). Special educational needs and the concept of change. *Oxford Review of Education, 16*(1), 55–66.

Dyson, A. (2001). Special needs in the twenty-first century: Where we've been and where we're going. *British Journal of Special Education, 28*(1), 24–29.

Florian, L., Hollenweger, J., Simeonsson, R. J., Wedell, K., Riddell, S., Terzi, L., & Holland, T. (2006). Cross-cultural perspectives on the classification of children with disabilities. Part 1: Issues in the classification of children with disabilities. *The Journal of Special Education, 40*(1), 36–45.

Gregory, S. (2005). Deafness. In A. Lewis & B. Norwich (Eds.), *Special teaching for special children? Pedagogies for inclusion* (pp. 15–25). Maidenhead, UK: Open University Press.

MacKay, G. (2002). The disappearance of disability? Thoughts on a changing culture. *British Journal of Special Education, 29*(4), 159–163.

McLaughlin, T. (2000). Philosophy and educational policy: Possibilities, tensions and tasks. *Journal of Educational Policy, 15*(4), 441–457.

Norwich, B. (1993). Has "special educational needs" outlived its usefulness? In J. Visser & G. Upton (Eds.), *Special education in Britain after Warnock* (pp. 43–58). London: David Fulton.

Norwich, B. (1996). *Special needs education, inclusive education or just education for all?* London: Institute of Education.

Nussbaum, M. (2000). *Women and human development: The capabilities approach.* Cambridge, UK: Cambridge University Press.

Oliver, M. (1996). *Understanding disability: From theory to practice.* Basingstoke, UK: Palgrave.

Perry, J., Macken E., Scott, N., & McKinley, S. (1996). Disability, inability and cyberspace. In B. Friedman (Ed.), *Designing computers for people: Human values and the design of computer technology* (pp. 1–30). Stanford, CA: CSLI Publications.

Pogge, T. (2004). Can the capability approach be justified? *Philosophical Topics, 30,* 167–228.

Ree, J. (2000). *I see a voice: A philosophical history.* London: Flamingo.

Robeyns, I. (2003). Is Nancy "Fraser's" critique of theories of distributive justice justified? *Constellation, 10*(4), 538–553.

Robeyns, I. (2006). The capability approach in practice. *Journal of Political Philosophy, 14*(3), 351–376.

Sen, A. (1992). *Inequality reexamined.* Oxford: Clarendon Press.

Shakespeare, T., & Watson, N. (2001). The social model of disability: An outdated ideology? In S. N. Barnartt & B. Altman (Eds.), *Research in social sciences and disability: Vol. 2. Exploring theories and expanding methodologies* (pp. 9–28). Oxford, UK: Elsevier Science.

Terzi, L. (2004). The social model of disability: A philosophical critique. *Journal of Applied Philosophy, 21*(2), 141–157.

Terzi, L. (2005a). Beyond the dilemma of difference: The capability approach on disability and special educational needs. *Journal of Philosophy of Education, 39*(3), 443–459.

Terzi, L. (2005b). A capability perspective on impairment, disability and special needs: Towards social justice in education. *Theory and Research in Education, 3*(2), 197–223.

Terzi, L. (2005c). *Equality, capability and social justice in education: Re-examining disability and special educational needs.* Unpublished doctoral dissertation, Institute of Education, London.

Terzi, L. (2005d, May). *Equality, capability and social justice in education: Towards a principled framework for a just distribution of educational resources to disabled children and children with special educational needs.* Paper presented at the Workshop on Normative and Quantitative Analysis of Educational Inequalities, Université Catholique de Louvain, Belgium.

Thomas, C. (1999). *Female forms: Experiencing and understanding disability.* Buckingham, UK: Open University Press.

Thomas, C. (2002). Disability theory: Key ideas, issues and thinkers. In C. Barnes, M. Oliver, & L. Barton (Eds.), *Disability studies today* (pp. 38–57). Cambridge, UK: Polity.

Thomas, C. (2004). How is disability understood? An examination of sociological approaches. *Disability and Society, 19*(6), 569–583.

Tomlinson, S. (1982). *A sociology of special education.* London: Routledge & Kegan Paul.

16 Concluding Thoughts

On Perspectives and Purposes of Disability Classification Systems in Education

Martyn Rouse, Kelly Henderson, and Louis Danielson

As can be seen from the collection of papers in this book, the classification of children who experience difficulties in learning is a highly complex and contested process that evolves slowly in response to new demands, new science, and professional insights. It is carried out in different ways in different places, for a range of different purposes and it can be justified by many and various intentions. The classification of children and youth who experience difficulties in learning exists not only within education but also across service sectors, such as health, vocational training, and the judicial system, adding further complexity to the process.

Like all complex systems, current classifications of disability and special educational needs consist of a series of procedures and structures that are supported by specialists. A substantial infrastructure supports and sustains current classification processes, including professional beliefs, training, certification and accreditation, and the test publication industry. These systems are not only complex; they can also result in "institutional inertia," whereby the industry of assessing and classifying children to receive special education takes on a life of its own. Self-interest and deep beliefs about key constructs, such as what constitutes a disability or special education need, are remarkably resistant to change, even when the original underpinning assumptions or purposes have been challenged. Thus, as noted in Chapter 1, *a* way of understanding a process can become *the* way of knowing about it.

This book has focused on current issues of disability classification of children for educational purposes. In drawing on international and cross-national work in education, it considers how current systems are working. For example, in the United States, the Individuals with Disabilities Education Act is intended to guarantee access and equity in education for children with disabilities, but the procedures for determining eligibility for the additional services and due process of law that guarantee a free and appropriate education depend on a judgment that a child has an impairment that interferes with learning, and is in need of such support. In other words, it assumes that children with disabilities are different as learners from other children their age. Other countries follow a similar pattern, though they differ in terminology and eligibility criteria.

Riddell (Chapter 8) reminds us that the study of classification systems is crucial because it reveals a great deal about dominant discourses and the underlying relationships of knowledge and power. The ways in which a difficulty is described is closely linked to how it might be dealt with. Further, as Pullin (Chapters 6 and 7) warns, disability classification systems can be misused in order to gain a particular advantage or additional resources. For example, individuals (and their families) may have incentives to acquire disability status if the benefits outweigh the potential costs of any stigma associated with the disability. These trends can be seen in the huge increase in requests for additional time in examinations or modified assessment arrangements, raising complex questions about equity and equal opportunity.

The classification of those who experience difficulties in learning traditionally, however, has been based on the concept that these difficulties rest within the child as some form of disability or "special educational need." The contributions to this book review the historical and cultural context in which classification systems in at least three countries have developed and remind us that all systems of classification are located within particular professional, educational, cultural, historical, legal, and policy frameworks. As the contributors demonstrate, the mechanisms by which children are identified as having special educational needs vary widely. Yet nationally and internationally, there is a need to communicate in some consistent and comparable manner about the characteristics and needs of various subgroups of learners, if the goal of "Education for All" is to be realized.

INTERNATIONAL COMPARISONS

Most educational researchers now agree that children with disabilities and those who are identified as having "special educational needs" are best served when the focus of intervention is on the student's learning and participation rather than his or her impairment. Yet the use of medical categories of disability in education persists in many countries, and even countries that do not use medical categories of disability in education still classify students with disabilities as having "special" or "additional" needs as a means of ensuring and controlling access to education, and for rationalizing the distribution of additional resources. The question is not whether a disability classification is needed in education but what form should it take and how can it be improved and monitored.

As various authors in this volume note, the medical categories are not as clear and precise as many people would think. Ebersold and Evans (Chapter 3) point out that there are huge variations in the numbers of children identified with apparently "measurable" categories such as blindness or physical disability in different countries. For example, there are 43 times more blind students in Poland than in Greece, whereas Belgium has 343 times more students with physical disabilities than does Italy. These differences in the proportion of children classified as disabled reflects differences in national policies and the modes of allocating additional resources rather than the "true" incidence of any particular disability.

In addition, as Hollenweger (Chapter 2) notes, some international comparisons such as the Organisation for Economic Co-operation and Development Programme for International Student Assessment (PISA) specifically exclude children with disabilities. Given that disabilities are defined differently and at different rates in various countries, it would be prudent to be cautious when making judgments about the efficacy of national education systems based on such comparisons. Such prudence is required not only with regard to comparability of data on special needs education but also issues of access and inclusion of all learners in international assessments. There is usefulness in exploring the different ways in which countries classify children and respond to their needs. Doing so makes it possible to scrutinize some unquestioned assumptions that lie at the heart of many current practices in one's own country. It also helps with understanding the numbers that are reported in international comparisons of student attainment and participation.

FUTURE DIRECTIONS

Collectively, the papers in this volume suggest that the time has come to ask whether schools are still justified in using disability classification systems as part of an effort to reduce disparities in access, to improve equity and achievement among students, and, if so, to what extent are they defensible? What criteria might be used to judge or justify a classification system? Is it possible to have a disability classification system that does not rely on medical categories? What, if anything, might replace them? How might developments that emphasize capabilities and functioning meet the requirements of equity and the fair distribution of services and resources?

The fundamental reason for any system of classification is to make sense of complexity, to explore similarities and differences between individuals and groups. As the organization and delivery of services to children and their families is undergoing radical reform in many countries with the merger of education, health, and social services into integrated children's services (see for example, Wedell, Chapter 4), the implications for classification systems are profound. These include the need to develop a common assessment framework and joint training of professionals.

This book has explored the ways in which classification systems are evolving in several countries, but further work on this topic is required if we are to understand the powerful impact that classification and categorization have on the way we understand and respond to children's difficulties in learning and participation, not only in school, but also as active participants in a civil society. Given the increasing recognition that many learning needs are associated with educational, social, and economic factors, it would seem sensible to develop systems that have the capacity to understand difficulties in the social and the educational context in which they occur.

Although there is a need to communicate in some consistent and comparable manner about the characteristics and needs of learners, including those subgroups of children who have been identified as having special educational needs, there is also a need to reflect on the discourse of classification and to ask whether it serves its intended purposes. Moreover, the need to communicate reliably about groups is further complicated in many countries by racial, linguistic, and economic issues. Students of racial and ethnic minorities and students who are nonnative-language speakers are overrepresented in certain disability categories (as well as in more restrictive educational placements) in the United States. Similarly, in the United Kingdom, ethnicity and socioeconomic status appear to play a role in identification of special educational needs status and in resource provision (see Dyson & Kozleski, Chapter 11). While new large-scale data sets might help to illuminate some of the relationships between race, language, poverty, and special needs status, it would be unwise to assume that they will be capable of answering all questions. The usefulness of these data sets is dependent on the quality of the judgments of those who design, collect, record, and enter the data.

If classification systems are to reflect current developments in education, there also needs to be a review of the ways in which professionals are prepared and supported to work with these new systems. There will be little progress without the development of professionals. Hardman and McDonnell (Chapter 10) have reviewed developments in teacher preparation in the United States and Norwich (Chapter 9) in England has looked at how new classification systems might inform professional knowledge. It is clear that teacher preparation and continuing support is a crucial element not only in development of classroom practice, but also in the development and use of new classification procedures.

The final section of the book considered new approaches to the classification dilemma. In Chapter 14, Speece raised the criteria (reliability, coverage, logical consistency, clinical utility, and acceptability to users) for assessing the adequacy of classification systems first presented by Cromwell, Blashfield, and Strauss (1975) in the first volume by Hobbs. She used these to reflect on current developments such as "Response to Intervention" (RTI) in the United States that are designed to reduce the demand for classification by intervening before failure occurs. RTI is an approach that is consistent with the notion that successful classroom practices can reduce the incidence of disability and special needs by providing teachers with insights into children's strengths and learning needs. Similar approaches have been introduced in England as part of the national primary strategy. As Norwich (Chapter 9) argues, classification systems in education must acknowledge the complexity and nuance of individual learner characteristics in order to design effective pedagogy.

The field has made considerable progress in recent years and in many ways disability classification and special education share a common history. One of the original intentions of Alfred Binet's testing of children more than 100 years ago was to identify children who were not capable of benefiting from mainstream schooling, many of whom ended up in special education. More recently, children were classified to protect their rights as part of the struggle for access and equity in education. By focusing on children's deficits, however, these approaches had unintended negative consequences, many of which have been explored in this book. It is time to consider what should replace them. New approaches to disability classification, such as the *International Classification of Functioning, Disability and Health* (ICF) described by Simeonsson, Simeonsson, and Hollenweger

(Chapter 13), and the capability approach as described by Terzi (Chapter 15), point toward new conceptualizations for classification frameworks that have the promise of meeting many of the needs for defensible systems. Nevertheless, much work remains to be done.

The aim of this book was to initiate a consideration of new knowledge and developments in the area since the Hobbs Report (1975). Although *The Futures of Children* inspired the symposium that led to this book, it does not complete the task of a systematic review of classification in education nor does it fully update the comprehensive work that was done in the 1970s. Rather, it begins to consider the role of disability and special needs classification systems in the evolving context of current international educational reform movements that are based on the development of systems of schooling that are more inclusive, more focused on learning outcomes.

NOTE

Opinions expressed herein are those of the authors and do not necessarily reflect the position of the US Department of Education, and any such endorsement should not be inferred.

REFERENCE

Cromwell, R. L., Blashfield, R. K., & Strauss, J. S. (1975). Criteria for classification systems. In N. Hobbs (Ed.), *Issues in the classification of children: A sourcebook on categories, labels, and their consequences* (Vol. 1, pp. 4–25). San Francisco: Jossey-Bass.

Index